'Theatrical, confessional, masterly descriptive, it is hard to find one word to sum up the achievement. *Position Doubtful* leaps straight onto the shelf occupied by the great accounts of inland Australia.'
—Roger McDonald

'Kim Mahood is an astonishing treasure: an accomplished artist and writer who is equally well-equipped to navigate both Aboriginal and settler Australia. Her lyrical yet unsentimental memoir is a story of honoring the knowledge that two cultures have mapped upon each other, a lesson the entire globe needs to learn.'
—William L. Fox
Director, Center for Art + Environment, Nevada Museum of Art

'The rich pulse of country makes the heart quake with recognition. Mahood belongs to country and it blesses her with that most refined human sensitivity, doubt. She is not tempted to improve or judge the communities of her country because she prefers to love them, the whole buckled, lovely and jumbled chaos of the land. *Position Doubtful* has the scale and delicacy of desert, and records genuine Aboriginal voice and emotion.'
—Bruce Pascoe

'*Position Doubtful* is a remarkable, intelligent and mature work. As Mahood writes of — quite literally — building a map that is geographic, social, and cultural, you feel that she has, ever so gently, shifted your view of the world.'
—Sophie Cunningham

LONDC

D1461571

T

POSITION DOUBTFUL

Kim Mahood is a writer and artist based in Wamboin, near Canberra, whose 2000 memoir, *Craft for a Dry Lake*, won the NSW Premier's Award for non-fiction and the *Age* Book of the Year for non-fiction. Her artwork is held in state, territory, and regional collections, and her essays have appeared in *Griffith Review*, *Meanjin*, and *Best Australian Essays*. In 2013, she was awarded the Peter Blazey Fellowship for a non-fiction work in progress, and was shortlisted for the Elizabeth Jolley Short Story Prize. In 2014, she was awarded the H.C. Coombs Fellowship at the Australian National University.

POSITION DOUBTFUL

mapping landscapes and memories

KIM MAHOOD

SCRIBE

Melbourne • London

Scribe Publications
18–20 Edward St, Brunswick, Victoria 3056, Australia
2 John St, Clerkenwell, London, WC1N 2ES, United Kingdom

First published by Scribe 2016

Quoted material on p. 1 from *The Way to Rainy Mountain* by N. Scott Momaday,
reprinted with the kind permission of the University of New Mexico Press;
on pp. 147–8 from *Tragedy Track: the story of the Granites* by F.E. Baume,
reprinted with the kind permission of Hesperian Press; and on pp. 295–6
from *Representing Place: landscape painting and maps* by Edward S. Casey,
reprinted with the kind permission of University of Minnesota Press.

Text design by Sandy Cull, gogoGingko
Printed and bound in Australia by OPUS Group

Scribe Publications is committed to the sustainable use of natural resources
and the use of paper products made responsibly from those resources.

9781925321685 (paperback)
9781925307740 (e-book)

A CiP data entry for this title is available from
the National Library of Australia.

This project has been assisted by the
Australian government through the
Australia Council for the Arts, its arts
funding and advisory body.

Australian Government

scribepublications.com.au
scribepublications.co.uk

For Pam, Margaret, Dora,
Patricia, and Anna

CONTENTS

THE REMEMBERED EARTH

Once in his life a man ought to concentrate his mind upon the remembered earth, I think. He ought to give himself up to a particular landscape in his experience; to look at it from as many angles as he can, to wonder upon it, to dwell upon it.

—N. Scott Momaday, *The Way to Rainy Mountain*

Imagine the document you have before you is not a book but a map. It is well-used, creased, and folded so that when you open it, no matter how carefully, something tears and a line that is neither latitude nor longitude opens in the hidden geography of the place you are about to enter.

You flatten it gently in the wind, find stones to weight the corners, but it is bigger than you thought: there is another fold, and another. The wind makes it impossible to open it fully, the seams are tearing, and it is apparent that if you try to look at it all at once you risk the whole thing coming apart.

The map has been annotated by more than one hand. There are marks, almost rubbed away, which have been traced over so that information will not be lost. Along the frayed creases where the map has been folded, it is no longer possible to read what is inscribed there. So you fold it into manageable sections, and search for familiar locations. It's a while since you were here, and things are not where you left them. Or maybe it's your point of view that's changed.

Skeleton Valley, Running Dog Creek, Smoke Hills — the names have found their way to you along a whispered thread of folklore. And there are others whose rhythms suggest a song — Jarluwangu, Kaliyaka, Manyjurungu. On this map, many locations are described as 'Position Doubtful'. If you could fold the map out fully, if it was not so fragile and the morning was still instead of windy, you could chart your course from one 'Position Doubtful' to the next, beginning from the place where you are standing.

How many of us still feel the grip of place — the long span of a life traced out in the growth of trees planted by someone you knew, a family history measured in memory and change, the sudden clutch of knowing that it will end, life and memory both, that love and sorrow cannot be separated? To learn the names of trees and grasses, the times of their seeding and flowering, the glimpse they offer into the grand slow cycles of nature, is to see your own life written there, and passing. To know the geography of a place is to know why we have always made stories in which our own human stuff is indivisible from the stones and creeks and hills and growing things.

This is a kind of love story. It is an unrequited love story, because it is between a person and a place, and a place doesn't love you back. But perhaps that isn't entirely true. Perhaps it's like loving God, and what you get back is a reflection of what you put in. Apart from the deep and unequivocal love I have for my family and close friends, there has been no other love in my life as sustained as the one I have felt for a remote pocket of inland Australia.

The love I feel for the place has something in it of the passion and hunger of an affair of the heart — a physical sensation in the body, a disturbance of the organs, a disorder of the mind. When I'm there, I'm alive with an intensity I feel nowhere else. But to live there permanently would require a sacrifice that I'm not prepared to make. And so I return, year after year, stepping back into the self the country has held in trust while I've been away. Each time, I wonder how I could have forgotten what it feels like to be there, how I could have left it behind.

For more than twenty years now, I have been returning to a tract of country that extends across the Tanami Desert to the edge of the East Kimberley. What began as a pilgrimage to revisit the country where I had spent my late childhood and teenage years morphed into annual journeys that have included artist field trips with my friend Pam Lofts, visits to the cattle station that had been my family home, volunteer work in the art centre at Balgo Aboriginal community, an artist residency at the Tanami mine, and map-making expeditions and environmental projects with the Walmajarri custodians of Lake Gregory. Over this period, I have become gradually enmeshed with the traditional owners of the region.

The place that had occupied an almost mythical status in my childhood was made both ordinary and infinitely complex as it became a necessary part of my life. This remote, mysterious country has become the centre of my enterprise as an artist and writer. Why this has happened continues to tease my mind. Every year, as I make preparations to leave behind my orderly life on the outskirts of Canberra and follow my well-worn track across the country, I wonder what I'm doing, whether any of it amounts to anything, and how I can hope to sustain it, both financially and physically. And every year, at a certain point, I stop asking the questions and start packing the ute.

I am onto my third in a series of second-hand Hilux dual cabs — a model robust enough to stand up to the attrition of the Tanami road corrugations and the directives by my Aboriginal minders to 'keep going, keep going' across trackless stretches of spinifex and wattle scrub. My travelling kit is pared down to the essentials that have been established over a couple of decades of trips. I always plan to get special built-in drawers, but there is never the time or the money, so it's the same battered milk crates — the red one for the spare oil and tomahawk and cable ties, the blue one for the camp oven and the galvanised bucket and billies — the same set of stacking plastic drawers for the cooking equipment and basic foodstuffs, the same toolbox with its eclectic collection of tools, all of which have at one time or another proved their usefulness. I am onto my second swag cover and my third folding table. I haven't yet got around to replacing the folding chair with the broken leg attachment, which is fine if I take care when I sit down, but there's a danger it might collapse under one of the large Aboriginal ladies who snaffle it when my attention is diverted. I wrestle the second spare tyre into place on the tray, wondering how much longer I'll be able to do it. Ditto for heaving up full jerry cans of fuel and water. But I'll face that when I have to, which is not yet.

The suitcase of clothes, the plastic crate of books and art materials, the laptop and portable document box, the dog bed and the dog — I'm onto my third dog — all go into the back seat, goodbyes are said, and this settled life begins to loosen its hold.

The first day is all about making miles, putting enough distance behind us to begin the process of entering the other life. The route I take depends on the time I have, whether or not someone is travelling with me, and what the weather conditions are like. If time and weather permit it, my preferred route is through Broken Hill, turning north at Yunta to Leigh Creek and up the Oodnadatta track, through Dalhousie and Finke, and along the old Ghan route to Alice. But that track is an expedition in itself, not to be done in a hurry, and more often than not I take the shortest route out through Mildura and Renmark, Peterborough and Port Augusta, and up the Stuart highway. I love the drive through South

Australia, which is a form of space travel, a reminder of the scale and existential strangeness of this country.

The hours of driving through that particular landscape are hours in which I revisit the cultural disjunction within Australia, a gap that is both geographic and psychological. Retaining an embodied sense of this is central to what I do, since the gap between the urban, Eurocentric, aspirational, heavily populated south-east corner of the continent and the remote, predominately Aboriginal, barely sustainable, thinly populated pocket of desert is the space in which my writing and my art practice are made. This is the improvised life I have chosen to live for the past twenty years, straddling two worlds, settling in neither, trying always to keep alive the awareness of the other world in the one I currently occupy.

What drives me is not a desire to help, to fix or change, but to understand something about my country. The desert took up residence in my psyche when I was very young, in an impersonal, obdurate sort of way that made it impossible for me to form lasting attachments to any other place. A unique set of circumstances has given me privileged access to one of the least-known parts of Australia, and I have set out to learn it in as many of its manifestations and strata as I can discover. It has become the primary relationship in my life, an affair that roller-coasters from heartbreak to euphoria, although in recent years it has become less volatile, settling into the steadiness of commitment and familiarity.

+ + +

Among the documents that have drawn me back into the country are maps I have inherited, copied, stolen, made, and made up, along with maps I have been given, shown, and told about. I first came across the term 'Position Doubtful' in the account my father wrote of an expedition he made across the Tanami in search of a stock route in 1962. He describes the first days navigating west from the Tanami Road:

> The next day dull conditions found us travelling on our Balgo bearing between sandridges towards a rugged sandstone hill. This was the best landmark for thirty miles around, but it wasn't marked on our aeronautical map. As this was only thirty miles off the Tanami Road it didn't auger too well for the rest of the trip, particularly as the only landmark marked anywhere near our route (another fifty miles on) was marked Position Doubtful.

The aeronautical map he refers to is in my possession, and the landmark is there, with '(PD)' printed under the name McFarlanes Peak. The term lodged in my mind as a metaphor for the way in which white Australians move through and occupy the country, especially the less accessible parts of it. And while the advent of satellite technology has given us the tools to find and map geographic locations with great accuracy, it seems to me that our position in relation to the remote parts of the country is more doubtful than it has ever been.

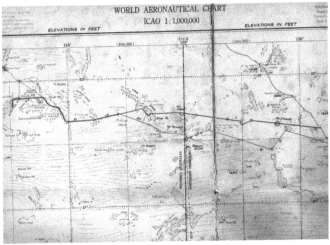

It doesn't escape my attention that landmarks along the route marked on my father's map are named for the wives and children of the expedition members. My own name is there, attached to a point at the southern end of the Lewis Range. I have another map, more recently acquired, that shows the traditional names for the places the expedition passed through. Rolled up on the floor of my studio is an unfinished painted map of the same area, made with the help of the Tanami traditional owners, on which both sets of names have been inscribed. My desire to learn the old names, to pay attention to the overlay, is connected to my own name being inked onto the aeronautical chart in my father's neat hand. Exploration and colonisation are part of my heritage.

One of the outcomes of my father's 1962 expedition was the establishment of a cattle station on the grasslands and mulga flats that lay between the sand-ridges and spinifex sand plains. Called Mongrel Downs, as an ironic nod to the assumption that the country was good for nothing, it became my family's home during the sixties and early seventies.

Some time ago, sorting through a trunk of family artefacts, the kind that can't be thrown away but serve no apparent purpose, I came across a map I had made in my early teens. Drawn with coloured inks on canvas, it is an obsessively detailed document of the topography and geology of the part of the Tanami that encompassed the family cattle station and surrounding region. I'd forgotten that I'd made it. But when I unrolled it, I remembered the hours I'd spent during the sweltering January afternoons of that summer, the airless silence of the room in which I worked, the ticking of the corrugated iron roof, the way the heat turned us all into introverts. The grubby sweat-marks my hands left on the canvas were still visible, along with a grey stain where I had spilled a bottle of Indian ink and painted it out with gesso.

I was a little shocked to realise that my preoccupation with maps and map-making went back so far, and that a fourteen-year-old girl had spent the best part of her summer holidays laboriously copying old geological charts. There is no evidence of creative flair, although in retrospect it might qualify as a treasure map, since the geological features it describes have since been discovered to contain some of the richest gold deposits in the country.

There are few placenames or roads on it. This is not a map designed to help you find your way. Instead it depicts contour lines and ancient watercourses, tectonic profiles and Cambrian sediments. I have no recollection of what that girl was thinking about when she wrote *Carpentarian Proterozoic, gossanous sandstone, phyllitic greywacke* next to the legend of coloured squares that corresponds to the coloured shapes on the map. She didn't grow up to be a geologist or a palaeontologist or a cartographer. I think she liked the way the coloured shapes fitted together, the way they suggested that some mysterious pattern underlay the country. And I think she liked the reverberations the words gave off — *porphyritic, sub-lithic, adamellite* — glittering, inscrutable words that belonged to the earth, and could not be used for other things.

Pinned to my studio wall is a hand-drawn map I began several years ago. Its geography is easy to identify if you know that part of the country. I know it well enough to draw a fair facsimile from memory. Its template is based on the flow of water — a river that runs south-west until it encounters the dune fields of the Great Sandy Desert and becomes a terminal lake system; an eroding sandstone plateau that once formed the floor of a Gondwanan sea; patterns of ephemeral lakes, both saltwater and freshwater, that reveal a network of ancient waterways. This map has no roads and, again, few placenames. It is annotated with words in which the topography is represented as metaphor — Erasure, Testimony,

Improvisation, Vertigo, Threshold, Lacuna, Undertow. Some days, trying to discover where to go next, I see through it into limitless, shimmering space.

In recent years I have made a number of maps with Aboriginal people, designed to reveal common ground between white and Aboriginal ways of representing and understanding the country. Based on topographical maps and satellite imagery, they are painted on canvas the size of groundsheets, robust enough to withstand being laid out on the ground, sat on, rolled up and tied to the roof rack. The information marked on them is a mixture of Aboriginal knowledge — traditional camp sites, the birthplaces of individuals, the tracks of ancestors — scientific information about ancient shorelines and archaeological investigations, and the template of bores and paddocks and tracks and boundaries that represent the cattle stations and stock routes of white settlement. They serve different purposes — aboriginal, scientific, testimonial, environmental — depending on when and where they are used. Often there is a mismatch between my interpretation and the Aboriginal interpretation of their purpose.

My own map is an attempt to track this faultline. Its scribbled threads of geography and metaphor represent my own uncertain search, my attempt to infuse the physicality of landscape with the poetics of western psychology.

In 'A Literature of Place', Barry Lopez writes, 'I am someone who returns again and again to geography, as the writers of another generation once returned repeatedly to Freud and psychoanalysis.'

In its broadest definition, geography is the interplay between humans and place. Like Lopez, I believe geography shapes who we are and how we think, and the time I've spent in this remote tract of desert among both its original inhabitants and its second-settler latecomers has only served to reinforce that belief.

The river on my map has two names. Its ancestral name of Tjurabalan is associated with the beings whose activities created the river and the surrounding landforms, while the less imaginative Sturt Creek was attached to it by the first white men to explore it. My own names for it are Erasure and Testimony, in reference to the accounts of a massacre that took place on its banks.

Below the point where the river forks and spreads into a delta of anabranches and ephemeral claypans is the word Amnesia. The clear line of the river, for which people hold an equivalent clarity of knowledge, diffuses into a zone of indeterminate edges and contradictory stories. Jurisdictions are contested, names and memories misplaced. As the divided channels of the river take shape again to fill the lake basins, memory also gathers form and conviction. Placenames, traditional and European, proliferate. Creation stories abound, as they do along the river. People claim clear affiliation to particular locations, and the country is rich with stories. The Walmajarri people, for whom it is their traditional homeland, still live here. The terminal lake system has dried out and refilled for millennia, a Palimpsest that has been erased and re-inscribed many times.

Clustered around the eroding tableland that forms the Balgo Pound are Vertigo, Anomie, and Mosaic. The community of Balgo is where I had my first extended encounter with desert painting and with the intense, unsettling reality of remote community life, both vertigo-inducing in their different ways.

A hundred kilometres to the east is the abandoned homestead of Ngulupi, once the centre of a successful cattle operation developed by the Mission. Sites of abandoned human occupation are rife with metaphor, and Ngulupi offers plenty. One of them was provided by my friend Pam Lofts, who made a number of artists' field trips with me, and for whom the outstation was rich pickings.

She called the work she made *Threshold (might be somewhere)*, and I can't improve on it as a metaphor for the contradictions roosting in the doorways of the abandoned dwellings.

Further east again is the 'mongrel country' of my childhood, a landscape of grasslands and mulga and occasional low hills, spinifex sand plains and sand ridges, and broad fossil waterways filled with the sediments of that worn-down country. The Lacunae that mark the map here are the ephemeral lakes and claypans typical of the Tanami, where water is more often a palpable absence than a presence, an intermittent manifestation that presents an alternative to the inland sea and its association with the Jungian unconscious.

+ + +

After my first pilgrimage to the Tanami in 1992, following the death of my father, I didn't return for several years. Instead I left the life I had established in North Queensland and went south, seeking out a different artistic environment, exploring some of the challenges the journey had raised. But I did go back several times to Alice Springs, re-forging a connection to the town and its surrounding country, picking up links from my past and discovering the community that had developed in the previous two decades.

Shortly before the first Tanami trip, I had shared an exhibition space in Sydney with Pam Lofts. She was a redhead when I met her, a weather-beaten beauty with a black retriever called Sam who sat sphinx-like in the gallery space watching Pam arrange the rusted metal artefacts and drawings and scrolls of text that comprised her installation. During the days that we spent installing our respective exhibitions, we discovered intersections and affinities in our art practices, and a shared preoccupation with the desert. My work, *Encampment*, was a diorama of wrapped figures and makeshift structures that had their origins in the myth of desert exploration and heroic failure. Pam's installation, called *Memories from the Desert*, documented her experience of time spent in Balgo working on a book about the lives of six women who had grown up in the Great Sandy Desert. She was about to buy a house and settle in Alice Springs, and invited me to use it as a base when I travelled through the Centre. So began a friendship and artistic partnership that was to span the next twenty years.

It was through Pam that I encountered the community of people who had been drawn to Alice Springs because of its proximity to Aboriginal Australia. Many of them were involved in the industries that had grown up around the Western Desert painting movement, the native title and land rights movements, and the health and cultural organisations that proliferated through the seventies and eighties. And there was a core group of white artists, of whom Pam was one, who brought a new sensibility to interpreting the desert. I was not entirely comfortable in this new community, but I no longer belonged to the old town of truck drivers and stock inspectors and station agents, or to the station people who came in from the bush for race meetings and the annual show. I still knew their language, I could visit and make a fair job of fitting in, but I couldn't sustain it. The two worlds didn't intersect. The ground between them was occupied by the Aboriginal people, who were linked through land and history to the pastoralists, and through self-interest and social politics to the artists and lawyers of the Alice Springs new wave.

Pam's house was a hub of visiting artists and friends, with her presiding at its centre like a radiant, irritable master of ceremonies, making us feel at once welcome and intrusive, essential to the creative energy she wanted to bring to the town, always on the brink of overstaying our welcome. Because she worked at home, she found the constant presence of other people an obstacle to getting her own work done, but a day without visitors would bring her out of her house looking for company.

Pam and I started making field trips to the eastern and western MacDonnell Ranges, and south to the edges of the Simpson Desert — walking, drawing, gathering materials, making transient sculptural works, developing the patterns that would carry us through more years and bush trips than we could have anticipated. Out bush, the domestic tensions of the house disappeared, and we developed an easy routine of work and talk. Breakfast, and Pam's morning coffee-making ritual — which took longer as her standards rose — was a time for conversation, as were the evenings over a bottle of wine and hand-rolled cigarettes. We talked of what the country meant to us and why we felt compelled to explore and interpret it. Although our work and the preoccupations that drove it were different, we shared a passion for the elusiveness and contradictions of the country, recognising each other as fellow travellers of the desert's difficult terrain.

The country around Alice was rich in possibilities, but we both had unfinished business with the Tanami. We applied for and got Australia Council funding to cover the cost of travel and materials, and embarked on the first of many projects that would take us back to the Tanami again and again. To begin with, we skirted the fringes of the Aboriginal world, touching down briefly in the disorder and squalor of the community camps to visit people, or to go on hunting trips with the Warlpiri and Ngardi custodians of Mongrel Downs. At some point it had been renamed Tanami Downs, but most of the local people still used the old name. The hunting trips were pure pleasure — hanging out with people in their own environment, walking, looking, paying attention. This wasn't so different from the way we spent our time as artists.

The communities, on the other hand, were confronting,

exhausting, and intimidating, and they produced in me an itch of discomfort I knew I'd have to scratch. I needed to go back to the source, to spend time among the people whose culture had been shaped by the desert, whose minds and bodies were the product of thousands of years of adaptation.

After years of passing through, of evasions and equivocations, the opportunity presented itself. Friends of mine were managing the Warlayirti art centre at Balgo in the south-east Kimberley, the community that had been a Catholic mission in the days when it had been my family's nearest neighbour. In exchange for voluntary work, I was offered a place to stay and the chance to explore some of my own preoccupations. It was a way of doing it without doing it too hard. I'd have my own vehicle, could take off when I chose, camp out, paint, abscond. I arranged to spend several months there, sub-let my studio, packed my swag and Slippers the dog into my battered blue Hilux, and drove across the continent to the junction of the Tanami and Great Sandy Deserts.

VERTIGO

Balgo, 2001

You can stand almost anywhere on the rotting sandstone rim of the Balgo Pound and feel the gut lurch of falling through time as well as through space. Although the drop in most places is no more than fifty metres, it taps an ancient fear of falling off the edge of the world, and the howl of sailors as their ships sail into nothing. This eroding plateau, high above the lacy grasses and ironstone gravels of the pound floor, was a seabed once. On days of blue distance, looking south, the remnant peaks and mesas resemble the waves of a turbulent sea.

The first thing I do when I arrive is visit the sorry camp, where Margaret Bumblebee and her family are in mourning for one of Margaret's sons, stabbed in a pub brawl to which he was a bystander. Margaret and her mother, Dora, are Ngardi people, whose country includes the southern part of Tanami Downs. Because of my childhood links to that country I have acquired the status of a family member. It's a year since I last saw them, when we went hunting together on the station, and they are happy to see me. There's no sign of Margaret's daughter Patricia, and somebody tells me she's over the border, NT-side.

I don't understand all the protocols of sorry business, and am uncomfortable with the ritual hugging and wailing, but I manage a modest display. Margaret and Dora are not permitted to leave the sorry camp, and are subject to traditional food prohibitions, so they are dependent on others to bring them the food they are allowed to eat.

—Hunt a *lungkurta* for me, Dora says.

Lungkurta, the blue-tongue lizard, is allowed, but not the other goannas, or beef. Fish is also acceptable, so I go to the store and buy tins of tuna, and a tin of Log Cabin tobacco for Margaret. Dora chuckles when I mime how I tracked the tins of tuna through the bush for her, chased them down and clubbed them with a crowbar.

—Bring me some more tomorrow, she says. *Lungkurta* next time.

I slip the tobacco to Margaret when no-one is looking, and she palms it into her pink vinyl handbag. There's not much chance she'll be able to conceal it for long, but she might get a few chews out of it before it becomes common property.

The art centre, run by my friends Tim Acker and Erica Izett, is a long, brown building on the western perimeter of the community. Beyond the fence that encloses the centre and a quadrangle of sand, the low wattle scrub extends to the graveyard where, in a certain light, against a backdrop of navy cloud, the white metal crosses look like a scene from Monty Python's *Life of Brian*.

Because the art centre is self-sustaining, earning a substantial income through the sale of paintings by its pre-eminent artists, it has been able to create its own governing structure and to make decisions based on the directives of its board members, who are all Aboriginal. There's an immense sense of pride and ownership among the Balgo artists and their families. But all of this is contingent on the commitment and energy of Erica and Tim, who work twelve-hour days, and on Erica's charismatic enthusiasm that attracts and sustains volunteers who, like me, put in months of unpaid labour. There are two other paid staff — Catriona, who works in the art centre, and Jo, who has been employed to co-ordinate the opening of a recently built culture centre. While the art centre is a commercial enterprise, the culture centre is to be a keeping place for traditional artefacts and a space in which to record and share knowledge and stories. I'm soon part of a close-knit team, the first of several that will be forged in the following years, with friendships honed by the extreme nature of shared experiences. It is the flip side of the poisonous antipathies that can also arise in these hothouse environments.

Erica pours herself into the place with profligacy. She is perpetually on the edge of exhaustion, a willing conduit in the negotiations of other people's complicated lives. The cry of 'Nungarrayi!', her skin name, begins from the moment she walks in the door, and echoes relentlessly until she leaves the building, when it is replaced by 'Where Nungarrayi?'

Skin names are part of the kinship system that designates where a person fits into the network of relationships and obligations which hold the society together. In the past, only very young white children were incorporated into this family system, but it has been extended in recent times to include those *kartiya* (whitefellas), like Erica, whose work brings them into close contact with Aboriginal people. The logic behind awarding particular skin names can be somewhat inscrutable, and may include subtle obligations of which the *kartiya* are ignorant.

Erica's job as director of the art centre is a balancing act, looking after the interests of the painters who produce the art and the buyers who purchase it, which involves everything from overseeing the mixing of preferred colours for particular artists to catering for the fly-in fly-out buyers. Among the photographs and reminder notes on her noticeboard, she has transcribed quotes from various sages about how to behave better, to be kinder and more generous, and to see the best in others. Erica, the most generous of women, says she is too busy to remember how to behave well, and needs to be constantly reminded. The quotes taped to her lavatory wall are longer and more prescriptive, assuming a longer attention span.

Tim is tall and quiet and competent. He's a little disengaged, as if he's paying attention to an alternative commentary only he can hear. Among the many challenges he faces in his role as the art centre manager is the application of a goods and services tax to the production and sale of the paintings. In these early days of the tax's implementation, the artists may be required to submit quarterly business activity statements to the tax department — a proposition so surreal that most of Tim's intellectual circuitry is caught in the perpetual loop of trying to distinguish the intractable from the impossible.

I camp on the verandah of Tim and Erica's house while I set up a living space in one of the art centre storerooms. The morning breeze carries the smell of sewage, and across the road a smouldering fire gives off the stink of burning plastic. An empty pram and an adjustable office-chair frame it in faintly sinister parentheses. In the foreground, lean dogs scratch and skulk, and dark people in bright clothes saunter, sit, and loiter, in a slow eddy of interaction and avoidance. The quiet is ripped open by the truncated screams of a camp dog under attack by its fellows — a glissade of syllables as precise and shocking as a spray of blood. The cur bolts in the direction of the store, pursued by the pack.

There's evidence everywhere of the whitefella siege mentality

— the high chain-link fences and padlocked gates around their houses, the alarms and locking devices on their cars, the welded steel cage around the petrol bowser. Next to a sign claiming Balgo as a 'Tidy Town', an empty cage designed to hold discarded aluminium drink cans is surrounded by an ironic pile of cans and other rubbish. Since I arrived I've been watching the progress of a pram cartwheeling in frame-by-frame animation across the community, shedding seat, wheels, and handles until it is reduced to a skeletal hieroglyph. Finally someone runs over it, and it lies in the road like a squashed bug.

I take on the job of stretching and priming canvases, for which there is endless demand. On a good day, an established artist can complete a painting, possibly two, and it requires production-line efficiency to prepare the canvases, decant the paint from large drums into small containers, photograph the finished work, record the associated story, catalogue the painting, remove it from the stretcher frame, and begin the process all over again. Apart from recording and cataloguing, which are Catriona and Erica's domain, I share all these tasks.

The senior painters work with extraordinary focus, but Eubena is in a category of her own. Day after day she sits on the floor of the art centre and covers big canvases with sweeping organic forms, swabbing on the paint with a broad, frayed brush. She works from an internal geography that manifests itself in an almost automatic sequence of marks and notations. To some extent, the same process is evident in all the older painters, but Eubena seems to absent herself from her surroundings, disappearing into the work. She is charged with a mysterious force, working fast and rhythmically, as if her physical being is travelling across the ground of the canvas. She doesn't speak, doesn't acknowledge the cups of tea we bring her, ignores suggestions that she should stop and eat something or go home because it's time to close the art centre. She makes no distinction between linen and cotton canvas, best quality or ordinary paint. That is our job — to watch every move, and to make sure the materials are of the highest quality, her preferred colours are already mixed, and she has everything she needs. She churns them out, signature works, the same painting over and over. And why not? It's the same bit of country, and the *kartiya* are willing to buy anything she paints.

There's fierce demand for the paintings from collectors and dealers. Eubena supports an extended family network who make frequent claims on her for cars and money. From time to time, when the humbug becomes unbearable, she charters a plane to fly her down to the tiny outstation in the desert near her ancestral home. This is preceded by her visiting Erica in a state of agitation, ranting and muttering until she has built up a head of steam intense enough to make the decision to leave. At these times her appearance is alarming; her extraordinary head like an Aztec carving, her eyes set so far back that only a sliver of bloodshot white is visible. She crouches at the end of the dining table, her voice rising into strident laments. Erica sits close and embraces her, and the old woman lays her head on Erica's bosom and murmurs like a sorrowful child.

I understand little of my conversations with Eubena, but I make sounds of acquiescence and encouragement. She has designs on my vehicle, and I come out of these conversations unnerved by the prospect that I may have agreed to sell it to her. Language, or its lack, is a constant thread in the web of crossed wires and compromises of daily intercourse. The old painters were born in the desert, and didn't encounter whites until they were adolescents or young adults. We converse with them in whoops and exclamations, a child-like language of mime and exaggeration. For people like Erica, to whom it comes naturally, a great bond of affection is forged. To me, whose currency is words, this behaviour feels artificial and patronising. I sometimes wonder if these people think the *kartiya* are a race of demented children.

Kartiya means white, but it might as well mean stranger or outsider. Skin names notwithstanding, one does not cross the barrier of whiteness. I struggle through half-understood conversations, even with people whose English is good. We rely on goodwill and humour to get us through.

Tjumpo believes the art centre belongs to him. He was one of the last of the desert people to come in to the Mission. Drought caused his people to abandon their country on the edge of the great salt lake, but to all intents and purposes he lives there still, his old mind marooned in the enchantment of heat and light. He haunts the art centre at all hours. Though the scale of his paintings taxes his physical frailty and his increasingly senile brain, he can't leave them alone. The dimensions of his memory have no boundaries. I suspect that faced with a canvas twice the size, he would continue to paint his shivering rectangles until they faltered off the edge.

Tjumpo's geometric renderings of the salt-lake country where he was born are vertiginous fields of energy, triggering the cognitive shifts that happen when faced with the peculiar absence of perspective produced by the salt lakes. There's a quality of heatwave and mirage one gets just standing in front of them. That isn't the whole of it, of course — there's some deeper organising principle at work that eludes me. He does a white painting, starting with a black ground, like the black mud beneath the salt surface, and paints the whole thing in shades of white. When I look at it, the subtle modulations of tone that run through it, it makes me feel that I occupy different levels of light, held simultaneously in more dimensions than I'm used to. It's like being suspended horizontally above expanding lines of energy, at the centre of which a small black rectangle tilts at gravity like a cosmic negative. It is almost impossible to look at.

A planeload of buyers is flying in, and we are all co-opted into the flurry of preparation that precedes their arrival. There's a re-hang of paintings to show the new work to advantage, and unstretched canvases are laid out on large tables. Works by Eubena and Tjumpo, Helicopter, Lucy Yukenbarri, Nyumi, and Boxer Milner — the much-in-demand elder painters whose work graces collections all over the world — are grouped together. Then there are the mid-range artists and the emerging artists whose work can be purchased for a bargain price by someone with a good eye.

Erica rushes about, directing operations. She thrusts a roll of paintings at me.

—Napurrula darling, put these away somewhere.

—I thought selling them to buyers was the point.

—They're for the big competitions. There's a couple of buyers in this lot who won't take no for an answer, so it's easier if they don't see the paintings in the first place.

I take the canvases to the storeroom where I now have a bunk bed and a work table, and stash the roll under my bed.

Tim collects the buyers from the airstrip and brings them to the art centre, where they are offered morning tea. The woman pilot is also a successful dealer, and she doesn't waste time on the morning tea, but makes straight for the pile of canvases on the premier painters' table. After half an hour of examining the paintings, one of the buyers saunters towards the section of the art centre that contains the kitchen and bathroom, as well as the two rooms that serve as accommodation and storerooms. When she sees me following her, she indicates that she needs to visit the toilet. I wait behind the door of the paint storage room and watch as she comes back along the corridor, glances about furtively, and sneaks into my room.

—Excuse me, I say, that's my bedroom.

She looks startled, but continues to scan the room, and shows no signs of leaving it.

—I thought this was a storeroom, she says.

—It is, I say, but it's also my bedroom, and either way it's private.

—What's that? she says, pointing to the roll of canvases under the bed.

—That's a roll of rejects, I say.

Against the wall is a large primed canvas on a stretcher frame, and I pick it up and manoeuvre her through the door with it. Naked greed is something I'm not familiar with, and the sight of it is hilariously disgraceful. The buyer, who is short and round, scuttles ahead of me while I make shooing noises and shake the canvas at her. I lock the door once I've got her out of the room. Erica shoots me a glance, and I give her the thumbs up.

Catriona and I walk out of the art centre, laughing, and into the path of a payback party setting out to avenge the killing of Margaret's son. They have pulled up near the verandah in a tray-back truck, their faces erased with white ochre. The dead man's brother-in-law is painted up and sitting in the doorless cabin, his massive body in its coating of white ochre dignified and terrible. We avert our eyes and hurry past. But the image stays with me — the monstrous ash-coloured body in the doorless cabin of the truck, the mask-like faces of the women hunkered down on the back among bedding and crowbars. There is an irreconcilable core here that we blunder around, peripheral and irrelevant.

Walking side by side, Catriona and Jo look like a pair of exclamation marks, one dark-haired, one fair, both stick thin. Jo has a single-minded focus that will brook no distractions. Behind a dry, self-effacing humour she is wound tight, marching through an impossible spectrum of tasks, munching through chocolate bars and Minties, her brain ticking like a metronome; this is done, this is still to do, that must be planned.

—This culture centre is built on Minties, she says.

Jo, Catriona, and Erica all ingest energy as pure sugar, in the form of chocolate and sweets, which they must burn up instantly, because there's not an ounce of fat on any of them.

Erica suggests I help out with the women's mosaic that is being laid down at the entrance to the art centre. The enthusiasm for it has petered out until only its instigator, Lucy, is left day after day sticking down the bits of broken tile. I'm happy to sit on the concrete slab breaking tiles and mixing grout while Lucy tells me stories of the mission days when she was a girl.

—We knew how to work then. If we don't work, we get a good hiding. Those old nuns used to lock us in the dormitory, try to stop the boys coming around.

Lucy wheezes with laughter. Her de facto, Frank, stops by every couple of hours in an ancient van, chauffeuring a group of old men for whom he has taken responsibility. His fair skin is greasy with ingrained grime, his eyes an anxious lambent green. He speaks a coarse Kriol with a flawless ear for the inverted consonants of Aboriginal English.

—Dem pucken fetrol snippers, he says. Dey fin platten de fattery in my ban.

The old men shuffle their frail stick limbs to climb in or out of the van. Frank buzzes around them like an angry insect, his voice ratcheting up several notches of outrage as he explains that it is only through his concern for their welfare that they ever get to go anywhere.

An encounter with Frank is the verbal equivalent of falling into a cement mixer, but he assists the old men with exquisite gentleness, shepherding them, anticipating obstacles, taking the arms of the blind and lame to negotiate the steps. Frank's childhood was spent on a mission where he encountered a rarefied form of Jesuitical Catholicism that his simple and hungry soul absorbed at the expense of all other forms of social behaviour. He understands injustice in ways inaccessible to people like me, and his concern for the old men is obsessive and altruistic. Through the staccato racket of their protector's commentary, they totter and smile with impervious sweetness.

—I bin pick 'im up in the Roebuck pub, Lucy remarks. Might be I'll take 'im back soon.

The story the mosaic depicts, as far as I can make out, is a generic women's account of finding, gathering, and preparing bush food. There are sandhills and waterholes and coolamons and camp sites; but if there is a larger organising principle to the story, Lucy is keeping it to herself. She designates certain sections for me to work on, and I fit my part of the pattern together like a jigsaw, spending hours sorting through the fragments for the right colours and shapes. In the end, my sections are heavy looking, too tidy, without the airy spaces that float around Lucy's designs. Lucy sticks her bits of tile down with arbitrary style, and fills the gaps with grout, creating a pattern full of air and light.

While we work on the mosaic, the men paint a *Tingari* ceremonial mural on the side of the building — a vast web of linked sites that represents the conceptual terrain they carry with them from the homelands they have left. Senior painter Tjumpo has his own wall and his own assistant, a Catholic volunteer called Daniel who has come north to explore his relationship with God and blackfellas. I watch Daniel filling in neat circles around Tjumpo's blobs and swathes, tidying up the exuberant energy of the old painter's marks.

It's what we do, I think. *We try to tidy them up, we can't seem to help it.*

The circles drip and run, and Daniel dabs ineffectually at the congealing paint, making ugly smears. Tjumpo examines the mess Daniel has made, laughs, and takes a loaded brush and slaps it over the botched area with painterly authority, to which Daniel concedes with good grace.

As it nears completion, I wonder again about the provenance of the mosaic. There's something ad hoc about the way Lucy works, as if she's making it up as she goes along. And it is slowly emerging that Lucy is not quite accepted by the Balgo population. She is better educated than most of the locals, having completed her secondary education at boarding school and trained to be a bilingual teacher.

I piece together her backstory during the hot, meditative afternoons while the two of us glue and grout, and Lucy murmurs a monologue of the defining events of her life, a meandering tale of displacement and resilience, of husbands and children and provisional adjustments to circumstance.

—My people are Jaru, Lucy says.

—I went back to my country, but I didn't know my language.

—I couldn't speak for my country, so I came back here.

She works intermittently in the adult education centre, teaching people how to write in Kukatja, the language that has become dominant among the half-dozen languages people brought with them from their respective countries. In recent years she has turned her hand to painting, producing odd hybrids of naturalistic images of birds and animals embedded in fields of dots. To my eye, they are decorative without being naïve, lacking the abstract forcefulness of the mosaic. The process that has triggered in me an obsessive tidiness has loosened and leavened Lucy's style.

Erica tells me that Lucy's mosaic is driven by gender politics, to balance a men's mosaic on the art centre verandah that describes the activities of two ancestral brothers as they travel across half a continent. The men's story represents a powerful dreaming track that passes through the country of all the significant language groups, and was completed by the men in a sustained collaboration over several days. But the women's mosaic is a diplomatic compromise that lacks an anchoring narrative to enlist the authority and sustain the involvement of the local matriarchs.

Walking to Erica's house at lunchtime, I encounter one of Frank's old men escaped from his minder and lying on his back on the path between clumps of high grass. He is chuckling to himself, and smiles at me when I bend down to help him up.

—Can't get up, he says. I bin fall down on my back like a beetle.

I get him to his feet and help him back to the pensioners' house, where he's greeted like a returning warrior by the rest of the old men.

—Thank you Napurrula, they call. Thank you for bringing back our brother.

On a day when the mosaic is almost finished, there's a flurry of interest from some young women, who descend like a flock of noisy birds. I've developed a proprietorial attitude towards the mosaic, and would prefer to drive them away, but Lucy is delighted. She invites the girls to help, and they set to with enthusiastic anarchy. In an hour the thing is done, the last spaces filled and smeared messily with grout, which I scour off as the girls rise screeching and flap away, leaving Lucy ecstatic and me shell-shocked.

Completed, it's beautiful. What the girls have done lends my sections of the work a compressed intensity that opens out into a gaiety of broken colour. The mosaic lacks the stark integrity of the men's dreaming story, but it has an ambiguous delicacy in which Lucy's breathing designs weave around my obsessively rendered details, the whole thing irradiated by the mad energy of the girls.

+ + +

Patricia comes through the door of the art centre and stands very still, casting her eyes over the long room. Her hair stands out in a dusty fuzz, its colour obscured by traces of red ochre. She is very dirty, her clothes a grimy, indeterminate grey, and she smells of smoke and meat and sweat. She brings with her into the orderly environment of the centre a pulse of something unsubdued, intransigent, on high alert. The side of her mouth is swollen, as if she has been hit.

When she sees me, she smiles.

—I heard you was here, she says. I drove all night. The car broke down but some tourists came past and helped me.

I had not expected to see her, having heard on the community grapevine that she had left her husband and was living with a white man in Katherine. I rush to embrace her, embarrassing her, and the gulf opens for a moment, and closes again. I step back.

—When did you get here?

—Last night. I heard you was here, she says again, and I feel helpless in the face of whatever it is that she expects of me. Between us hovers something that is not quite friendship, which stems from an awareness of the ambivalent ground we occupy. Our shared connection to country carries with it some form of mutual obligation, the nature of which I am uncertain. Within the intricate structures of the kinship system, Patricia is my daughter. My skin name of Napurrula, acquired as a baby on the Warlpiri settlement at Hooker Creek, makes me Dora's daughter and Margaret's sister. The serendipity of being a Napurrula means that I belong to the skin group with traditional links to Tanami Downs. The site where I was 'born' has been pointed out to me. Nothing I say alters this story.

Patricia is literate in three or four languages, including English, but this has not displaced her pre-literate sensibility, endowing her with an unsettling, turbulent perceptiveness from which she escapes into monumental drinking sprees. She looks tired, a little heavier and more shop-worn than the last time I saw her. She has come back for her brother's funeral, which is to take place in a few days.

—Where are you staying? I ask her.

—Women's centre. Come and see me later.

There is a tough intelligence in Patricia, of a kind that is accessible to whites and makes her popular as a negotiator, although there are some who don't trust her. They suspect her of having an agenda of her own, and in this they are probably correct. All the knowledge she has learned from her grandmother, born in the bushman days, and from her mother, first-degree law woman anchored in the immutable authority of the desert, has been invested in her. She has a task to do, straddling the irreconcilable worlds she was born into. To make of those incompatibilities some manageable compromise is not enough for her. What she wants is not clear, but I know that I figure somewhere in her plans.

Later, when I visit her at the women's centre, she asks me to take her family on a trip back to Tanami Downs.

—We should visit all the places, she says. Places we didn't go since I was born. You should know that country Aboriginal way.

—Yes, I say, I should.

With the funeral over and the sorry camp finished, Margaret and Dora are keen to go hunting for *karnti,* a type of yam, so I take the day off and we head out in my Hilux, along with Tjama, Maudie, and Nanyuma, nicknamed Shorty, who is not much over four feet high. The ground is too moist to show the cracks that indicate the presence of the underground tubers, and only Dora, old desert woman, can find them. Margaret sets some country alight, and the wind springs up suddenly as if unleashed by the fire, black smoke boiling up out of the spinifex. I am worried for Dora on the other side of the burning ground, so Margaret knocks the top off an anthill with her crowbar and stands on it.

—Maybe I cooked my mother, she says. Then she chuckles and points in the direction of the road.

—That Shorty one coming up the road look like anthill running along.

We look in the direction Margaret indicates, and there's Nanyuma coming along the road, her bobbing head barely clearing the height of the windrow, with Maudie wheezing along behind her.

They arrive panting and cross, having had to scurry out to the road to escape the flames, and four-foot-six Nanyuma threatens six-foot Margaret with a hiding. When Dora makes her way back across the tract of burned ground with her billycan full of *karnti*, the story is retold with much laughter.

—Naparrula was worried, Margaret says. He think might be I cooked you.

I think how different it would have been if three elderly white women had been out there in the path of a raging spinifex fire. These women are my role models for ageing — fierce and fearless and funny.

When I drop them back to the women's centre, Patricia is lying unconscious beside the gate. Up close, she stinks of alcohol.

—Should I get somebody? I ask, but the women shake their heads and motion me to leave. Driving away, I glance back at the group by the gate and see Margaret take hold of her daughter's limp hand, raise it, and lower it again with a kind of helpless sorrow.

I have been working in the art centre for a month when Eubena decides to take one of her breaks back in her home country. There's a spare seat on the plane, and the pilot has to return to Balgo to refuel, so Erica suggests that I hitch a ride and see some of the country to the south.

Seen from the air, Balgo looks like one of J.G. Ballard's post-apocalyptic fictions, the sort of place in which his stunted archetypes play out their end-of-the-world hallucinations. A cluster of tin roofs surrounded by dead cars occupies a tract of dusty red earth, at the centre of which the blunt spire of the church gestures upwards like a clenched fist. To the west lies the graveyard, invaded by wattle and the porcupine spinifex hordes of *Triodia basedowii*. Rows of white crosses, constructed from steel pipe so that they won't be devoured by termites, mark the stony grave mounds on which bright artificial flowers vie with the purple candelabras of *Ptilotus exaltatus*, a colonising pussytail that thrives on disturbed ground. At an equal distance to the east, like a counterweight, is the rubbish tip, stinking and smouldering and haunted by scavenging dogs. To the south, not visible from most parts of the community but felt as a kind of ambient vertigo, the fretted edge of the ancient sandstone shelf gives way to the eroded moonscape of the pound.

I'm transfixed by the great mosaic below — the parallel scars of the sand-ridges, which resemble the cicatrices of traditional body scarring, running east-west in a geographic code of wind and time; the silver swatches of ephemeral water that lie between the dunes after this season of excessive rain. The land is patterned with transparent shadows — old fire-scars over which the flexing weave of spinifex casts a subtle contour of dots. As we approach the outstation, the smoke of several fires becomes visible, and the new scars of recently burned ground. The smoke rises in a dark plume until it encounters an atmospheric layer into which it flattens and spreads, making visible the masses and currents of the air.

There's no-one waiting to meet the plane. Eubena and the two old ladies who have accompanied her settle in the shade under the wing with their baggage, while the pilot checks the aircraft. At ground level, the country appears flat, covered in low vegetation and spinifex. Apart from the colour of the soil — a rich, oxidised orange stippled with the purplish-black of varnished ironstone — the landscape is nondescript. But the weeks of watching the painters at work have refined my perception. The ground itself has become mysterious, nuanced with meaning.

I walk to the edge of the airstrip and stand under the vaulting air, turning slowly to take in the full circle of the horizon. The pilot and his plane are one entity, the women crouched under the wing another, and I am a third. The thread that connects us is tenuous, almost non-existent. If I walk a few metres, just beyond the range of vision, it will snap. The possibility fills me with an edgy excitement.

A ribbon of dust signals an approaching vehicle. When it arrives, Eubena wraps her wiry arms around my waist and lays her head on my shoulder. The embrace is difficult to interpret — it's not affection, but it is a leave-taking of some kind. Her old body feels bony and tough. The young man at the wheel nods perfunctorily at me while I help the women into the back and stow their bundles.

On the return flight, the sun dissolves the western horizon and detaches the silver discs of water from the earth, so that they float in the same dimension as the tiny aircraft. The light is golden and diffused, and we rush through it in a roaring silence. When I step out of the plane, I have a curious sense of the desert as a presence in my body, as if in my trajectory across it I have absorbed it, and must now carry it with me.

One of my jobs at the art centre is to photograph the finished paintings for cataloguing, using a digital camera, and learning the basics of cropping and adjusting images. My understanding of digital technology is primitive and experimental, but there's something about the relationship between the pixellated image and the use of dotting that provokes me to borrow the camera and take photographs of the surrounding landscape. There's a correlation between the spectrum of saturated digital colours and the vivid acrylic colours preferred by most of the painters. I sit up at night and tweak and crop my photographs on the art centre computer, until I've created fractured landscapes of intense pinks and magentas, lemony greens and cyan and cobalt blues. This manipulation of photographs is a new tool, and it's appropriate that I should discover it out here. And timely, because the authority of the paintings to which I'm being exposed every day is infiltrating my own perceptions to an alarming degree. They make such perfect sense, Tjumpo's layers of light, Eubena's shimmering weave of tracks. These embodied representations of country threaten to overwhelm whatever tentative intuitions I'm trying to formulate, teasing out the root of the difference between how I've been taught to interpret the world, and this other multi-layered response to the physicality of place. It's not so much a visual landscape as a place, a pattern, a story. If you spend enough time you begin to feel the patterns of the country you are walking on. It's there, under the feet, under the skin. It ripples and shudders, so that the story you tell is subtly altered, the pattern you make is stretched and distorted, and something else shows through.

I think about what Eubena and Tjumpo bring to their painting — childhoods in which the land was the supermarket and cathedral and school and pharmacy and playground, and white men were still a rumour of ghosts. The same ghosts, who turned out to be dangerously made of flesh and blood, later provided the means by which a new vocabulary of country could be written in paint on canvas — a set of notations drawn from a shared consciousness and channelled through the skills of particular individuals, so that the work has the authority of an embodied, collective expression. It's difficult, in the face of this sort of authenticity, to give weight to my own work. It's only the fact that I can't leave it alone that keeps me gnawing at this particular bone.

At the end of each day I collect the small plastic containers left by the artists, and recycle the paint into jars of separate colours. Until now I've always painted in oils or watercolour, disliking the strident colour and plastic texture of acrylics. But this paint is of the best artist's quality, and wastage offends the frugality forced on me by years as a struggling artist. With Erica's permission, I claim the recycled paint, along with offcuts of Belgian linen. Using stretchers of a popular eighty-by-thirty centimetre format, I stretch and prime several small canvases. The format is counter-intuitive, because I plan to use the canvases vertically to explore ideas about the horizon. After walking around them for several days with no idea of how to begin, I load them into my vehicle with a selection of paints, water, Slippers the dog, and a thermos of tea, and drive down into the pound.

There's no shade, and the flies are active, but the discomfort triggers in me a kind of desperate energy. The edge of the cliffs breaks against the sky like a wave. I score it in with hard strokes of the brush, an emphatic horizontal that differentiates my approach from the local Aboriginal concentration on ground and surface. This seems important. Although my own perceptions have undergone all sorts of modifications, I know that the horizon is more than a visual dimension. It is as much a symbol in its way as the concentric circles and lines that indicate sites and routes, and it's a symbol to which I can lay claim. The horizon is one of the perceptual faultlines that runs between white and Aboriginal ways of understanding country. There's an assumption among white observers of traditional Aboriginal painting that the horizon is absent. But it is omnipresent, hovering in the space around the paintings. If you sit beside the painters while they work, you feel the horizon all around you. The strangeness is in our habit of hanging the paintings on walls, which must provoke a sense of vertigo, seeing the ground so precariously tilted. Desert paintings are not closed. Laid on the ground, they become part of the earth, open-sided, leading off to connected journeys.

I try to catch the mysterious blur of the cliffs to the south-east and the black smear of a burn scorched into the spinifex, the bleached light and passages of impenetrable shadow. The hot, flat colours and the plastic finish of the paint are repellent, and the speed at which it dries makes subtlety impossible. My distaste opens onto the canvas in fractured forms that are both disturbing and exciting. The paint has to go on fast without mixing — magentas and oxides and acid greens and crimsons.

The pound defies definition. It's about wind and stone and emptiness and light and heat. I imagine a series of vertical panels with almost nothing in them — hard surfaces, empty space, horizon lines. But the underlying forms are feminine. Beneath the sandstone cap of the plateau, the collapsing rubble spills down in voluptuous curves, like a chorus line of full-skirted dancers spinning in a long arc from north to south. The hills are breasts topped with stony nipples; the yellow grass makes lacy patterns at the base of the cliffs; the spinifex softens the contours of everything with a spiky fuzz. Everywhere is pattern and repetition. Perspective, created by the receding and diminishing hummocks of spinifex, has a hallucinatory quality.

This country displaces assumptions, resists meanings. All the ideas I've brought with me are made insubstantial by the reality of the place. The country is green and full of strange light, which makes it difficult to see.

A large satellite transparency, purchased for the art centre and installed by Tim on a lightbox designed for the purpose, generates immediate and sustained interest among the older painters. It shows a vast tract of country that includes Balgo and most of the traditional lands of Balgo's resident population. Tjumpo identifies his lake and begins to track his way across the map, naming sites and describing their characteristics, invoking the ancestors who made them and singing wavering fragments to himself. Eubena, returned from her holiday in the deep desert, is brought in by one of her daughters. She peers for a moment at the illuminated expanse of country before breaking into a radiant smile and touching the map with long, articulate fingers. Watching the two old people, the tender precision of their hands that have a creature intelligence of their own, tracking the contours of their dreaming across this piece of contemporary technology, I wonder that they can read it so easily. Erica says the old people talk about flying over their country in their dreams.

People gather and confer. Young people who have never visited their family homelands are brought in and shown the architecture of their bloodlines. Tjumpo can't stay away. Time and again he sets down his brushes, levers himself upright from the canvas on which he is working, and makes his way back to examine the luminous replica of his country. Neither can I leave it alone. I stand beside the old man and wonder what he sees. What I see, with a kind of astonished recognition, is a design wrought on the earth by water, fire, and air. It is all movement, the wind made visible in the fine corduroy of the dunes, as if a master calligrapher has taken up a brush and swept it, every hair separate and distinct, in parallel strokes from right to left. Across the grain of the wind, the ancient waterways nudge through the dune fields like the ancestral snakes to which they are attributed. Within their contours, the salt lakes are strips of ragged lace, the ripped hems of petticoats uncoiling from dancing girls. The fire scars sweep across the country like the shadows of carnivorous birds.

Catriona and I move out of the art centre and down to the 'motel', with its view of the cliffs mediated through several layers of weldmesh verandah and chain-link fence. The kids have broken in at some point, because someone has scratched 'get pucked' on the wall in the lavatory. It makes me chuckle and think of the homilies on Erica's lavatory wall every time I see it.

Mostly we have the place to ourselves, but visiting tradesmen and consultants stay here from time to time. The tradesmen travel in matching pairs. The Telstra technicians are stocky and rotund, with tattoos and ponytails. The plumbers are leaner, laconic, as if the effluvia they deal with has clogged the outlets for all but the most basic communication. The architects wear glasses, and ask questions about Aboriginal art, and watch ABC television rather than the commercial channels preferred by the others.

Sitting in the partial shelter of the motel verandah, the wind ripping past in a cold gale, I watch the morning parade of vehicles go past. The first gives off a nasty clunking sound, and I can see something rotating in the vicinity of the diff. The next goes by fast in a cloud of dust, emitting a high-pitched whine, a long-haired yellow dog standing on the bonnet with its muzzle pointing into the wind. The third is driven by manpower, four grinning young men pushing while the driver hangs a lazy arm out of the window. He waves, a slow ironic salute, and I wave back. Beyond the road, in the spinifex at the edge of the pound, a boy in a bright-red jacket rides a bicycle, bouncing and flying across the tussocks with joyful exuberance.

This flawed, volatile place is a hub around which the energy of the desert swirls, a company of people who in the past would have gathered in such numbers and from so many directions only at times of major ceremony. Created in the beginning by the good intentions of its Pallottine Catholic founding fathers as a refuge for displaced people, it was displaced from one location after another, to fetch up finally on this brink.

Established as a refuge from the frontier, it became itself a kind of frontier, the vanguard of an attempt to save heathen souls. The heathens, whose souls belonged to specific locations and could not be given up, said and did what was required of them to gain access to the reliable food supply, and began to perfect the art of passive resistance. Rumours penetrated into the deep desert, and by increments it emptied, its people mobilised by curiosity and the prospect of food and novelty. Of those who came in of their own volition, some stayed, some went back to their country and used the Mission as a fall-back when their own resources were scarce, and some preferred the stations, in spite of the hard work and harsh conditions, because they did not interfere in the spiritual and cultural practices that people brought with them.

This autonomy came to an end with the establishment of the dormitory system, which operated between 1951 and 1973. Children were taken from their families and installed in gender-segregated dormitories. In the spirit of government attitudes of the day, the Mission implemented a program that assumed the right to take children from their families and educate and train them. In order to stay close to their children, the adults curtailed their wandering, with some settling permanently at the Mission, and others coming and going on a regular basis. For most of them it meant that life in the remote desert was over. The incarceration of the children in the dormitories produced a literate generation, a generation that emerged with a work ethic compatible with white expectations and a range of skills to which this ethic could be applied. The methods that achieved this result were authoritarian, often to the point of cruelty, and achieved at the same time a fracture in the social and cultural life that has never healed. The dormitory system broke the family structures and severed links to language and country, and could not in the end provide enough to replace what it had broken.

The stamp of the Mission is still strong, although Balgo ceased to be a mission twenty years ago. Sometime in the early seventies an enlightened priest took notice of the fact that in the past half-century there had been few converts to Catholicism, and understood that coercion and the banning of traditional practices did not produce enthusiasm for conversion, and only drove the traditional practices underground. The subsequent opening up of the Catholic ritual to include elements of Aboriginal tradition saw a flowering of inter-cultural religious activity and a rush of baptisms. As a result, a union evolved between the Rainbow Serpent and the Holy Trinity, a confluence of iconic contradictions that even a religious sceptic like me finds irresistible, a hybrid spirituality that rests as much on the theatre of its rituals as on the seduction of its teachings, not to mention a mutual pragmatism. But more than that, the common ground is in the stories, especially the Old Testament stories with their violent, prophetic characters, their retributions and betrayals, their arbitrary and punitive laws, which have the same persuasive authenticity as the Dreaming. Maybe what people need now are contemporary stories with the same mythic force, to show them how to live in the modern world.

And the Catholics are still here. They're the constant factor. Every new government claims it's going to close the gap between white and black Australia, and throws money and rhetoric at the problem while achieving little, and meanwhile the Catholics step into whatever breach is opened up — educational, medical, spiritual. They patch up the bodies and the souls day after day, year after year, educate the children after a fashion, and bury the ubiquitous dead, whose names they know and whose lives they've borne witness to.

Erica, Catriona, Jo, and I make a trip with a group of senior women south into the desert to gather materials and stories for the new culture centre. Among the women who accompany us are Tjama, Payi Payi, and Marti, whose stories Pam documented, in collaboration with the first Balgo women's co-ordinator, Sonja Peter, in *Yarrtji: six women's stories from the Great Sandy Desert*. The women are custodians of the Nakarra Nakarra dreaming track, a section of the Seven Sisters itinerary that crosses continents and cultures. The Seven Sisters travel under many names — the Greek Pleiades, the Hindu Krittika, the Swahili Kilimia. In Australia they have as many names as there are languages to speak them — in the western desert they are called Minyipura, Kungkarangkalpa, Jakulyukulyu. Among the Ngardi and Kukatja they are the Nakarra Nakarra.

On the way south we call in to a small outstation and collect the local custodians, an extended family of big powerful women and slender flighty men. They move as a single entity, like homing torpedoes. Set them in any direction and they are unstoppable, pointing out the *Tjukurrpa* everywhere, gathering bush tucker and bush medicine, setting fire to the spinifex, digging for goannas, demonstrating the uses of termite mound and the technique for making bush sandals. Erica asks if they can make a number-seven boomerang, a lethal hunting weapon that cartwheels along the ground. The wood must be cut from the junction between the trunk and root of suitable trees. Within minutes several cork-barked hakeas have been partially wrenched from the ground, examined, and all but one rejected. This is dug and crowbarred up, and the appropriate section chopped out.

—I hope you're taking karmic responsibility for the trees being sacrificed to this culture centre, I say to Erica, joking, and she looks stricken. Later, I see her trying to set one of the trees back in the ground and pack the displaced soil around its roots.

Payi Payi sits near me on the crest of a dune and begins to sing. She is short and square, and wears a viridian jacket with pink stripes and a plum-coloured velvet skirt. Against the oxide red of the sand she glows like an iridescent beetle. Around her the parrot-shaped green flowers of *Crotalaria cunninghamii* nod their beaks in sentient appreciation, and the yellow spikes of sandhill grevillea rear like antipodean triffids above the sheaves of seeding spinifex. At the base of the dune is a billabong, full from the recent rains, its surface a glinting shiver of light. The men have lit the spinifex to flush a goanna, and the air smells of burning resin. The crackle of fire and the distant sound of children's voices play counterpoint to a larger silence. I am sharply aware of the solid squat powerhouse of the woman beside me, the translucent perfection of the green *crotalaria* flowers, the luminous fine grains of sand that cling to my fingers, the light that seems to penetrate the surfaces of flesh and plants and soil, isolating them in a radiant clarity. Payi Payi's song travels along my nerves like neuralgia, triggering an inchoate sense of what it was like to live always in this light and silence. A moment of déjà vu strips my mind of all but an intense aware-ness of *being* this place. The experience is gone almost before it registers.

The hills of Nakarra Nakarra are astonishingly feminine, like a cluster of breasts garlanded with dwarf native pine. We pick our way across their curved slopes while the women recount the events that brought the Seven Sisters to this place. I have a curious sensation of walking in the shared mindscape of the women who have brought me here. They are themselves in the here and now, and they are the sisters that exist as features of the landscape; simultaneously individual modern beings and the embodiment of ancient collective presences manifest as the sacred geography of their world. That world is shaped and imprinted with encounters between the Nakarra Nakarra and the Wati Kujarra, the two ancestral brothers with whom the sisters skirmish in a gendered landscape charged with the pressure points of pursuit and escape, deceit and challenge. The women steal sacred objects from the men, they flee, they return, they succumb. Sex occurs, though whether it is rape or complicit is difficult to tell.

At dinner camp, Catriona and Jo do a mad chook dance — two skinny white girls flapping their elbows and lifting their bony knees, squawking and shrieking with the wild pleasure of the past few days. The Aboriginal onlookers think it's hilarious.

A hot Sunday stillness has fallen on the community, penetrating even into the air-conditioned sanctuary of the art centre. The canvases crowding each other on the walls bring the surrounding country inside more pervasively when the people are absent, the arbitrary boundaries created by the rectangular format turning them into fragments excised from the landscape. I've locked the doors in order to spend the afternoon painting. I'm desperate for silence, for privacy, for the space to process the images accumulating behind my eyes. There's a hammering on the door, and shouting. I recognise Tjumpo's voice, and ignore it. Whatever is troubling him is not my business. The art centre is closed, and my time is my own. Later, I learn that one of the senior men, using power tools to make traditional artefacts, had sliced his thigh, and it bled badly. He is gracious when I apologise for not opening the door to Tjumpo, who was seeking help for him.

—I thought it was kids, I say, although this is not true. I can't tell him that in that particular moment nothing had mattered more to me than the need to shut out the world he occupied.

Most mornings, I walk with Tim and the dogs to the edge of the pound and inhale the shudder of vertigo as a bracing reminder of the faultline on which we live. The horizon shifts in and out of focus — now near, now far, a mirage in the blue air. A moment of inattention and you're falling, into the gap between ways of being and knowing, into someone you don't recognise.

ANXIETY AND DESIRE

Tanami, 1996

Pam was always good at titles. *Anxiety and Desire* was what she called the body of work she produced from the first two field trips we made to the Tanami, and it flagged the ambivalence with which her whole artistic oeuvre was inflected. She had moved to Alice Springs and established a home there because it brought her closer to the traditional Aboriginal world and a landscape that both unnerved and attracted her. The country aroused in her an existential longing that was assuaged to some degree by spending time in it, but she was troubled by its inherent discomforts and hazards. Among the work she produced for *Anxiety and Desire* was a series of exquisite large drawings of *Solanum diversifolium*, a bush tomato that bears fruit encased in spikes. One of the most important and prolific bush foods, it is almost impossible to pick without drawing blood. Of the varieties of *Solanum* with fruits that aren't protected in this way, several are poisonous, and if eaten will make you sick.

Pam's experience of the country had been mediated through her contact with Aboriginal people, and her work focused on the incompatibilities between white and indigenous ways of inhabiting the land. She believed that the right of white people to belong in country that was already occupied was compromised, and was troubled by her own desire to find a way to live in a place for which she felt a deep affinity but to which she did not belong. She brought to her art practice a sensibility trained in theories of deconstruction and post-colonialism, and saw the imposition of white, predominantly male, culture — in the form of cattle stations and mining — as inherently destructive. While her empathy lay with the Aboriginal culture, there was plenty about it that troubled her, too, especially in its contemporary, dislocated, and violent manifestations.

I was after something different — the rediscovery and remaking of my own track among the multiple tracks that inscribe the Tanami. That my track included a childhood associated with the colonising cattle-station culture made for some challenging moments between us. I could step into the persona of someone for whom the station world was natural and familiar — although it always cost me something to take it on — and while Pam appreciated the access it gave us, she was never quite reconciled to the fact that I could do it. My familiarity with the country, and the practical skills I had acquired growing up in it, allowed us a freedom of movement that would not otherwise have been possible, and the irony of this did not escape her. Neither did the recognition that Tanami Downs now belonged to the Warlpiri traditional owners, who maintained a proud proprietorial investment in its continued viability as a cattle station.

+ + +

The first Tanami trip was the toughest, when the fundamental differences in our philosophies of country came into play. This was Pam's first encounter with cattle-station culture, and it reinforced all her preconceptions and prejudices. In the four years since my initial visit, the Tanami Downs' management had changed, and the incumbent manager was a truck-driver from Queensland with a drinking problem and a cache of guns hidden out in the scrub. We arrived shortly after a domestic upheaval from which his wife had fled in the night, apparently in fear for her life, having taken shelter at Rabbit Flat Roadhouse before clearing out for good. There was a much younger woman ensconced in the homestead — a foster-niece or some such vaguely incestuous connection — who appeared to be taking the place of the departed wife. Whether her presence had contributed to the wife's departure wasn't clear, but seemed likely. She was a robust, extroverted girl, who told us a graphic story about her previous boyfriend having been decapitated by a helicopter, though she turned out to be something of a fabulist.

The manager was friendly enough, but it was clear that our visit had exacerbated the already volatile tensions crackling between the various members of the household. He was a weather-beaten man in his early fifties, and seemed to know something about cattle, but his struggle to point out directions on my map suggested that he was illiterate, and made me wonder how he managed the paperwork. He invited us to call in to the stock camp on our way to the border, and Pam was keen, although I knew she would find it shocking.

Negotiating the station that year was hard even for me. I wasn't disturbed by the cattle work or unduly alarmed by the stories of guns and midnight escapes, which were of a kind with the world I'd grown up in, but the situation on the station was not typical.

It was an extreme version of the way things could be, and I recognised the tensions that accompany excessive alcohol and emotional incoherence. As for the cattle work — the branding and castrating and earmarking, the killing of an animal for meat — those things are part of farm and station life, and every child who grows up on the land is familiar with them. Pam had none of that early experience to mediate her encounter with a world she was predisposed to distrust and fear. She was shaken by our encounters at the homestead, appalled and sickened by the blood and stink and singed hide at the cattle yards. I felt responsible for her discomfort, and defensive about the culture that had contributed so much to my own identity.

But the country provided respite from the human undercurrents. This would hold true across the years, and was something we came to take for granted.

We made a base camp at Lake Ruth, or Mangkurrurpa, the large freshwater claypan that had been a focal point for my family when we lived on the station. It was dry, covered in a fine white crust of bleached water weed, and we camped on the western edge in a stand of *Melaleuca glomerata*, the narrow-leafed ti-tree that grows everywhere that water flows or gathers in the Tanami. Pam walked, familiarising herself with the location, hunting and gathering materials and ideas. She commented on the motorbike and cattle tracks that scarred the surface of the lake, but the white silence of the lake basin, the twisted, sprawling ti-tree, the receding horizontals of lake edge and ti-tree scrub and spinifex plain and skyline took the edge off her remarks.

At the eastern end of the lake, I dug a shield-shaped hollow in the lake bed, and mounded the displaced earth into its mirror image. The earth was dark-red under the white surface, and the twin shapes looked like a wound. The hollow mirrored the form of a coolamon, a container made from softwood or bark to carry food and babies. I had been carried in just such a cradle, made for me by an Aboriginal woman soon after I was born. Although I knew it could open me to accusations of appropriation, I felt no constraints about using the form. In traditional culture the lake is a red-ochre site, a place of healing, and I lay down in the hollow and felt the earth on my naked skin, imagining the membrane melting away until the cells of my body and the grains of soil shared the same substance.

From Mangkurrurpa we went west to Bullock's Head Lake, where I had scattered my father's ashes four years earlier. It was dry, as it had been on that earlier occasion, and the spectacular blue-green and purple samphire *Tecticornia verrucosa* flourished on its cracked clay surface. In a clear space away from the samphire, I dug another coolamon in the sand-coloured clay, and used ashes from our campfire to coat the mound and line the hollow. Afterwards I photographed my cast shadow framed by its gothic arch.

Pam continued to walk and photograph and collect, absorbing each location, waiting for something to trip the creative trigger. She told me that my purposeful approach demoralised her, but I reminded her that I had a previous visit and a whole backstory to draw on.

The following day we drove to Balgo, which was more familiar ground for Pam. She had spent a good deal of time there during the years of recording and transcribing the stories for Yarrtji. We sought out Tjama and Marti and Payi Payi, who were delighted to see Pam, and sent us to camp in the women's compound.

—You'll be safe there, they said. Too many sniffers in town.

Petrol-sniffing among the young people was endemic, and although my vehicle was diesel they could still rifle through our gear in the hope of finding something to steal or eat. A padlocked gate and a two-metre fence with barbed wire around the top enclosed the compound, which consisted of a large shed and a small ablution block, currently out of order. We were woken at intervals by the fighting of camp dogs, and by the shouts and cries of restless humans. After the first night we were given permission to camp in the pound, and found a sheltered spot among trees near the dam. There was a horse graveyard nearby — the bones of fifty or more animals scattered on the red-gravel flat, evidence of dry times when they had bogged in the muddy slime of the drying dam and been dragged away, and shot if they weren't already dead. The coolamon I dug there was token, since I didn't have the crowbar that was needed to make more than a shallow impression in that stony ground. And the pound is not the sort of place with which to claim affinity on a personal scale. It's a desert cathedral, constructed of windy light and arrested movement, a stillness tense with the trapped energy of deep time.

Two days later we travelled further west to Mulan, home to people I knew from the station times. The community is located a few kilometres north-west of Lake Gregory — called Paruku by its Walmajarri custodians — a vast system of fresh and brackish lakes at the northern edge of the Great Sandy Desert.

Margaret and Dora were staying in Mulan — Margaret's husband had recently died, and the family had moved away from Balgo for the time being. When we called in, they directed us to one of the favoured camping sites on the lake shores, and we drove through miles of yellow grasslands to a spit of white sand that divided the largest of the basins from a deep lagoon.

Those days at Paruku were spent in a kind of dream. It was as if we had stumbled upon the inland sea of the European imagination. Drowned and fallen acacias provided firewood, and in the evening the brolgas flew across the sunset in stately formation, or posed on the shoreline like arcane symbols waiting to be translated. Pam hung swathes of muslin from the trunks of the drowned trees that clustered in the shallows, so they looked like the masts of buried ships. I found the pelvis and backbone of a bullock that had been dismembered for meat and picked clean by birds, and laid it in a coolamon I dug by the lake edge. This one I coated with red pigment, so that it became twin red ellipses on white sand by blue water.

Ngulupi, 1997

The station was less volatile when we called in the following year. The truck-driver, along with his guns and personal demons, was gone, and the manager who had replaced him was a young single man whose mother was visiting. We sat with her on the lawn in the late afternoon, sipping red cask-wine with ice, and talking about the country.

—I love this country, she said. People don't understand. There aren't words to describe it.

Our time was limited, and we both wanted to visit the

abandoned homestead at Ngulupi outstation, just across the border. Pam was still searching for a theme compelling enough to develop a body of work. She had called in to Ngulupi with some Aboriginal women years earlier, when it still functioned as an outstation and cattle enterprise attached to Balgo. My connection went back to its establishment in the sixties. The place was cross-threaded with the strands of people's lives, many of whom I knew, and I wanted to sift through the residue to see what I could discover.

We approach Ngulupi circumspectly, camping several kilometres from the homestead on a clear patch of ground surrounded by soft grasses and scattered acacias. Small red anthills cluster in the tall grass, massing up against the road like a crowd waiting for a parade. Pam takes a ball of red wool from her artist's toolbox and wanders off among the anthills to wind lengths of wool around their peaked tips, so that they appear to be wearing red caps. The effect is comical and a little sinister — a cabal of pointy-heads gathering for some mysterious purpose. While she is engaged in this, I collect firewood from a stand of mulga a short distance along the road. Fresh camel prints follow the road, and a snake track crosses it in a series of calligraphic arcs. The lowering sun turns the grasslands a vivid gold, and skeins of light thread through the branches of the mulga, glinting on the webs of golden orb-weavers. This is soft country, cattle country, where a vision flourished for a time, lost its momentum, and died.

In the morning there is a fine frosting of ice on the swags, and the red-capped anthills watch us like primordial garden gnomes while we stir the fire into life and Pam brews her morning coffee. We roll our damp swags and prepare to travel the last few kilometres.

The silence begins as we pass the empty stables and cattle yards, growing in intensity as we approach the cluster of buildings. It has substance and volume, as if an accumulation of absences has formed a vital element of the place. It occupies the gaps between the outbuildings, and reaches a pitch in the stone house that gives the settlement its designation as the Homestead.

The place is full of restless ghosts, unsettled and unsettling. The texture of the air is different from the last time I was here. It had been denser back then, lying heavily in the corners of the rooms, gusting damply along corridors, saturated with the emanations of its human occupants. It had smelled of cooking and cigarettes and beer and sweat, and the petty irritations of people living too close to one another. There had been the perpetual background hum of the generator and the murmur of television soaps from the master bedroom, punctuated by the pterodactyl shrieks of a caged white cockatoo. Now the air has no weight, and smells of dust and sunlight. There is damage, but not much — a shattered window, some torn flywire. You could move back in with a bit of tidying and sweeping, if you didn't mind the ghosts.

The crimson flowers of the bougainvillea that flourishes along the eastern verandah have bleached and drifted through the torn flywire, rustling underfoot like the husks of discarded conversations. At one end of the verandah, dozens of boxes of condoms, still neatly packaged, bear witness to a government safe-sex education program that made it this far before it foundered. Traces of the last occupants are everywhere in the abandoned paraphernalia of ordinary life, as if they had packed up a few essentials and walked out ahead of some impending catastrophe. It feels both voyeuristic and necessary to make an inventory of what they have left behind. On the verandah is a heavy toolbox with its owner's name stencilled on the side. At the last it must have been too big and awkward to take. In the kitchen above the sink a bouquet of plastic flowers still shows faded colours beneath a coating of grime. A large metal cooking pot that I last saw full of stewed salt beef sits empty on the laminated tabletop. An electric sewing machine is framed by an open window.

After photographing the abandoned rooms, Pam goes off to explore the outbuildings and community houses, but I'm not yet done with the house. I know the people who built it, and most of those who have lived in it since. I know who owned the toolbox and the sewing machine. Fragments of my own past are here, scattered among the detritus of those other lives.

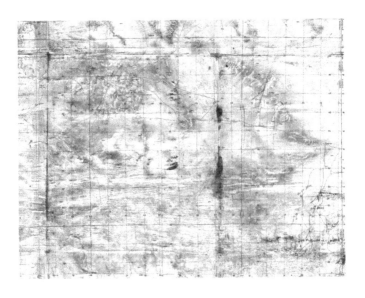

In the room that served as the office, a filing cabinet spills manila folders and mouse droppings. A pink tail-tag is taped to the wall alongside scrawled phone numbers. Among the debris on the floor is a map that, when spread out, proves to be four topographical charts taped together and laminated in soft plastic. Much used, and in places held together only by the laminate, it shows the area over which the Mission once held jurisdiction, the cattle stations that abut the mission boundary to the north-west, and the topographic features that shape the region. Ngulupi, with its radiating fence-lines and tracks marked on the plastic in blue pen, is compressed into the south-east corner, an anomaly of grasslands and mulga sandwiched between salt lakes and spinifex plains. The date of printing on the maps is 1968. They show tracks and placenames that have disappeared from more recent editions. Old road, people say now, when we cross the junction of a fading set of wheel-tracks. Old Mission. Old Station. Things are superseded quickly out here. Old Homestead, they will call this place soon, although it is not much over thirty years since it was built.

Although it wasn't built for religious purposes, the architecture of the house reflects the same aspiration as the church and the parish buildings of the Mission. The dressed stone walls are freighted with a European aesthetic, designed to withstand the desert gremlins that incubate in minds prone to introspection. The corridors terminate in arched stone doorways that frame the brilliant outdoor light, and the dark internal rooms open onto cloister-like verandahs.

In the bedrooms, my sense of transgressing is stronger as I encounter something stalled and claustrophobic. Among the abandoned items of clothing are a pair of black patent high-heeled shoes and a yellow nylon blouse. Together these garments trigger an image that feels like memory, of a woman standing before a mirror in the embalmed light of mid-afternoon. Although I have imagined her, she is as vivid to me as the real women who lived in this house. Her baffled misery flows out towards me like smoke, and I can smell her body odour, of nicotine and sweat and cheap shampoo.

The real horror is outside, though time has taken the edge off it. When the water failed at the bore, the stock came looking for water around the homestead. Two horses have fallen into the mechanic's pit in the workshop, their remains interlocked in a fretwork of ribs and vertebrae, still held together with sinew and scraps of hide. Outside the workshop, a perfect horse skeleton lies undisturbed, vulnerable as an exposed grief, pale grass growing up through the brackets of ribs. In the bathroom of one of the small prefabricated houses, the mummified remains of a cow presses the bone socket of an eye to the open metal louvres that ventilate the lower wall. Its dimming gaze would have registered the outside world as it died, trapped by the door it must have knocked shut when it sniffed out the water in the lavatory bowl.

Before we leave, Pam appropriates the high-heeled shoes and some branding irons she finds at one of the outbuildings. I keep the map.

+ + +

The prevailing story of Ngulupi is of shame and embarrassment and failure. There are rumours that cattle had been sold illegally to cover unpaid wages; that the last manager had done time in prison as a result; that the management of the outstation had been handed over to the traditional owners, who had walked away and left the stock to perish. The gaps in the story are manifold and troubling. It smacks too much of the irresponsibility of blackfellas, their casual incompetence and thoughtless cruelty. Another failed enterprise, another source of shame and sadness.

It's more complicated than that, of course.

Established in the era of a tough and practical priest on the only pocket of country within the Mission boundaries suitable for raising cattle, Ngulupi first prospered under pragmatic competence, and more recently failed under absentee incompetence. At its peak it ran six thousand head of cattle, supplied beef for the Mission, sustained a herd of quality horses and trained a generation of Aboriginal stockmen. The Kersh family, who managed Ngulupi from its beginnings in 1965 until 1973, built the homestead of quarried stone and established the infrastructure of bores and paddocks. They were people with a background in cattle-raising under remote conditions — good Catholics committed to the well-being of the Aboriginal families who worked with them.

In the space of thirty years, the Ngulupi cattle enterprise flourished and foundered. That it operated successfully for most of those thirty years before collapsing in so ugly and definitive a way suggests more than ordinary mismanagement.

The seventies brought the great upheaval of secularisation, when the drive towards self-determination for Aboriginal people resulted in the Church being reduced to providing pastoral care. Prompted by the changing circumstances and the need to educate their growing family, the Kersh family left Ngulupi in 1973 and returned to eastern Australia. For a time the cattle operation was handled by competent and experienced managers, but as control of Balgo passed through a sequence of increasingly disengaged management structures, responsibility for the station eventually fell under the jurisdiction of an administrator based seven hundred kilometres away in Kununurra. His knowledge of cattle-raising was based on figures that assumed predictable calving rates, predictable seasons, predictable markets, and predictable Aboriginal staff — a set of fallacies that quickly dismantled the hard work of his predecessors. Wages and bills were not paid, normal maintenance costs were not met. The station was left in the hands of its Aboriginal owners who, lacking the skills to make the necessary management decisions, walked away. People, both black and white, knew what was happening, but no-one took responsibility and no-one took action. The ugliest part of the story is the abandonment of the stock, resulting in the slow deaths of hundreds of horses and cattle as the windmills broke down and no longer pumped water to fill the tanks and troughs.

It is the kind of event that, in less remote circumstances, would have raised serious animal-welfare issues and resulted in criminal charges. But out here on the edge of nowhere, it slipped under the radar. The political ethos at that time supported the devolving of responsibility onto Aboriginal traditional owners. What happened at Ngulupi encapsulates the evasions and dishonesties of the period, and the refusal to acknowledge that the Aboriginal people of the region might not have been prepared for the responsibilities that were handed over to them. There were capable stockmen among the Aboriginal people, but no-one with the necessary management skills or the will to take control. The details of that era have faded in the minds of the local people, leaving only the memory of yet another betrayal.

Ngulupi and the cattle enterprise were collateral damage in the deliberate destruction of a functioning, albeit flawed, Catholic system. More poignantly, the last manager of Ngulupi, a local man who had grown up on Billiluna and managed cattle stations in the Territory, was jailed for selling cattle to pay the stockmen's wages. Scapegoated for the systematic incompetencies of the community management, left to take the rap by the traditional owners who had encouraged him to sell the cattle on their behalf, he emerged from his months in prison bitter and heartbroken, and left the region for good.

+ + +

Ngulupi captivated Pam. The abandoned settlement provided the point of entry she had been struggling to find. For her, it represented the failed enterprises and cultural impositions that the missionaries and cattlemen had foisted on Aboriginal people — a cross-cultural crime scene to which she could apply her forensic methodology of documenting and interpreting evidence. The out-station was a perfect midden of material objects and metaphors: branding irons, ear-marking pliers, spurs and bridle-bits designed to establish control and ownership over animals; theatrical set-pieces that included dead horses and broken-down cars and pink baby-jumpsuits; high-heeled shoes and sewing machines that inferred a dislocated feminine presence; dim, graffiti-scrawled interiors slashed with sunlight. She saw it as emblematic of all that was wrong between white and Aboriginal cultures, and applied her own style of cultural critique to it — not constrained, as I was, by knowing many of the people who had lived there.

The appropriated branding irons inspired the fabrication of a set, each brand sporting a single letter that, when arranged in a semi-circle with their curlicued handles turned inward, spelled the words ANXIETY AND DESIRE. In the exhibition of that name, the high-heeled shoes acquired a set of budgerigar wings, and perched, poised for flight, on the wall. Earlier, filled with pebbles from the ironstone gravels on the floor of the Balgo Pound, they had minced across that same terrain with an air of tipsy bravado.

IMPROVISATIONS I

Mulan, 2004

I said no at first, when Julianne Johns rang to invite me to Mulan to help set up a women's refuge and culture centre. Julianne, the eldest daughter of Rex and Anna Johns, belonged to one of the founding families of the Mulan community. Her father had worked as a stockman on Mongrel Downs in the sixties and early seventies, and Julianne was born during one of the periods when the Johns family were based at the station, so our connection went back a long way.

I didn't want the responsibility or the entanglement. Women's business wasn't my thing — nor was the drudgery of writing submissions, or anything to do with money or buildings. And I was uncomfortable around the new generation, who were more dependent than their parents on white people, and more resentful of them. They seemed tricky and sullen, losing themselves to alcohol and drugs at a frightening rate, lacking the will to take responsibility for their lives. I was more comfortable with the old people, who knew themselves and how they belonged in the world, and with whom I shared the knowledge of a different time.

My time in Balgo had convinced me that I didn't have the temperament to work for extended periods in a community. The ambient tensions of daily life, the robust disorder always threatening to overwhelm the tiny pockets of order one managed to establish, the sense of forever being on the fringe of something impenetrable, exhausted me. The relentless sociability of the culture prised open my self-containment and revealed its limitations. I reverted to making artist trips with Pam, revisiting familiar sites, teasing out how to represent the country and my relationship to it. I continued to visit the people I knew in Balgo and Mulan, but I was content to accept that I lacked the moral fibre for community life.

Then Julianne rang to tell me that Rex had died. Before long they would all be gone — the people who had grown me up, taught me how to be in the country, been proud when I mastered some new skill. Something in me couldn't let it go. It felt as if my own history had delivered me into the lives of people who identified me as someone who might have a reason to say yes. I said I would take the job, trusting my instinct to move towards the thing I wanted to resist.

Mulan was a much smaller community than Balgo, with a population of Walmajarri people living on their traditional country beside the vast, mysterious lake that was their playground. I came to the community with a set of credentials that linked me to the families who had established it, and relationships that stretched back over two generations. It would be different from the multilingual melting pot of Balgo.

What I remember of those months in Mulan is the rain. There were storms most days, although it was May and leading into winter. The water lay in the road in long orange puddles, reflecting the clouds and power lines and circling hawks. The last of the old rainmakers had died in Balgo, and in the days before his funeral the sky turned thick and grey, leaking rain like a grieving spouse. People said there would be a big rain after the old man was buried, and then nothing for a long time, and that is what happened.

On my first day I am approached by a round, smiling, middle-aged woman wearing a striped beanie who hugs me and says, 'My name is Fatima. I'll be working with you.' Behind her is a larger, younger, rectangular woman, impassive as a rock until she smiles, which is as startling as if a rock had smiled. Fatima, I learn later, is also called Veronica and Kanpirr, which is the name of a bush-medicine plant, but mostly she is known by her surname, Lulu. The big woman with her is her second daughter, Karen, who is referred to by her initials, KL. They move on, leaving me feeling vaguely ambushed, although I can't say why.

Later, Rex's younger daughter, Rebecca, takes me to the clinic where she works, saying she has something of her father's she wants to give me. Wearing a pair of white cotton gloves, she takes a black felt Akubra from a box and puts it ceremoniously into my hands. It is stained with dust and grease, with a strip of white plastic doing service as a hatband. I wonder if Rebecca wears the gloves for reasons of hygiene, since this is a medical clinic, or whether it is to protect herself from the numinous aura that clings to the hat. I think of my father's hat, still sitting on the filing cabinet in my mother's office, an avatar of absence. I'm very moved to be chosen as the custodian of the hat.

Among the people I encounter when I arrive in Mulan is Shirley Brown. I had met her when she was a shy seven-year-old and I was seventeen, and then briefly at a women's ceremony at Billiluna twenty years later. She looks just like her father, Malley Brown, who was the head stockman on Mongrel Downs for most of the years we were there. During the 1950s her grandfather, Len Brown, was the white manager of Billiluna Station, where most of the

Mulan families grew up. She has only recently come back to live in Mulan. On an afternoon soon after my arrival, we drive out to Parnkupirti Creek with three of her children and her grandson, James. We sit by the channel and she talks about what has brought her back.

Her mother, Bessie, was promised, Aboriginal way, before she took up with Malley Brown. Malley was identified as being wrong skin through his mother, Betty, who grew up on Moola Bulla, a government-run cattle station and institution for mixed-race children. Cultural prohibitions were brought to bear, and after Shirley was born Bessie was given to her promised husband, Bill Doonday. While Bessie was out bush giving birth to her second daughter, Shirley's half-sister May, Malley found Shirley alone in the camp nearby and took her to his parents in Halls Creek. This was around the time my father offered him the job of head stockman at Mongrel Downs. And so Shirley's fate took a different direction. She was brought up in Halls Creek and Alice Springs by her grandparents, and eventually lost touch with her mother and her country until after her first son was born. I recognise in her something of what drives me — unfinished business with people and country.

For several weeks the four-roomed demountable that is to become the Mulan women's centre sits in a shallow red sea, and when the water dries up I take photographs of a bedraggled Mickey Mouse staggering across the curled eggshell clay, trousers around his knees and a deranged smile stitched to his face. I'd found him on the floor of the demountable, which is in moderately good condition, although all the windows and mirrors have been smashed. I spend my days cleaning out the broken glass and debris, replacing the windows with perspex, fixing bolts to the doors. Lulu and KL visit me from time to time, KL driving the green Gator used to ferry elderly people around the community. Sometimes they are accompanied by Monica, a white-haired matriarch of great good humour and legendary hunting skills. These are the women behind the plan to establish the women's centre, which, as far as I can make out, is to function as a refuge, a place to store cultural objects, and a place where women can gather to paint, make baskets, and gossip.

Most of the time I work alone, which suits me. It's a peaceful location, screened from the community by wattle scrub, with a view of low hills and spinifex and termite mounds. Once the plumbing and electricity are installed, it might serve as alternative accommodation for me. The community manager's house, where I'm staying, is the default motel in the absence of visitor accommodation, and I find it difficult to keep track of the flow of people who come and go. Many of them will become my friends, but at first the house seems like a revolving door through which moves a stream of strangers. Never at my best when I don't have a private bolthole, I am beginning to feel the lack of somewhere to retreat.

Lulu and Monica want to go to Balgo to visit the art centre and the women's centre there. I have heard that Margaret and Dora are living at the women's centre, so I'm keen to see them. I drive around to Monica's yellow house and toot the horn. She comes out with her small white dog, Jakamarra, at her heels.

—Are you ready?

—*Yuwayi*, just got to turn off the kangaroo tails.

She shovels the coals away from the tails she's cooking in a shallow pit in the yard, covers them with a piece of tin held down by rocks, and gets in the back seat with Jakamarra. We drive to Lulu's house, where she is waiting out the front in a state of high dudgeon because someone has pinched the starter motor from her son's vehicle. The car is sitting on makeshift blocks, all four wheels removed, with no battery (someone else stole that), and a few other essential bits of the motor seem to be missing as well.

—Did it go? I ask her.

—No, she says, but now it really won't go.

She gets into the front seat and says we need to go to the shop before we leave. KL decides to come, and gets in the back with Monica. At the shop, Wendy Wise sees a space in the back seat and also decides to come. Lulu gets out and goes into the shop. Monica gets out and goes into the shop, comes back, and gets into the car. KL gets out and goes into the shop, Wendy gets out, Monica gets out, and then gets back in. I start the motor and begin to drive off slowly. They run for the car, two fat ladies and one skinny one. All of them get in, and we leave town.

In Balgo, I take the women to the art centre, and stay to chat with Sam and Stephen, the couple who have replaced Tim and Erica. It's their second year in the job, and they are grappling with the problem of carpetbaggers buying paintings directly from the artists. Convincing people that it's in their best interests to sell their work through the art centre, against the lure of cash in hand, is a constant challenge. Although the centre pays considerably more, the money is not available until the work is sold, and, for some artists, sales are rare.

Lulu has money business to negotiate, so I leave the women in the art centre and go in search of my friend John Carty, who is embarked on a PhD on the Balgo painters and their art. He has recently moved to one of the parish flats — a decaying set of demountables belonging to the Church — and is 'renovating' it in preparation for the arrival of his girlfriend, Jess. When I get there, he is attempting to remove a camp dog and her new litter of pups from underneath the verandah of the flat, where she has established herself and her family. It is well known among the camp-dog population that *kartiya* are more reliable food resources than blackfellas, and this one has staked out John as a potential owner.

—I'm not falling for it, he says, and the long-nosed red-speckled bitch gives him a limpid canine smile.

—Of course you're not, I agree.

John, known to everyone as Jakamarra, is in the barefoot and full-bearded phase of his evolution as an anthropologist, revelling in the daily adventure of interpreting life and art in Balgo.

—What made you choose Balgo? I ask him.

—I always felt like there was something missing from the culture I grew up in, he says. When I came out here for the first time, things suddenly made sense.

Lulu and the others are waiting for me when I return to the art centre, and they direct me to the house occupied by Judith, the current co-ordinator of Kapululangu, the Balgo women's cultural organisation.

—Those ladies always growling her, Lulu says. Sometimes even they hit her.

—Who hits her? I ask, but Lulu shakes her head.

—She's mad one, that one, she says.

Margaret and Dora are in the co-ordinator's house watching a video. They greet us with pleasure, but the video continues to absorb them, and soon Lulu, Monica, KL, and Wendy settle in to watch it with them. Judith is on the phone to some kind of support hotline.

—They come into my house whenever they feel like it, I hear her say. They treat me like I'm their servant.

I head across the road to the women's centre, where Patricia is in sole occupation.

—That mad crow over the road is trying to get me out, she tells me.

It's good to see Patricia, although she's looking a bit rough around the edges. We catch up on where she's been, and discuss how to find the money to pay for an extended family trip to Tanami Downs. Although there have been short trips with a few people, it has so far been impossible to organise the resources and the time to make the big trip Patricia wants. And I feel a subtle reluctance to commit to the plan, knowing how much work and effort it will entail. The phone rings while I'm talking to her — an official call of some sort — and I leave her to get on with whatever business she is transacting. When I look in later to say goodbye, she is still on the line. A camp dog sneaks through the door behind me, and Patricia reaches down, picks up a stone and hurls it with dead-eye accuracy at the hairless brindle cur. She leans back in the rickety office chair with the demeanour of a high-powered executive, and gives me a brief dismissive wave.

Patricia goes about her business, tracing the strands of her various involvements and responsibilities. Kartiya laws, she breaks whenever necessary. They have no deep hold on her, though the punishments are an inconvenience. To break the church laws gives her real discomfort; she feels the sorrow of Jesus at her constant failure to live up to His expectations, to live in His presence. Traditional law is the hardest of all. She is strong for the Law — her mother and grandmother have made sure of that. But she keeps running away from her husband; she can't stay with him for long before the violence breaks out between them, and in this her family is no help to her. To be beaten is what happens, especially if you are as outspoken and recalcitrant as she is.

To wait your time is the Aboriginal way. Life will arrange itself around you, and your turn will come. Men die before women. Wisdom accumulates in you along with knowledge, and power of a kind. But she can't wait for that. Things are changing too fast; no-one is sure any more what is important and what is not. The holders of the old knowledge are passing away, almost all gone now. She feels the world coming loose around her, wild and dangerous without the old forms to hold it in balance. She hears the whispers and anger, she knows she risks punishment from those more powerful than she is, but she can't help herself.

On a chilly afternoon, Lulu and Bessie send Shirley Brown to fetch me and Petrine McCrohan, who is in Mulan to help develop sustainable tourism enterprises. Shirley says we are going out to the lake so we can be mudded — the formal welcome that is also insurance against going unrecognised by the Lake Snake, who is a manifestation of the Rainbow Snake, and family to the pair of ancestral snakes who assisted willy-wagtail in his campaign of vengeance for being overlooked at a gift-giving ceremony. The two snakes, cousins of wagtail, flew in a cloud of dust and rain to the ceremonial ground and swallowed all the people, bringing them back and spitting them into the lake at two sites that are said to revolve like water going down a plug hole. It doesn't do to ignore the *genius loci*, but I wished the women had chosen a warmer day to perform our welcome. By the time we have collected everyone, it is four o'clock, getting colder and windier and damper by the minute.

The water level is very high, as it has been for the last few years after several heavy wet seasons. We head south from the community along the eastern edge of the lake. There is no real border between land and water here, but an indeterminate zone that changes imperceptibly from mud to water, where brolgas make stately salutations to each other among the drowned spikes of *Acacia maconochieana*, a salt-tolerant wattle that grew up around the central basin of the lake during the decades when it was almost dry. The Walmajarri attribute the dry years to the displacement of the lake people from their country. They say that only when the land was returned to its traditional owners did the rain come back.

At the edge of a small creek we get out of the vehicles, and Petrine and I are told to roll up our sleeves and the legs of our cargo pants and stand in the water, which is freezing. Lulu does the honours, plastering grey mud on our arms, legs, faces, and hair, while Bessie and the others call out to the snake and tell him what is going on. Bessie bestows on me the name of a deceased ancestor, whose *kartiya* name is Violet Campbell, near enough to Violet Crumble to appeal to me as a pseudonym. From now on, the snake that lives in the lake will be able to smell me and will know not to do me harm.

On the way home, we stop near Parnkupirti Creek to collect bark from a fire-scorched *tinyjil* tree, the white coolibah *Eucalyptus victrix*, and Evelyn Clancy tells her late husband's dreaming story — of the two dingoes who made the lakes, ending their journey with the creation of the Parnkupirti watercourse and going into the ground near Comet Bore. Evelyn is Jaru — she grew up on Sturt Creek Station and was given as a child-wife to a much older Walmajarri man, a senior custodian for Paruku and its major creation story. She is recently widowed, and it is only later that I understand that this performance is a reassertion of her status as a traditional elder for Paruku.

Petrine is one of several people who become part of the network of *kartiya* friendships forged during this first visit to Mulan. There is also Tanya Vernes, who works for the World Wildlife Fund and is collecting resources with the traditional owners for a dictionary of Walmajarri plants and animals. Peter Lockyer is an architect-builder embarked on a project to establish a local building team in Mulan. Everyone calls him Lockyer because someone called Peter has recently died, so the name is *kumanjayi* and can't be spoken. This is Lockyer's second annual three-month stint, and his partner, Sandra Bowkett, and their long-time friends, Phil Bourne and Kate Lewer, come to visit for several weeks.

Lockyer is committed for the long haul, and plans to return to Mulan every year to maintain and develop the building team. His is the kind of practical model that takes into account the need to maintain a life apart from the community, but builds the community into that life. Drawing Kate and Phil into the same orbit is part of his master plan, and they are already half-persuaded.

It's clear that my own business with Mulan won't be finished with the completion of the women's centre. Already suggestions are being made and plans laid for another project. The implications of this are something I'm not ready to look at just yet.

Before I leave Mulan, Pam drives out from Alice with Wendy Teakel, a friend and artist colleague, and we camp for a couple of days at the southern edge of the lake, before heading to Tanami Downs to spend some time at Lake Ruth. On the way through Balgo, we call in to the women's centre so Pam can see Tjama, and for me to say goodbye to Margaret, Dora, and Patricia.

Shortly after we arrive, Patricia's husband appears at the gate of the compound, too drunk to be inhibited by the fact that it is off-limits to men.

—Slut! That's a word for you, he bellows. I'm bleeding in my heart for my wife. I hear she's gone off with a *kartiya*. I'm finished with you, slut!

He's a big man, and his face is greasy with emotion. Patricia stalks off and picks up a crowbar, with which she begins bashing at a jammed door. The man's bloodshot eyes swing over to the old women, who drop their heads and turn their faces away, more from the shame of his violation of their place than from fear. His eyes light on us.

—Fucken *kartiya* come here and rip us off all the time. We didn't invite you to come here. I voted for this women's centre, so I can come here. I don't give a shit.

He shakes his head as if he's smacked into something and is trying to regain his bearings.

—You know me, Tjampitjin. I've never ripped you off, I say.

—We invited them, Tjama says at the same time, which seems to galvanise him towards Patricia. She squares up to him with the crowbar, solid and fearless. His eyes swivel past her as two vehicles draw up, disgorging uniformed men with what appear to be guns in their hands, and he turns and walks away quickly out of the gate.

The dogs understand the men's purpose before the humans do. Animals which a moment before have lain about in the dust like dead things bolt towards every available cover.

—Morning, ladies. Mind if we come in and spray the dogs?

—*Yuwayi*, Patricia says, you can spray them if you can catch them. She jerks her head after the departing figure of her husband.

—You can spray him, too.

The lame and the diseased, as well as the robust and the healthy, dash to the far corners of the compound. Some of them find holes in the fence and scurry into the spinifex. Among much shrieking and laughter from the women, the health team rushes after the dogs within range and blasts them with chemicals.

There's a hiatus while Margaret's big brindle pet, Choclat, has convulsions. Tjama throws water from a billycan onto the twitching animal.

—He always have fits when you spray 'im, she remarks.

Dora lays about with her walking stick, beating off dogs as they emerge from their hiding places and set on the disabled Choclat, and the chief dog-man takes the opportunity to spray the attacking curs. When the men have departed and the chaos has settled, Patricia puts down the crowbar, with which she has successfully un-jammed the door.

—I need to take a shower, she says.

On a flat stretch of road, a carload of Aboriginal people pull over and make a small fire. They have come out past the boundary of the community in order to drink a bottle of rum that has been smuggled in by one of the women. The fire is necessary to keep the wandering spirits at bay, although the moon is not far off full, and already high in the sky and casting black shadows. The drinking is purposeful: the intention is to get drunk. A small child wanders between the adults, and eventually crawls into the lap of one of the women and falls asleep. They drink until the bottle is empty, then cram back into the car, leaving the fire burning. On the way back, the driver misjudges a bend in the road and loses control. The car slides and rolls, and a woman is thrown from the open window, breaking her neck. She dies instantly. The child is badly injured.

My home base during these years is a mudbrick house on a thirty-acre block excised from a property called Manar, one of the first sheep stations established in the Braidwood area, an hour's drive from Canberra. It is beautiful and isolated, and the rent is cheap. My frugal electricity needs are met by a bank of batteries fed by solar panels, and I cut firewood from the fallen snappy gums brought down by winter storms. Rainwater is harvested from the roof into a large storage tank, and is pumped into the overhead tank that provides water pressure to the house. I earn a survival income by teaching two days a week during university semesters at the art school attached to the Australian National University.

Returning home after two days of teaching, I check the phone for messages. John Carty's voice on my answering machine is choked with sobs.

Patricia's dead. She was killed last night in a rollover. Call me.

I don't feel much to begin with. What happens in that other world occurs in a parallel reality that I have to re-enter before I can absorb it. I sit for a while, imagining John making the call from the art centre in Balgo, seeing a different light from the one outside my window. Margaret will be distraught, bleeding from where she has bashed her scalp with a rock, and Dora will be hunkered down, stripped to the waist, immobile. Shock and grief will be shuddering through the community; already the dead woman's name will be banished, and she will be referred to only by her skin name, Napangarti. There's a photograph from my last visit pinned to my noticeboard, of the five generations together — Dora, Margaret, Patricia, Beverly, and Cherelle.

I pick up the phone to call John.

Getting from Canberra to Balgo for the funeral proves complicated. Having established that Pam also wants to go and is prepared to drive her vehicle to Balgo, I fly to Alice Springs, and we make camp the first night about four hundred kilometres along the Tanami road. The next morning, Pam's vehicle blows the radiator when we stop to gather wild hibiscus flowers for the grave. Fortunately we are close to the Granites goldmine, and we limp into the mine workshop, where the mechanics diagnose a probable cracked head. The current managers of Tanami Downs, Jim and Stacey Napier, are going to the funeral, so with the help of the Granites staff I contact the station and organise a rendezvous. A young woman drives us out to the end of the haul road, a twenty-kilometre stretch of well-maintained bitumen along which the haul trucks carry the gold-bearing ore from the pit to the mill. Stacey meets us at the improbably named Penguin corner, and we spend the night at the station, leaving at first light in the Napiers' Ford to drive the three hundred kilometres to Balgo in time for the nine o'clock funeral.

When we arrive, John passes on a message that we are to go directly to the sorry camp to pay our respects to Margaret, Dora, and all the mothers and grandmothers who will not come to the church. The camp is at the house of Margaret's son David, where thirty or so women are huddled, hair shorn, faces and bodies plastered with white ochre. We move among the mourners, shuffling on our knees first to Margaret, then Dora, embracing them, going through the motions of ritual grief, being directed with subtle gestures to the next person who must be acknowledged, and the next, the lamentations falling and rising as we make our way through the assembly. As we leave the sorry camp, a force passes through the white-ochred bodies of the women that lays them down like rows of fallen tombstones.

The church is packed. The entrance has been smoked and the coffin carried in amidst a great surge of wailing. People are still filing in and arranging themselves as best they can, propped against the wall or sitting on the floor.

It's hot, the air barely moving under the ceiling fans. People start to make their way to the front of the church, and offer their tributes to the dead woman. Faxes and emails from friends and relatives are read. Dogs wander in and out through the open doors, and children scamper between the pews. The procedure unravels along the line of its own particular logic.

There's something raw and desultory about it all. The hot cluster of bodies, the sprawling dogs, the gusts and eddies of grief, the stark reach of the surrounding desert, all feel true to those old stories with their violent, prophetic characters, their retributions and betrayals. The gathering is probably closer to the Old Testament world than the Christian one that overlaid it.

After the tributes, the priest moves in front of the altar.

—Napangarti was a Christian, he says, and she didn't carry her faith lightly. She challenged me about how the Christian faith could be compatible with the traditional world she was raised in. She struggled with it. Struggle was in her nature. Napangarti knew her weaknesses, she struggled with them also, and often she didn't win that struggle.

He's talking about the rip-roaring binges Patricia went on from time to time, when she cut a swathe through the community, and when anyone she bore a grudge towards kept out of her way.

—She carried a great responsibility on her shoulders, straddling two worlds and interpreting them to one another. It was a difficult task, and there were times when she wanted to throw it down and walk away. But she never did. She carried it, and she made all our lives richer for doing so. To lose her is a loss not only for her family and community, but for all of us, and for the future.

I imagine Father Matt, with his Irish terrier's face, going round for round with Patricia in the battle for her soul. It would be a soul worth winning, out here in Old Testament country, and she would have joined the battle with enthusiasm. I remember the first time I met her — that disturbing intelligence circling and testing, curious, resilient, suspicious.

When the priest returns to his seat near the altar, there's an outbreak of wailing at the front of the church, a gut-wrenching howl of individual grief, quite different from the haunting pitch of ritual grieving. I feel sorrow break out over me like a fever.

A man comes forward, shining with sweat, very black in his white shirt, black trousers and tie. He positions himself behind the coffin and begins to speak.

—My auntie, he says, my auntie never had a disagreement with anyone.

This is so patently untrue that a shudder of attention runs through the congregation.

—My auntie was a good and kind person. She was a Christian woman.

He goes on in this vein, transforming the recalcitrant fibre of Patricia into a mushy facsimile.

—A drunkard shall never get into heaven! he shouts. Drunkenness and fornication are abominations in the eyes of the Lord!

Given that Patricia's death was the result of drinking, and that she had lived for a time with a man who was not her husband, this should be a major breach of taste, but no-one seems fazed. He is a minister of the Assemblies of God church, and this is the sort of thing they say.

I'm clammy with heat and hunger and the evolving surrealism of the service. A blood-distended tick attempts to scale the timber leg of the pew in front, and through the open side door of the church I can see two dogs copulating unhappily. Pam catches my eye and looks away, mouth twitching.

Someone begins to sing in a rich, pure voice, a hymn I recognise, though the words are in language. Their meaning rises up from some buried place — boarding-school days, long ago. When the hymn is over, two young men bring out a ghetto blaster to accompany the home-made lyrics that they perform with varying degrees of finesse, until Father Matt's intent expression gives way to a practical exasperation.

—It's getting hot, he says, meaning, *We still have to bury her.* In the intensifying heat out on the stony plateau where the graveyard is located, a thawing corpse will not be a good thing.

Pam and I pick our way through the wattle and spinifex to the graveyard, carrying our bundles of plastic flowers. A bobcat is parked not far from the open grave, ready to fill it in when the graveside rituals are done. In their uniform of white shirts and black skirts or trousers, the family mourners make a black-and-white tableau against the red ground and blue sky.

Father Matt stalks about the open grave in his cassock and sandals, a yellow plastic jerry can standing at the ready. On the side of it someone has written 'holy water' with a black marker. The ghetto blaster has been brought from the church to provide backing for a middle-aged couple with a guitar who sing a country gospel song about saviours and sin and seeing the light. Meanwhile the early-afternoon light hammers down on us, hard and hot and shadowless. Family members file past the coffin, some of them dropping to lie full-length on the wooden lid. The rest of us follow, offering our final goodbyes. I can't believe she's really dead. That sort of presence, that much *power,* can't just disappear.

But it can, and it has. The coffin is lowered into the grave, we throw gravel and leaves and holy water onto it, and the bobcat wakes and grumbles into action, trundling forward to shovel raw earth into the hole, coating us all with a red veil of dust.

Still the gruelling procedure isn't done. Back at the sorry camp, there's the ritual distribution of tea and flour and blankets, along with a ceremonial reckoning to establish responsibility for the death, which we have been summonsed to witness by one of Patricia's brothers. Stacey hands out sandwiches and cold drinks, and we stand on the outskirts of the ritual business — a strange and unnerving process, the outcome of which I don't learn until much later.

All I want to do is crawl onto the tray of the Napiers' Ford and sleep, but we must go through the hugging and wailing again with Margaret and Dora, take our leave of John and Jess, and drive back to the station. Jim decides to take the bottom road, which is shorter but slower, involving numerous close encounters with kangaroos, bush turkeys and cattle, and a tyre change in the dark when a slow leak turns into a fully-fledged puncture. It's after ten when we arrive at the homestead, by which time the exhaustion has transformed into a hyper-alertness that requires a couple of hours of debriefing before any of us can sleep.

SEARCHING FOR THE INLAND SEA

Lake Ruth, 2000

After several trips to the Tanami, Pam and I had established a co-operative working relationship in which Pam photographed my work and I played the characters in her photographic scenarios. I would ask Pam to photograph me crouching among the anthropomorphic hummocks of low termite mounds, my body covered in red mud, or half-concealed in a shield-shaped hollow dug in the side of one of the massive cathedral mounds. And Pam would ask me to wrap myself in maroon velvet and pose among piles of bones, or to wear the Hawaiian shirt she found among a bale of second-hands at Ngulupi, and stand in the prow of a tin boat with binoculars and a map. I had lent myself to these ironic scenarios without feeling implicated, until the boat was incorporated into them.

+ + +

The boat, which at that point I believed to be the same one my father had brought to the desert during the time we lived there, continued to grip my imagination. Abandoned at the edge of Lake

Ruth, it floated off on journeys of its own whenever the lake filled, and the first thing I did when we made camp was to search for it. If there had been a heavy wet season and high water, it might be stranded in the ti-tree on the northern dune, or foundered on the eastern rim of the lake basin, drawn along on the undertow of the palaeo-channel.

Years later, sorting through a box of family photographs, I came across a picture of my brother sailing the boat that belonged to our time at Mongrel Downs, and I experienced a vertiginous bolt of memory. The craft in the photograph was a small wooden yacht, far more elegant and streamlined than the clumsy tinny that provided me with my metaphor of journeying. After the initial shock, I was amused. I had needed a boat as a metaphor to carry the story I was telling, and unreliable memory had done the rest.

+ + +

On this visit I plan to fill the boat with the fine white fur that coats the lake surface, the residue of a delicate weed that has dried and bleached, turning the claypan into a shining blank. My intention is to drag the boat a short distance and empty it out, as a metaphor of my personal history.

—Why don't you drag it across the lake before you empty it, Pam suggests, and I'll take photographs.

The idea of shifting the private gesture I was in the habit of making into something less personal and more symbolic appeals to me. I am not quite done with the habit of exploring my own psychic baggage, but I'm getting a little tired of it. I put on the black anonymous outfit and white face-paint of the mime artist, and we spend the afternoon choreographing scenarios in which I drag the boat with a length of sisal rope wrapped around my waist, and Pam takes photographs from afar and close-up, to create the illusion of distance and effort.

The photographs show a black-clad figure dragging a white boat across a white landscape. The horizon is an unbroken line, and the sky a pale, clear blue. The distant figure draws closer and moves past and away, like a penitent or an apparition. The work we made that afternoon lifted something from me, and laid in a piece of grit around which much of our subsequent friendship was formed. For Pam the performance represented a post-colonial folly, a Fitzcarraldo moment in the Australian desert, but for me it was something else. When Pam claimed the work as her own, since she had suggested the dragging of the boat and had taken the photographs, I didn't quibble. The beautifully composed images were the result of her fine photographer's eye, and as art objects they belonged to her.

The value for me lay in the physical sensation, the weight and resistance of the boat, the texture of the sisal rope, the brittle weed crunching under my bare feet, the white glare of the afternoon light. There was no irony, only the act of participating in something impersonal and archetypal. In all the personae I have worn before and since, that solitary androgynous figure feels the most authentic. The figure dragging the boat becomes a metaphor for the making of a story — the blank space, the uncertain direction. The boat is no longer my boat; it belongs only to the country, and to whatever stories it accumulates along the way.

This disjunction between the image and the performance would occur several times over the years, when I took something from the act of performing that was at odds with Pam's intention for the photographs. Although we never spoke of it, I'm sure she knew this, and even appreciated that it brought a quality to some of the photographs that belonged to the unreconciled space between us.

Four years after the first boat performance, we re-enacted it, this time with Lake Ruth filled to the brim, and the strip of sand and ti-tree where we usually camped transformed into an island. I paddled the tinny with my long-handled shovel, and Slippers the dog was my navigator. The photographs Pam took show the pale edges of sky and water bisected by a narrow strip of land. The colour above and below is a deep indigo, although the sky lacks the inky depths in which the boat and its occupants are mirrored. Slippers glares into the camera with alarmed yellow eyes, while my alter ego paddles in slow circles.

Lake Ruth, 2005

The lake is once again dry, and the small, moisture-deprived, desert flies force us to take refuge in our mozzie domes, which we drape with wet sarongs as a makeshift form of air-conditioning. In the heat of the day, we sit inside our domes reading and drawing while the flies seethe over the wet towel with which I have covered the Esky containing our perishables.

Pam has brought a bag of props and costumes, and wants to do a photo shoot beside the desiccated remains of a camel that has died at the edge of the lake. The props include black lace gloves and pointy-toed stilettoes, and an ultramarine-blue satin skirt with lilac net petticoats. I agree to participate, but playing out Pam's scenarios provokes something recalcitrant in me. I get the point of the character Pam wants me to inhabit — a feminist critique of the white male myth of exploration — which rouses my resistance to theoretical positions. But I can't resist the costumes and the absurdity, and at her best Pam brings a sublime silliness to what we do.

When I put on the full skirt and high-heeled shoes, I feel in some obscure way like a female impersonator, or the impersonator of a feminised self who has never existed. In the outback culture of my youth, women who wore flamboyant clothes and obvious makeup were mocked by both women and men. I suppose it was an acknowledgement of their power, and their danger. It had surprised me to discover, sometime in my teens, that putting on a skirt acted as an instant signal to attract the attention of men. It couldn't possibly be that simple, I thought, to be transformed from androgyny to sexual desirability by the donning of a single garment. If it was true that men were so easily manipulated, then to wear a skirt seemed like a form of cheating.

Pam also dresses up — in a tail coat and a pair of black shorts with orange spots — and sets up the camera on a tripod with a timer so we can both be in the frame. The sprawling, hide-covered skeleton of the camel, with its twisted neck and death's head grimace, is the central motif. But it is soon evident that Pam is happier behind the camera than in front of it, where she becomes a self-conscious ham. And it frustrates her to have to keep resetting the timer. Her preferred technique is to take dozens of shots, hoping that among them will be one that captures something unique. I'm quite happy, once I've made the transition, to teeter about in the sand pretending distress at the loss of my camel, and swiping at the flies with a plastic flyswat. The overturned boat is nearby, and I sit on its hull and throw layers of skirt over my head in a simulation of despair.

The Napiers, who have managed the station since 2002, come to the camp in the evening with slabs of Tanami Downs steak, which Jim barbecues while the boys tear about on the moonlit circle of the lake bed. In their rough-housing they break through the dry surface to a layer of grey mud that unleashes a salty stink, as if the lair of an old subterranean beast has been breached.

The heavy wet seasons of recent years are changing the character of the lake, leaching salts up from the groundwater. A few kilometres to the south, a salt lake marks the course of a palaeo-channel, one of the ancient waterways that shape the subtle topography of the Tanami. I have long had a wish to visit it, and Jim offers to take us there the next morning.

Jim Napier is the most resourceful and good-natured of men, always ready for an expedition to help me look for some inaccessible place, or to facilitate a trip with traditional owners to visit a soak-water or a dreaming track. He forces Pam to re-calibrate her view of the outback male. Solidly built, with straight black hair and a round, cherubic face, he has a schoolboy's enthusiasm for adventure, coupled with superhuman competence and a relentless physical stamina that he has passed on to his three sons.

The boys are a trio of self-reliant child-adults — when I first meet them, the eldest, Brock, is about eight, Jamie six, and Dusty three or four, and all are excellent motorbike riders and an essential part of Jim's team of stockmen. Jim's wife, Stacey, gives the edge to an otherwise ideal family, being a wild and truculent girl of extreme moods and appetites, and the centre of her family's universe.

The tyre tracks of the Napiers' Ford are broad and easy to follow, and my Hilux has no trouble negotiating the spinifex-hummocked sand plain, with its occasional stunted bloodwoods, scattered grevilleas, and *Acacia coriacea*, commonly known as dogwood. The anthills on the plain are small and crenelated, like urban skylines. Ahead of us the horizon feels unstable, as if we are approaching an edge of some kind. The sandy soil becomes littered with limestone pebbles, and the anthills morph into the massive conical forms of cathedral mounds. Abruptly, the salt lake is before us, a negative space boundaried to the south by another unstable horizon. I know from the maps I've studied that the lake decants from the eastern end into a long basin — a link in the chain of salt lakes that divides when it reaches a region of high dunes, one branch flowing east into the flat Tanami marshlands, and the other coiling southwest to Lake Mackay and the Great Sandy Desert.

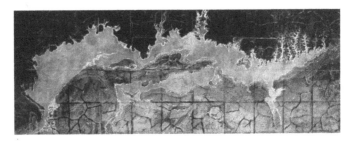

Between the salt lake and the limestone ridge where we have halted is a low red dune, an arc of sand created by wind and waves when the ephemeral lakes were substantial bodies of water. Stunted ti-tree grows along the dune, and red and gold samphire spreads out onto the salt crust, which is buckled and crisp. The southern horizon ripples with dissolving light, like wind moving through invisible fields of grass.

—We have to come and camp here, I say, and Pam nods, gleeful at the prospect. Photoshoots glint in her eyes.

Back at Lake Ruth, when the sun goes down and the flies finally leave us alone, we raise beakers of red wine to each other and speculate on a name for the character who is taking on a distinctive identity.

I consult my well-thumbed copy of *The Wildflowers and Plants of Inland Australia*.

—Eremaea means desert-lover. And there's a coolibah called Eucalyptus intertexta. How about Eremaea Intertexta. I wonder how that translates? Lover of deserts between texts? Love and the intertextual desert? It's very Deleuze and Guattari.

—Smartypants, Pam says. What about Eremophila.

—Too ditsy. She wears skirts and sandals, and trips around getting snagged on the spinifex. Cassia Desolata — now there's a name I could live with.

—Hallucinations of ice-cream when you've been in the desert too long.

—Senna Pod? Crotalaria? Caustic Vine?

We carry on in this vein for a while, until I switch my reference book to Latz's *Bushfires and Bushtucker*, and suggest *Triodia pungens*, the name of a common form of spinifex. Pam takes a liking to it for her own desert persona, as an alternative to Trudi Sparkle, which is her other nom de plume. We assume that 'pungens' means smelly, and only discover later that it means sharp, which is a better fit anyway.

I remember Violet Campbell from the Mulan mudding ceremony.

—Violet Crumble, I say.

—Violet Sunset, says Pam.

She had a look about her,
one of those travellers brimming with purpose,
the mote of a mission beaming in her eyes.

You've been — she said, lipstick mouth framing the question
— this way before. Have you seen
the sea they talk about? Blue miles of water, and the birds
flying at dusk in their thousands, with a sound like creaking doors.
White sandy beaches, and a lost tribe of fisher people,
taller by a head than the rest of us, and closer to God.

She showed me a map, fingernails clicking like red spears
along the route she had chosen.
—By my calculation, it's three days to the west, with ten miles
    of dunes,
and a clear run on the third day. The boat slows my progress,
rowing on still days up the sides of the sandhills.
It's hard going. My hair's a mess,
and my skin! I don't like to think about it.
When I get there, the first thing I want is a good wash.

I might have said — It's a long shot, sailing through deserts,
the next dune masquerading as a horizon,
the ground traversed unnervingly like the ground ahead,
and something strange occurring just outside the range of vision.
Days of monotony, punctuated by the surprised flight of birds,
and the sudden conviction that one has been this way before.

Instead, I told her that, travelling from the west,
I had no sea-sightings to report,

only an absence, obscured by light, and a shell muffled in red sand
that held the sound of breaking waves.

She shrugged, seeming not too disappointed,
re-applied lipstick, and set her sail to the wind.
—Between you and me, she said, bending out from the boat's
  cant,
—I'm starting to think it's the things you're not looking for that
  count,
if you only knew what they were.
Good to meet you, but I can't waste the breeze.
She waved, and trailing her shadow behind her,
went at a fast tilt into the west.

Later the same year, when cold weather has settled the bush flies, we camp at the salt lake. It is the July full moon, and we take our swags out onto the salt, and float all night on a mirror of white light. I wonder whether there is a psychic imprint on the human mind from a time when the earth was composed of salt flats and samphires — or maybe we carry a pre-human imprint from the proto-mammals who crawled out of the sea and began to evolve on the saline flatlands behind the coastal dunes. There's a sense of oceanic calm, of being an integral part of an impersonal cosmos. Sleep is impossible under the high-beam headlamp of the winter moon, and we are both awake to see it set, half a moon stained gold in the west by half a sun rising in the east. As the cold air warms up, a wind rushes through the ti-tree on the red dune with the sound of surf on a beach.

The lake surface is lifted in tunnels and corrugations of granulated salt, as if worms have crawled about under the crust, breaking through in search of light and air. Piles of droppings at the base of the red dune indicate the presence of a substantial rabbit colony — it must be near the northern limit of their range. As is our practice in a new place, we spend the first day wandering in separate directions, laying in the personal co-ordinates that best suit our individual processes.

Pam goes west, following the longitudinal arc of the lake. I cross the lake bed to the southern shoreline, beyond which the cathedral termite mounds are packed together like the conical mud huts of a vast African village. Termites are the major life form in the Tanami, and I have long been convinced by the theory of the Afrikaner scientist-poet Eugène Marais, in *The Soul of the White Ant*, that termitaria are composite animals that function as single sentient organisms. The conditions must be optimal for mound-building — clay-rich sand and sub-surface moisture and unlimited spinifex, mainly *Triodia pungens*, which the termites collect and store in the outer chambers of the mounds, where they grow and harvest crops of mould to feed the termite tribe. Bilby burrows at the base of the termitaria indicate an efficient food-chain hierarchy. Bilbies eat white ants, and it looks as if each burrow has a direct pipeline to a permanent food supply. I wonder why rabbits have colonised the northern shore, while bilbies hold dominion on the southern side.

In the late afternoon we get together for a photoshoot. Becoming Violet always costs me something, a relinquishing of the persona of competence and tough-minded intelligence that I have worked so hard to acquire. It had taken so little, when I was young, to be judged a fool because you were female. A wrong step and you were sliding down the slick hormonal slope of female instability, to be mired in the swamp of scorn and misogyny at the bottom. Before I can enter the light-hearted, playful state necessary for Violet to appear, I need to pass through a retrograde cranky stubbornness. Apart from my discomfort with the feminised and theorised aspects of the persona, I feel subtly coerced to discover something through the medium of Violet that I prefer not to know.

Pam understands some of this, and intuits more. She drags out the bag of props, and unzips it to reveal Violet's blue satin skirt glimmering under oddments of black lace and a pair of yellow duck-feet slippers. While I work my way through my resistance, Pam fiddles with her camera, an ancient Nikon to which she has a superstitious attachment. She has continued to use it, and slide film, long after the rest of us have switched to digital cameras, and is forever having to wheedle its temperamental malfunctions and hair-trigger mechanisms into good behaviour.

The western horizon shifts through a spectrum of gold and

orange and vermilion and pink and violet. Pam directs me to clamber up and crouch on the peak of a termite mound while wearing a navy dustcoat and the yellow duck feet. She is trying to capture something surreal that will transcend the clichés of her own feminist post-colonial enterprise; but without the skirt and stilettoes, Violet doesn't manifest, and I'm just a sitting duck on an anthill.

Violet sets up her tent on the salt lake, where it echoes the shapes of the termite mounds. The wind blows sheaves of lavender clouds from the west, and she takes off her shoes and cartwheels into the dusk.

Violet stands on the salt lake under the rising moon and feels the tidal pull of the inland sea. She hears the sound of waves breaking on the shore of a sea that dried up half a million years ago.

The inland sea is a desert of wind-blown dunes, a trace of salt in a place that nobody visits. Violet stands still as a pillar of salt and listens to the absent sea.

She hears the sound of termites mending the mounds and tending the queens, building sentient cities beyond the reach of the primate mind.

She hears the lives of the lovers she's left and the children she's never had.

She hears the sound of memories disappearing.

PALIMPSEST

Mulan, 2005

By the time I came to work in Mulan in 2004, the faultlines in the complicated tenure arrangements over Paruku were beginning to show. The pastoral leases of Billiluna and Lake Gregory had been purchased by the Aboriginal Development Commission for the Walmajarri Traditional Owners in 1978. The leases were then held in trust and nominally managed by the Aboriginal Lands Trust, while the Walmajarri set up a pastoral company and continued to run cattle on the land they occupied. In 2001, native title was recognised over the country under leasehold, and in the same year Billiluna and Lake Gregory, which continued to exist as pastoral leases, were declared an Indigenous Protected Area.

Billiluna and Lake Gregory stations operated on a 'hunt and harvest' basis, with local people killing animals for meat whenever they had the resources, namely a vehicle and a gun. The hunt-and-harvest approach was also applied to the annual muster, usually carried out by a contractor who took the major share of the harvest as live animals to sell.

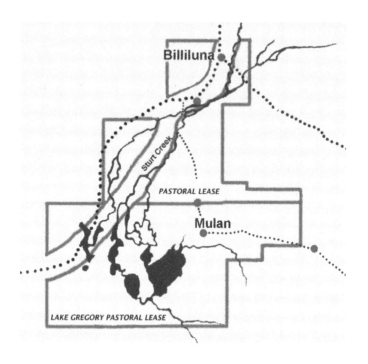

Meanwhile the Indigenous Protected Area, or IPA, the Aboriginal equivalent of a national park, occupied the same terrain, and the contradictions implicit in the relationship were becoming evident. The Paruku lakes system comprised an arid-zone wetland of great environmental value, providing a breeding ground and refuge for bird species of all kinds, and waterbirds in particular. It had been suggested for listing as a Ramsar site, a wetland of international significance, and the impact of stock, especially brumbies, was beginning to raise questions about the commitment of the traditional custodians to the environmental values they had pledged to support.

Some of these complications had emerged in my conversations with Shirley Brown, the first co-ordinator of the Paruku IPA, and with the current co-ordinator, Mark Ditcham — called Skinny

Mark to distinguish him from the other Marks living in Mulan. I wasn't especially au fait with the environmental issues, but it was clear that the IPA program offered real opportunities for the local people. And I knew things about the lake country that didn't seem to be on the radar of the traditional owners. Since the first of the ancient Aboriginal burial sites were discovered at Lake Mungo in 1968, I had been captivated by the developments in Australian archaeology. I knew that Jim Bowler, the geomorphologist who made the Mungo discoveries, had identified the Paruku/Lake Gregory system as an active equivalent of the Willandra Lakes system to which Lake Mungo belonged, and had made exploratory visits to Paruku through the seventies to the early nineties to learn what the northern terminal lake system revealed about ancient climate activity in Australia.

Shirley Brown knew nothing of the Mungo story, had only the vaguest idea of how the figure of 40,000 years of Aboriginal oc-cupation of Australia had been arrived at, and was thrilled to learn the link with her own part of the world. Skinny Mark was happy to support anything that enhanced the credibility of the IPA.

Shirley and I concocted a plan to invite Jim Bowler back to Mulan to travel around the lake, gathering and recording both scientific and traditional information. Petrine McCrohan was a long-time friend of Jim Bowler's daughter, and knew Jim and the family well. She gave me Jim's contact details and offered logistical support. When I contacted Jim and outlined the proposal, he said he would be delighted to come back to Paruku and revisit the sites of his previous explorations.

Luck and serendipity are on my side in putting the project together. A small budget comprising a grant from Lotterywest covers travel costs, supplies, fuel, and cultural payments. The in-kind support is astonishing. Jim Bowler, Petrine, Walmajarri-language specialist Eirlys Richards, film-maker Julie Bailey, and Broome-based anthropologist Catherine Wohlan all bring their skills to the project free of charge. John Carty brings the Palyalatju troop carrier and back-up anthropology skills for when a male is called for. Skinny Mark brings his team of rangers to set up the camp, collect firewood, take photographs, and play country music on the IPA troop carrier's sound system.

The other Aboriginal participants comprise the core of traditional owners that I will work with again and again as the years pass. Foremost among these is Bessie, premier traditional owner for Paruku, for whom recording and preserving cultural knowledge is paramount. Bessie's husband, Bill Doonday, is a Warlpiri man, but his long residence at Mulan, as well as the death of most of the men of his generation, has made him the male elder by default. Charmia Samuels has the same cultural clout as Bessie, with an equally authentic hereditary connection, and both speak high Walmajarri. Bessie's sister Lulu was educated in the Mission and writes Walmajarri, as well as Kukatja and English. She has a broad set of alliances, being a church elder and a member of all the local steering committees and boards, as well as being willing to work with *kartiya*.

Evelyn occupies a complicated position, as does Monica. Both have been married to senior Walmajarri men with flawless affiliations to Paruku, both have been recently widowed, and both are from elsewhere. Evelyn is a river woman, born and raised on Sturt Creek, with Jaru as her first language, although she speaks fluent Walmajarri. Monica is Ngardi/Kukatja, born in the bush south of Balgo. Both are beginning to have their status challenged, although they are probably the most skilled in traditional knowledge. In an unstable world in which the only thing you can definitively claim as your own is the country where you were born, territorial jealousies trump old friendships and alliances. But both women have powerful though very different personalities, and are not easily displaced. Monica's implacable good nature and Evelyn's volatile fearlessness have so far stood them in good stead.

Then there is little Anna Johns, Rex's widow, and wacky Wendy Wise from Wangkajungka, and Minnie Pye, one of the few women of her generation with a live husband, Frank Gordon, who made several trips down the Canning Stock Route as a young man.

Among the middle generation of women are Shirley Brown and her sister May; Lulu's two older daughters — Noonie and KL; and Anna's daughters, Rebecca and Julianne. They are only intermittently available, as they all work — in the office, the clinic, or the school — and are essential to the day-to-day functioning of the community.

There is a notable lack of middle-generation men who are willing to participate in anything that smacks of cultural business. The reasons for this aren't clear, but I suspect it's partly to do with the preponderance of women elders, partly to do with the perception that effective power lies within the *kartiya* domain, and partly a lack of confidence in taking on cultural authority.

It's my practice to use canvas groundsheets to mark the progress of my own trips, and this seems to me to be an appropriate way to record this new adventure. I clean out a workspace in the empty builders' quarters next to Skinny Mark's demountable, and before we embark on the field trip I make a map of Paruku, drawing a grid over a printed satellite image and scaling it up to fit a two-by-two-metre canvas. Drawing the visceral shapes of the lake basins, which resemble hearts and stomachs and foetal sacs, I have no intimation of how well I will come to know them.

The *kartiya* participants assemble, driving and flying in from west and east. I have a moment of panic at what I've orchestrated, but it's too late to do anything but behave as if I'm in control.

It takes the best part of a morning to get people, equipment, and supplies into the vehicles and out of Mulan, but by midday we are making our way south and then north-west around the main lake to Yunpu, one of the freshwater basins on the western side of the lake system. During extended dry periods the western lakes dry up, and maps drawn between the fifties and the eighties often refer to them as plains.

But the monsoonal activity in recent years has brought regular wet seasons and high rainfall, and Yunpu is a blue lagoon rimmed with white sand and sheltering ti-tree. We set up camp, the Aboriginal contingent spreading groundsheets and erecting tents in a tightly organised circle of family groups, the *kartiya* heading off with swags and mozzie domes to make solitary nests well away from the central camp. The *kartiya* behaviour provokes baffled head-shaking from the locals. Sleeping alone makes you vulnerable to attack from wandering spirits, and camping under the available tree cover limits the options for places to use as a toilet.

Flotillas of pelicans, whose Walmajarri name is *walany*, drift in the middle of the lagoon, and closer to the shore hundreds of *kipilyuk*, the wonderfully named wandering whistling ducks, paddle and dive. *Pirntiny*, the red-kneed dotterel, scurries in the shallows alongside *nirninirni*, the black-winged stilt. Evelyn has taken it on herself to educate me, and is vastly entertained by my attempts to pronounce the Walmajarri names. My mutilation of *wirarrawurru*, the name of the pink-eared duck, convulses her.

—*Wira-rra-wu-rru*, she says, breaking it into syllables for my untrained ears.

—Wiradthawoodu, I repeat, and she heaves with giggles.

—It's impossible, nobody can pronounce that, I say.

—*Wirarrawurru*, Evelyn says.

I roll out the canvas map, and everyone gathers for the business of setting down the names. Under the argumentative guidance of Bessie, Charmia, and Evelyn, I crawl around on the canvas, marking sites and place-names in chalk. Bessie has a long stick with which she points at the locations, or uses to poke me in frustration when I'm slow to grasp what I'm being told. Eirlys, the linguist, spells the names, and I begin to make the connection between the sounds of spoken Walmajarri and its formal orthography.

The shortcomings of my prototype map soon become evident. The first lesson in the overlapping of knowledge systems is that Aboriginal knowledge doesn't confine itself to the square dimensions of the canvas. Traditional jurisdictions extend to Well 50 in the west and to Jalyuwarn in the south. The ancestral dingoes who created the lake came down from the north and Kiki, the falling star, fell from the sky in the east. All these places and events are off the map.

—Puttem, I am told. You can fixem up later.

I puttem, and the edges of the canvas became congested with names that belong to the country outside the square.

The boundaries of people's knowledge are fluid, morphing and overlapping. The map is the ground on which the sites are marked, but each site has its attendant stories — dreaming stories and traditional ways of living, accounts of the station days and mission days and first-contact encounters. We record the stories as we go, on video and audio. Along with the names that are being pulled out of the collective memory are the genealogies locating individuals in the places to which they belong. People are familiar with this process, having been through years of native title consultations. I am yet to learn how fraught with risk this is.

Away from the ambient tensions and imposed routines of the community, the days move to a different rhythm. Everyone is in bed within two hours of nightfall, and is up shortly after sunrise. Breakfast is an extended, desultory process of tea-making and damper-cooking and conversations that weave between the cooking fires. The weather is mild and windless. We work on the map in the mornings, and hunt and fish in the afternoons.

On the weekend, families come out from Mulan to visit, and the presence of children generates a different energy — a glimpse of how life might have been lived on the lake shores in times of plenty. Among the visitors are enough middle-aged and younger men to warrant a special men-only recitation of the Two Dingoes creation story by Bill Doonday. Jim's white-bearded scientist status adds gravitas to the occasion, and John Carty is enlisted to mark the route of the dogs on the map. Lockyer and Phil and Kate, back in the community for several months, have come out for the day with their boys, and Lockyer and Phil are invited to join the men.

While the men participate in their secret men's business, which can't be recorded, Julie Bailey sets up her camera and films the equivalent group of women telling their stories. Bessie lays out the lines of descent, calling the names of the ancestors who lived as real people and are now part of the local cosmology, naming all the members of the living branches of family who have affiliations to the lake country. Lulu tells the story of *jintipirriny*, the wagtail who enlists the help of his cousins, the snake twins who live in the lake, to exact revenge for a slight he receives at a gift-giving ceremony. Spoken in Lulu's low, uninflected voice, the bloodthirsty tale of hubris, deceit, revenge, and slaughter reminds me of the Greek myths that captivated me as a child. This is no tidy moral universe where good behaviour is rewarded and mischief punished.

When the next generation speaks, the focus shifts. Bessie's daughter May describes the era of displacement and loss of language, when the families lived in Balgo, and she and her peers were educated in the Mission school and taught to speak only in English and Kukatja. She recounts the successful campaign to return to their country, and those first days of hope and enthusiasm. Shirley Brown's story is of being separated from her mother and her country, returning as an adult to rediscover and rebuild those relationships. Lulu's daughters, Noonie and KL, tell variations on the theme of spending weekends at the lake while being educated in Balgo, of homesickness during secondary schooling in Broome or Perth, of returning and settling down to make their homes in their own country. The Johns sisters are not present, and when I ask Julianne later why she didn't come to Yunpu, she says she hates camping out.

The central purpose of the map is to create a cross-cultural document that shows the interplay between Aboriginal knowledge and western scientific knowledge in a form that is easily accessible to both Walmajarri and *kartiya*. The Paruku system is a template of the progressive drying out of the post-Gondwanan landmass, when the vast, slow-moving rivers of that greenhouse world were choked and blocked by encroaching deserts. As ice age followed ice age, the waterways shrank and dried, and were reactivated with the return of wetter, warmer times, though with ever-diminishing rainfall.

Jim Bowler's explorations have revealed a series of shorelines on the western side of the lakes that indicate a progressive shrinking from mega-lake dimensions around 300,000 years ago to the current dimensions, a tenth of the original size, that exist today. The three significant shorelines represent intervals of roughly 100,000 years, and we drive out to the most recent of these, where Jim gives us a lesson in local geomorphology. On a clear patch of ground he draws a mud map to demonstrate how, with each phase of shrinking and refilling, the prevailing winds built a crescent dune, called a lunette, on the western shore of the lake. He points out shell and limestone evidence of recent and ancient floods, and shows us shells brought up from deep underground by termites and embedded in their mounds.

Jim says the terminal lake systems are like ancient rain gauges measuring the rainfall across millennia, providing tidelines and timelines for ice-age droughts and warm-weather floods. I prefer to think of them as palimpsests — surfaces on which successive texts have been written and erased, each erasure leaving traces of what was written before. The rains come, and the lakes fill and the sediments settle, layers of time measured in clay and sand and stone. The rains don't come, and the lakes dry out, and the winds bury some stories and uncover others. The rains return, and the lakes fill, and the prevailing winds build new shorelines that replace the old.

Stories are palimpsests, especially the story we are writing into the map.

After the weekend we pack up the Yunpu camp and set out for Well 50, the last-but-one of the wells sunk by Alfred Canning in the expedition of 1906, before he came upon the grasslands and bifurcated channels of the lower Sturt. Well 50 — called Jikarn by the Walmajarri — is at the limit of the lake people's country.

Our convoy of vehicles halts in the shade of a magisterial desert oak that dominates the crest of the broad red dune we have been labouring up for the past half hour. The dune is covered in buck spinifex and spindly mallee scrub, interspersed with flowering holly grevillea and the nectar-laden yellow spikes of Sandhill grevillea. The slope is not steep, just a steady gradient upwards to this point, where it flattens and begins to slope away to the west. It runs north and south, counter to the prevailing pattern of east-west sand-ridges that dominate this part of the country. Its massive size and transverse orientation give the clue to its origins, although, if we hadn't been told otherwise, most of us would read it as a sandy and unprepossessing bit of country to be crossed as expediently as possible.

But Jim has been briefing us throughout the trip with detailed interpretations of how and when the landscape was formed, so we know that we have reached the top of Paruku's original shoreline, created around 300,000 years ago by the waves of an inland sea. The sand would have been white back then, scoured from the lake floor and deposited on the western shore by the easterly winds that would also lay down the corduroy of dunes that define the Great Sandy Desert. I have collected zip-lock plastic bags of sand at every stop, to show how the colour darkens as we travel away from the lake and back in time. On this old ridge, the sand is a deep oxidised red.

Along with his original field notes and hand-drawn map with its notations and geomorphic hieroglyphs, Jim has brought a digital elevation map that shows the dimensions of the mega-lake and the raised outline of the transverse ridge on which we stand. This is where he drilled the core that brought to light the beach sands and shells of that first lake shore. The desert oak is there on the diagram: witness then to the scratchings and diggings of scientists; witness now to this motley group of blackfellas and whitefellas with our various preoccupations. Its needle leaves whisper us into silence as we gather on the carpet of leaf litter and cones beneath its canopy.

Charmia is one of the most senior and knowledgeable of the traditional owners. Her father, Roger, drew a map of the lakes and the northern Canning for the anthropologist Joseph Birdsell. His map is remarkable both for its detail and for its orientation, which puts south at the top.

—*Kurrkapi*, Charmia announces, touching the thick ridges of black bark and giving us the tree's Walmajarri name.

—This one *kurrkapi* is Japangarti skin.

And she begins to weep for all the human Japangartis who have died: the fathers and brothers and sons and uncles who share the kinship subsection and their brotherhood with the *kurrkapi*. The rest of the women join in, and after a while the wailing morphs into a song that Charmia leads, her feet planted wide, belly and lower lip thrust forward, beanie clamped low on her brow.

Having established the supremacy of ancestors and totemic presences, and placed science within the larger cosmological order of the Dreaming, the women bestow the kinship designation of Japangarti on Jim, effectively claiming him, his science, and whatever power and authority pertain to that science into the fold of the country. Jim is deeply affected, especially as Rex Johns, one of his first Walmajarri mentors, was a Japangarti. Although these days skin names can be handed out on the thinnest of premises, this one is genuinely significant, and we all feel it. We stand in the shadow of the ancient oak and feel the gravitational pull of a sea that no longer exists, and is all the more powerful for its absence.

A few kilometres to the south-west is Jikarn. As we make our way down the western side of the ancient dune, a low profile of flat-topped hills becomes visible, and the thin scribble of a creek flowing from the catchment of the hills to the foot of the dune, where it spreads out into a wide claypan studded with robust stands of mallee, tall enough to provide shade and firewood. The well itself is a little to the west of the claypan, visible as a depression marked by the remains of a rail fence, a hammered metal bucket and a rusting length of trough.

Old Frank Gordon, who travelled the stock route as a boy, runs his hands along the collapsing rail. He examines the heavy bucket, and shakes his head at the memory of bucketing up enough water to give five hundred bullocks a drink.

—All night, he says. Took all night for them bullocky to drink.

Today, at the well, it's Evelyn's turn to speak to the camera. She tells us the story of her husband as a young stockman walking away from the droving camp at Jikarn after a fight. The gist of the story, which Eirlys records and later translates, is the young stockman's encounter with a tree called *ngurlunyngurluny*, which followed him and caused him to climb into another tree for safety and to sleep in its branches. The next day, he continued to walk, digging for water at a soak, chewing tobacco to stave off hunger, until he reached a bore, where he rested.

At the bore, *pamarrngawurr*, a euro spirit guardian, threw little stones to let him know he was there.

—I know you, you're my cheeky brother, Evelyn's husband said.

—Wait till morning and I'll leave you some food as we head off, *pamarrngawurr* said.

The next morning, he ate the food *pamarrngawurr* had left for him. He saw camel tracks, which he had never seen before, and staggered on through sandhill country until he couldn't go any further and lay down in some shade, where two stockmen who had followed his tracks from Jikarn found him. They all rested, and the next morning they went east across the lake, which was dry in those days. On the east side they met the priest from Old Balgo, and he gave them a lift to the Mission.

After Evelyn's recitation, the party retreats to the shade of the claypan mallee near Jikarn for dinner camp, and the rangers have just got the fire lit when a Tagalong tour arrives — half a dozen vehicles of exuberant travellers on the last leg of their journey up the Canning Stock Route. They descend on us in their matching green polo shirts, and the team leader asks the women to dance for them. The *kartiya* among us cringe, but the women are not troubled. They confer, and agree to dance as long as they are paid. The travellers register disappointment at such crass materialism, but they negotiate photographs free of charge, and are mollified.

From Jikarn, the expedition returns to Mulan, and we continue to make day trips to the places people want filmed and included on the map. The first of these is a waterhole on Parnkupirti Creek, where the two ancestral dingoes went into the ground after creating the lakes. Bill Doonday directs me to drive along the dry creek bed until we get bogged, though not badly, and from that point we continue on foot. The creek banks are low and eroded, lined with prostrate *Melaleuca glomerata*, the toughest, narrow-leafed variety of ti-tree. As we approach the waterhole, drifts of salt cover the sandy bed of the creek, and Bessie explains that it is the sweat-trail of the dingoes. Slippers becomes agitated, perhaps sensitive to the presence of the ancestral dogs.

Doonday tells the public version of the dingo dreaming story, with Bessie filling in the gaps. When we check the film it looks wonderful — late-afternoon light, the red eroding banks of the creek with the white drifts of salt, and the two photogenic elderly people. Unfortunately, the sound has not come through. But the images conjured by the old man's voice stay with me, of the black dingo and the white dingo, a male and a female, full-bellied and weary from chasing and killing emus and making the lakes. They lope along the creek bed, tongues lolling, fangs bloody, sweat spilling from their flanks in salty streams. Exhausted, they slow down, walking, sinking, going in. Water fills the hollow left by their bodies, marking the place where they still rest today.

On an earlier occasion, Evelyn's deceased husband, Boxer Billiluna, recorded a concise and gnomic version of the story with Eirlys Richards. Boxer and Kilampi are brothers, and they identify with two rocks in the vicinity of Parnkupirti Creek. It is these rocks that Boxer is referring to when he says the two dogs put them down.

> The two dogs put Kilampi and me down at Parnkupirti Creek
> They put us down in the south
> Then we went eastwards
> The dogs took Kilampi and me to a place called Malarn in the east
> The two dogs with their bellies full went into the ground there.

On the final day before Jim Bowler's departure, we visit the site of the first Billiluna Station homestead, marked now by a set of steel stockyards and the remains of a tank and windmill. This is where Tiger Wirirr — father of Bessie, Rex, and Lulu — was blinded in an explosion when he was a young man. He and his cousin had been sent in from the stock camp to pick up supplies. It was common practice to keep dynamite for excavating wells, and there was a stack of it in the storeroom. The cousin dropped a lit cigarette, igniting the dynamite, and both men were badly injured. Tiger, unable to see, managed to get his cousin onto horseback, and they rode some twenty kilometres to Comet Bore, where people were camped. Their injuries were treated with traditional remedies — Tiger's eyes were plastered with mud. The cousin died, but Tiger recovered, although he was left permanently blind. He married a desert woman called Kitty Babala, founded a dynasty, and lived a long life.

The trip has reactivated Jim's interest in the story the lake country tells of ancient Australia, and he makes arrangements to return the following year to look for sites suitable for archaeological exploration. The artefact evidence suggests that human occupation in this area goes back a very long way, and there is a logic to the geographic route from northern Australia along the Victoria River to the Sturt, following the Tjurabalan dreaming path southwards along Sturt Creek to the terminal lakes of Paruku.

With the departure of Jim and the other *kartiya* members of the project, I set about adding strips of canvas to the map to accommodate the places that didn't fit inside the square. My tidy two-metre map becomes an unwieldy object four metres across at its widest — from Jikarn in the west to the trajectory of Kiki, the falling star, in the east — and three metres from the point where the ancestral dingoes enter from the north to the hills of Jalyuwarn in the south-east. As I resort to glueing the sections of canvas together, the whole thing being too big to stitch, I muse that bringing together the different ways of ordering knowledge was never going to be a seamless process.

This first Paruku map is the textbook from which I begin to learn the story of the lake and its people. I learn the jurisdictions of families and the totemic sites of individuals. The infrastructure from the station days is everywhere, in the form of windmills and cattle yards and fences, but the old way of life, before the station days, is still within the realm of living memory. The ancestors from whom people trace their descent are real people whose spirits occupy locations in and around the lake. The presence of the Mission is visible in the material ruins of abandoned settlements, less obvious but more insistent in the 'dormitory' generation educated by the nuns and priests at Balgo, and absorbed into the lingua franca of Kukatja.

Before undertaking the mapping project I was familiar with certain places, having camped, swum, and fished there, but the lake as a body of water and a system of waterways was inchoate. Having travelled with its custodians, and with Jim Bowler, I can begin to absorb it as a whole entity. To have the ancient geography interpreted simultaneously through modern science and the *Waljirri*, or Dreaming, lays down a template of country infused with multiple meanings. While I don't believe the creation stories in a literal way, they breathe animate life into the landscape in a form as potent and awe-provoking as the deep-time story Jim's science tells. They complement rather than contradict each other.

Bessie shows me a painting she made several years earlier, of Paruku in dry times, representing it as a large body of water fed by a river and surrounded by soak-waters. Explaining it to me, she can't remember the names of all the soak-waters, and orders me to get the big painted map. By identifying equivalent locations on the map she is able to orient herself and, with my help, identify the places she can't remember. Although her painting is diagrammatic, the sites are accurately oriented to one another. Bessie carries her country as an embodied map, laid in when she walked around the lakes as a child in the company of her grandmother. In putting together these two ways of conceptualising the same place, I experience a cognitive shift from which I will never entirely recover.

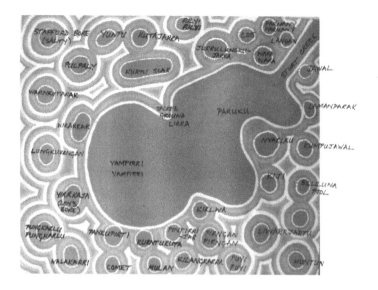

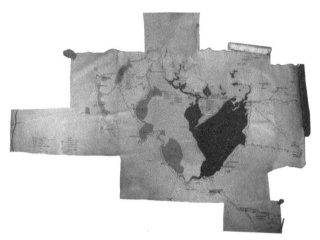

Later that year, when we exhibit the map and its associated stories and images in the Balgo culture centre, Bessie stands before it and makes an impassioned declaration in Walmajarri for the importance of language, culture, and country. Mounted alongside the huge canvas map are a copy of Jim Bowler's hand-annotated map of the successive shorelines, and the elevational map that shows the extent of the mega-lake as a green depression. So, too, are Bessie's painting of Paruku in the dry time, and her brother Rex's painting of flood time, with the same sites indicated on all of them. On the adjoining wall are the family trees of the two main clans that settled in Mulan. Julie Bailey has edited a CD of the material we filmed, which consists of people giving testimonial statements of their connection to country, footage of the sites we visited with Jim, the significance of places from the perspective of science and traditional culture, and a speeded-up hunting sequence to the tune of U2's 'I Still Haven't Found What I'm Looking For'.

To mark the occasion, the Mulan schoolchildren dance the story of Kiki, the falling star who came from the east and plunged into the lake, creating the deepest part.

TESTIMONY

Sturt Creek, 2006

After the success of the lake-mapping project, the Sturt Creek mob requested that a map be made of their country — the territory that occupies both sides of the waterway that charges the Paruku system. Sturt Creek, which alternates between a chain of permanent pools and a raging channel of floodwater several kilometres wide, is Jaru country, and the traditional homeland of several families who live in Mulan and Billiluna. Originally called Denison Downs, Sturt Creek Station was settled in the late 1800s, and continues to be part of the Kidman cattle empire.

Most of the Jaru people now living in Mulan grew up on Sturt Creek Station, receiving some schooling at Balgo during the Mission era, and returning to work as stockmen, gardeners, and domestics. Among the unintended consequences of the equal wages bill, implemented in Western Australia in 1968, was the displacement of extended family groups from their country, and the subsequent creation of a diaspora that saw the collapse of Aboriginal participation in the northern cattle industry. The Sturt

Creek families were caught up in this diaspora, with only a handful of the most competent stockmen retained as workers.

The river people had visiting rights to their country, but using them was dependent on the good graces of the incumbent manager of Sturt Creek Station. There was among this group a fierce undertow to get their country back, fuelled by their status as outsiders in the lake country, where many of them had retreated. And there was a story they wanted recorded and passed on while there was someone left with the authority to tell it — of a massacre on the river in the days when one law was being usurped by another, and neither prevailed.

The Sturt Creek mob mounted a pincer action in their strategy to achieve a trip to their country, co-opting me as the map-maker and suggesting to Jess, who was co-ordinating the women's component of the Palyalatju traditional-medicine project in Balgo, that the timing was right to gather the bush-medicine plants that only grew along the river. Neither Jess nor I were difficult to persuade. Between Jess's troop carrier and my twin-cab ute, we could take a dozen or so people — a manageable number — and spend a pleasant few days camped by one of the permanent pools on the river.

But in the time it took for me to rough out a prototype map, and for Jess and me to consult with the people who had initiated the idea, the trip had developed a momentum of its own, attracting a multitude of cultural organisations with various agendas to fulfil. The newly arrived co-ordinator of the Indigenous Protected Area, Wade Freeman, and the outgoing co-ordinator, Skinny Mark, offered logistical support and recording equipment. Yiriman, an organisation established to facilitate trips to country with elders and young people, suggested that the trip fitted perfectly into their brief, and offered the full scope of their experience and resources, which included the food for the trip and money for cultural payments. Jim Bowler, back to prospect for sites around Paruku suitable for further investigation, offered his scientific authority to support the push for a formal memorial site.

Given how rare it was to be overwhelmed with resources and enthusiasm for a project, there was nothing to do but stand back and let it happen.

+ + +

The old man in the passenger seat of my vehicle watches the country with deep attention, gesturing from time to time, calling the names of the places as they pass, turning his head to hawk gobs of mucous into a plastic bottle he carries with him for the purpose. His name is Boxer Milner, and he is frail and fierce, crippled from a car accident a year earlier that has reduced him physically but in no way diminished his authority and charisma. I have been elected to be his chauffeur over the next few days, which is both a responsibility and a privilege. One of his legs is almost useless. When I lift the intransigent foot into a position where he can manoeuvre himself onto his walking frame, he laughs.

—No good pucken thing, he says, disowning it, along with the incontinence that fills the cabin with an ammoniac reek.

—You better put something, he says, indicating the spreading damp patch on the car seat, and I dig a space blanket from among my camping gear and fold it on the seat, at which he nods approval.

—Pucken no good me, now.

—You're still boss for this country, old man, I say, and he grins.

—Too pucken right.

His language provokes shocked giggles and indrawn hisses from the back-seat passengers, Bessie and Lulu, who have become subdued as they leave the boundaries of their country and travel deeper into the old man's country. This has its advantages, since in normal circumstances they spend most of their time arguing with each other or telling me what to do.

We are at the tail end of a convoy of thirteen vehicles, behind the busload of pensioners who decided at the last minute that they wanted to come. The female driver is game, but inexperienced at managing a four-wheel-drive bus, and in consequence taking the rough track very slowly. I've chosen to stay behind the bus to ensure she gets through, since a breakdown with her cargo of mad, blind and lame old people doesn't bear thinking about. As the darkness drops around us the old man hunches in his seat, eyes fixed on the wheel-tracks lit by the headlights, with who knows what thoughts in his head. If he is in pain he gives no indication of it. Bessie and Lulu are silent as mice, and I know that they are afraid of the dark and the unfamiliar country.

I'm bemused at finding myself caught up in this excursion, since it's the kind of undertaking I do my best to avoid, being unsuited to the role of white slave and to the company of large numbers of people. From a modest plan to take a few traditional owners back to their country, this has ballooned into a major expedition, and I have reverted to my default position of finding one job for which I can be responsible, somewhere on the periphery of the action.

Driving Boxer Milner is a good choice. He is the storyteller, custodian of the words passed on from his father and brother. They will be recorded formally at chosen locations, but it is in the asides he makes as we travel that a different dimension of the story reveals itself: of the accommodations he and his people made after the event; of his career as a young stockman under the tuition of the man whose name is synonymous with the killings.

On the south side of the river is the new Sturt Creek homestead. I know this way of life — what it takes to educate children, maintain a homestead, manage land and stock, negotiate the vagaries of markets and drought and flood. And because I understand this world the old man approves of me, knowing I can properly appreciate the identity by which he still defines himself.

—I was head stockman, he says. Those whitefellas had to go behind. I was boss, in front.

Through the trees, the camp site is first visible as flickering firelight and the igloo shapes of mosquito domes, which have become the favoured shelter of Aboriginal people on these subsidised, *kartiya*-facilitated safaris. If it was not for the fleet of troop carriers parked at assorted angles on the outskirts of the camp, you might imagine you had stumbled across an ideal human community, tucked into the trees under an orchestra of stars, starting over in the grand adventure of creating its own society.

I find Boxer's family and deliver him, with his walking frame and folding chair, swag and medication, to the nieces who will care for him when he is not travelling with me.

—He needs clean trousers, I say, and somebody should take him to make *kura*.

I don't like his chances, but it's not something I can do anything about. They will manage between themselves, one way or another.

Meanwhile Lulu and Bessie have identified the mob with whom they will camp, and I'm directed to the patch that has been claimed for them within the social fabric of the camp. I drag mattresses, bags and blankets from the back of the ute, my ironic remarks about desert people travelling light being received with the disdain they deserve. Slippers beams a mad yellow stare from her cage as I remove the blankets under which it has been buried, and I reassure her she will be released soon, and fed.

I look for Jess, and find her at the camp of May Nungorrayi and Frank Clancy. It was May and Frank who initiated the idea of a trip back to their traditional country. Sitting on the edge of a grubby blanket, Jess is gnawing on a rib-bone and contemplating the extensive *kartiya* contingent without enthusiasm. Like me, she is overwhelmed by the dimensions that the expedition has taken on.

It's been a long, tough day, and when Jess hands me a charred and undercooked rib-bone I tear into it where I stand, ripping the burnt fat and bloody meat from the bone, smearing grease from ears to elbows. Slippers squeaks plaintively from the back of the ute, and I let her out and feed her.

In the morning it becomes apparent that this has been a camp site for a very long time. Stone tools lie everywhere on the grassy floodplain, under the spreading canopies of the white-barked coolibahs people call *tinyjil*. *Purkulpirri* wattle and the eremophila *wakila* grow further from the water's edge, where they are less frequently inundated. The remnants of an old crossing, washed out during one of the big floods, are visible at the edge of the creek, and the sound of the station generator travels across the water. This part of the river is permanent: a long, green stretch of water populated by spangled perch and catfish. Yesterday we saw kangaroos, emus, and bustards grazing on the river flats. The women have spoken about the pools where *pinanyi* grow, the waterlily tubers that are harvested and eaten. The place is a garden — self-sustaining, magical, worth fighting for, worth killing for.

When I rang the station manager to tell him of the traditional owners' intention to visit their country, he asked me to stress to them the risk of fire in the grasslands.

—The manager is worried about the grass getting burnt, so no hunting fires, I tell them at the morning gathering.

—Monica, that means you.

Monica is renowned for disappearing over the ridge in a puff of smoke, to return hours later with dead reptiles slung around her neck, scorched earth smouldering in her wake.

—What about you, Napuru? Lulu challenges me. You better look out for your cigarette.

—You're right. We all better look out for our cigarettes.

In order to make a plan for the day, everyone gathers near the main camp to discuss the various agendas attached to the trip. Each support organisation has its own set of desired outcomes: maintaining language; fostering health; facilitating cultural exchange between generations; recording stories; carrying out the bush-medicine and mapping objectives. For the traditional owners, it's a chance to re-visit country and re-affirm their relationship to it, and to spend a few days being provided with plenty of tucker and being driven to the sites of their own choosing, receiving cultural payments at the end. Among them is a contingent with their own fierce agenda — to get back their country — and this travels like a refrain beneath the other business of the trip. The revisiting of the massacre site, the re-stating of conception and dreaming sites, the re-telling of lives spent, work done and children born is all part of the plan of reclamation.

The consensus on this first morning is to visit the site of the massacre before travelling further afield. The old man is cheerful and sprightly. The blooming vigour of his homeland has seeped into him overnight, in spite of his neglected hygiene and physical infirmity. He stinks worse than ever in the reeking trousers, and I feel my own flesh contract at the thought of him sleeping in urine-drenched clothing and blankets through the chilly night. I help him into the car, and stow the walking frame and folding chair while he puts the makeshift sputum bottle carefully between his feet, where it can't tip and spill. Today he insists on being first, and we lead the procession of vehicles back along the track to the killing grounds.

The place itself is beautiful — a high point above an elbow of water on a bend in the river. In the dry season the river is a chain of long, deep, permanent waterholes. In the wet season the braided channels spread to a milky flood kilometres wide, creating the grasslands and coolibah floodplains that were once traditional hunting grounds, and later became frontier cattle country.

The bare remains of an old homestead mark the spot. The winter light scatters the leafy shadows of the drooping gums, and the grass is crisp and brittle around the sun-warmed sandstone of the fireplace. I carry Boxer's folding chair as he hobbles in a determined two-step with his walking frame, thrusting it against the shallow slope of the hill.

Wade is filming the old man's story, and there is some negotiation about where he should sit for his face to be clearly seen. It's a fine-boned, handsome face, topped by a thick thatch of white hair on which is perched a new, tan-coloured Akubra. Photogenic, confident, primed by the authority of the story he has to tell, he settles into his chair and grips the microphone, looking around to make sure his audience is present and captive.

Although he speaks mostly in language, it is apparent that he feels no obligation to spare *kartiya* sensibilities. The story is raw and straight, translated by his middle-aged niece Shirley Yoomarie, who stands behind him.

—I won't say the swearing, she says, above the staccato of 'puckens' and 'cunts' that punctuate the old man's delivery. His English has been acquired in a hard school.

+ + +

At the heart of frontier conflicts are two constants: the white men stole the Aboriginal men's women; the Aboriginal men stole the white men's cattle. That the country itself had been stolen is a different kind of story, for how do you steal embodied knowledge? How do you steal the webs and tracks of the Dreaming that tie place to people to culture to story? You can't roll up a piece of country like a carpet and make off with it in the dead of night. You can move your stock over it, you can fence it in, you can steal the livelihood of a people, but you can't steal the memories and the family histories and the conception sites that connect people to their country. These things persist wherever the people themselves persist.

+ + +

The story the old man tells on the sunny hillside, mediated through the voice of his niece, is of his people being rounded up and held in a stone enclosure called the goat-yard. They must have been tied up, or guarded, since when we walk down to inspect what remains of the stone walls it is apparent they were designed to hold stock, and that people could have climbed out easily enough. It was from here that the old man's father escaped, climbing over the wall and diving into the river. His name was Riwiyarra. In the old man's account, Riwiyarra walked under the water to avoid detection, and his escape was not noticed until he was seen on the other side of the river. The *kartiya* went after him on horseback, but Riwiyarra sang the horses and they became too weak to follow him.

—The prisoners had to dig a well, the old man says. When it was finished, the *kartiya* shot all the people and threw them down the well. They poured kerosene on them and burned them, men and mothers and babies.

—*Warra warra*, the old man shouts. Burned them to nothing, till there was only bones down the well they had to dig for themselves. They was digging their own grave. They didn't know that.

—My brother saw it happen, the old man says. He was young

fella, little kid. He was hiding in a dead bullock — those *kartiya* didn't look inside. He watched all those people getting shot, he saw the *kartiya* put them in the well, put the kerosene. He saw them throw the matches down the well. *Warra warra*, all the people crying, singing out. My father, his father, Riwiyarra, came back later and found him.

He tells the story, with embellishments, several times over, until he is satisfied that it has been heard. The ground is scattered with the remnants of settlement, and the women collect bits and pieces that they deem to be evidence — bullet casings and twisted wire loops that resemble manacles, although they are too big to hold the narrow wrists or ankles of Aboriginal people.

Later, the women describe cartloads of people being brought in, donkey carts loaded with the condemned. Like ants, they said, there were so many people. I don't believe that part of the story, although the image it conjures of the dusty road churned with wheel-tracks and the silent prisoners shackled to the carts is cinematic in its scope.

I believe the old man's story, but I don't feel it. When we go to the well, which was turned into a memorial in a ceremony carried out under the auspices of the local Catholic church some years before, it's the present gathering that touches my imagination. It's too rough for the old man to walk over, and he's worn out from the morning, so I drive as close as I can get across the stony ground and leave him to watch from the car.

We stand around the grave — fifty Aboriginal people and a dozen or so whites — all holding hands, and Jess begins to read the declaration of apology drafted for that earlier ceremony and left in a tin can at the foot of the cross. She breaks down after a few sentences and hands it over to Wade, who completes the reading without faltering. This is the moment I find unbearably moving.

I can't make real the terror, the murder, the burning, but this gathering holds something true, a moment to store against the future.

Next day, we all visit the homestead establishment on the south side of the river, the place where the Sturt Creek people grew up and learned the skills that mark them as station people.

Jess and I introduce ourselves to the couple who manage it, and their two small children. A fat Shetland pony watches morosely from the homestead yard, and ambles off in disgust when the Aboriginal kids descend on it. What follows is several hours of testimony to childhoods and working lives spent here: of working in the house, the laundry, the garden; of stock work and horse-breaking; of marriage and children; of holidays and coming home; and finally of the diaspora, brought about by the equal-wages bill that dispossessed all but the young, fit, competent stockmen. It is mind-numbing and riveting at the same time, the same story over and over, with individual variations, each person coming up to the chair, taking the microphone, delivering his or her statement of belonging.

Later, when we're on the road to look for one of the old station tanks, the lead vehicle, driven by Jess, slows and stops. Jess gets out and walks away to a clump of wattle, where she sits with her back turned to the line of vehicles that come to a halt one by one on the red-dirt road. I leave my vehicle and walk over to the trees. Jess is rolling a cigarette with an expression that suggests she is about to cry.

—I'm just having a *kartiya* moment, she says.

She lights the cigarette and inhales, exhales, with the concentration of a deep-breathing exercise.

—May and Frank keep arguing about which way we're supposed to go, yelling at me, 'Go this way.' 'No, go that way.' I can't stand it. I hate being in the lead.

I roll a cigarette and join her in the shade. Frank has got out of Jess's vehicle and is examining the road ahead for signs of a turn-off. No-one comes near us. Jess finishes her cigarette, composes herself, and goes back to the troop carrier.

—You better now, Napaltjarri? I hear May ask, her voice full of concern and sympathy, as I head towards my ute.

—Did you put out that cigarette, Napuru? Lulu says, and she and Bessie snicker in the back seat.

The track, when we eventually find it and drive along it for several kilometres, proves to be too wet to negotiate, so there is a laborious turning and back-tracking.

—Anyone sees our tracks, they'll think it's tourists, not traditional owners, I say, and the old man snorts with amusement. We drive out along a fence-line to a place where the old man says there used to be a set of yards. A few timber posts lying in the grass are all that remains of it. The fence, which has been built since the old man's time, cuts off access to the river a few hundred metres away. The old man indicates that he has something to say, and I unpack his walking frame and folding chair, and follow his instructions as to where to set the chair down. In the lengthening shadows of the afternoon, he grips the microphone.

—Old yard bin right here, he says. As he speaks, the plains brighten behind him in the lowering sun, and the shadows of the standing group stretch out towards us.

—Old yard bin right here. People trying to get away that way, along the plain. *Kartiya* bin round them up with horses. Three, four, five *kartiya*. That many *kartiya* bin round them up in one mob in one place.

—No get out. They puttem longa yard. They bin cleanem all the people.

—Five men, proper murderer. They bin shootem all here now. Whole lot finished, that lot *kartiya's* finished now. They not alive too.

—They couldn't get out.

—That's enough, that's finished.

—Finish now.

The time of day, the stillness of the plains, the rhythms and repetitions of the old man's voice, conjure the hoofbeats of horsemen and the thud of running feet. There are shouts, and dust, and the cries of the dying. The haunting is palpable, the silence trembling on the edge of sounds too ugly and remorseless to bear.

To my knowledge, no-one has told this story before, and no-one speaks of it again.

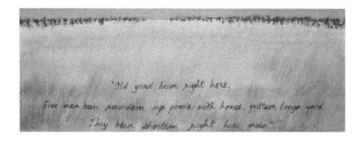

The following day, we visit the country where Shirley Yoomarie was born and which she is eager to show her daughters, who have never been here. She describes the *murungkurr*, who must be acknowledged and appeased when you are hunting.

—Little people, dwarfs, she says. You have to call out, *I'm hungry, I'm hungry*, so they won't hide the goannas and bush tucker from you. Sometimes they hide it anyway.

Nearby is a large earth-walled tank, known in the vernacular as a turkey nest, and several hundred recently weaned calves are stringing in from the plains to drink. They are big, strong Brahman calves, glossy and sprightly, and prove irresistible to someone's overgrown camp-dog pup. For a while there is a lot of dust and shouting, during which I drop my cigarette butt and then can't find it in the dry yellow grass. For the next few hours, as we drive back to the camp, Lulu and Bessie keep looking over their shoulders and claiming to see smoke. They think it's hilarious that I might be guilty of causing a fire I have been at such pains to warn people against. There is neither smoke nor fire, but there's also no joke that can't be pushed past its limits, and my carelessness has made their afternoon.

When I unroll the painted map of the river, everyone gathers around, calling for the old ones with the knowledge to sit beside me and oversee this transfer of the spoken story. Blind May settles her heavy body on the canvas, stretching out her crippled leg, its truncated foot like a bandaged hoof, and swings her wooden cane about to establish her territory. She prods me with it, then pokes at the canvas.

—What this place?

I move the tip of the cane until it rests on the spot where we are camped.

—This place is right here, right where you're sitting now.

This tickles the onlookers, but the old woman sights what little vision she has along the line of the walking stick, nods, and moves it to another spot.

—What this place?

I tell her what I know. Someone launches into a litany of the bloodlines associated with the river. This sets off a chain reaction that ripples through the assembly, with me at the centre of it, trying to make sense of the information coming from all sides. Jess grabs my notebook and writes down whatever she can extract from the rabble of noise. It's chaotic, impossible to decipher. May whacks her stick at whoever is in reach — mostly me, crouched and vulnerable, inscribing notes in chalk on the canvas.

—I can't do this, I say. We have to come back another time. Not now.

I leave them shouting and arguing around the canvas, and walk away to the river.

In the afternoon, when people have dispersed to fish and hunt, or sit together and tease out the minutiae of their connections to the river, I sit down with Boxer Milner and ask him to tell me the names of his country.

—Slowly, I say, as he reels them off, and he starts again while I pencil the names in the back of my notebook, twenty-six sites linked like beads on a string. I repeat them after him, my awkward pronunciation provoking scornful snorts, but I persevere. Once I can say the names properly I know how to spell them in the local orthography. When all twenty-six are recorded I read them back to him, and his hard, clever old face splits in a grin. This is his country I'm announcing, the names he can speak along the river from which his being takes its identity. In another time, we would be transgressing all kinds of prohibitions — that I, as a white woman, should have access to this sort of knowledge — but time is running out, and I represent a genderless entity with the mysterious skill of writing things down. In less than an hour I can reel off information he has learned over months and years as a boy, although what to me is a list of names annotated with brief asides — my brother was born there, old tank used to be there, my father found me in that place — to him holds the encoded cosmology of his kin.

My diagram in the notebook bears a marked similarity to the maps that represent urban underground rail systems, from which all but the basic routes have been excised. To get from A to B or X or Z, we don't need to know the multi-layered history of the places beneath which we travel. The map of the London underground reverses the process brought into being by the mnemonic codes of the old man's dreaming track, returning place to a tabula rasa through which we roar in a tunnel of artificial light.

I wonder whether the train drivers who spend their waking hours negotiating the great web of tunnels develop a troglodyte sense of orientation, whether their brains calibrate neural pathways that are specific to them, as do London taxi-drivers after years of memorising their city. No doubt this is changing with the advent of the GPS, rendering obsolete a highly specialised breed — an extinction that will go almost unnoticed in the plethora of more glamorous extinctions. So must have many specialised forms of consciousness flared and faded as the human brain alters to meet the requirements of its environment.

This is what strikes me as I write down the placenames for this old, pre-literate man, for whom each name is a code, a trigger that will activate a chain reaction of associations he will sing with his brothers that evening — the three old men harmonising with their clapping sticks, the rest of us falling away, mesmerised and exhausted, while the brothers see out the night in what will prove to be the last time they visit and sing their country together.

While the old man supervises my recording of his country, the teenagers, who have been forced by their parents to come on the trip, sit in the bus, sullen and resistant, plugged into their music devices and defying threats and pleas to come and listen, learn, participate. For many of the kids, the old man's knowledge has the same symbolic reductionism as the map of the train lines. What to the old people is knowledge — dense, profound, detailed and particular, providing both the information necessary for bodily survival and the moral compass to assist spiritual survival — to the young is becoming an incoherent stumble through a superstitious wilderness. The old fears of being punished for some inadvertent transgression still trouble them, but the means by which to manage those fears, the ceremonies through which the spirits can be acknowledged and propitiated, are losing ground.

Back in the community, I drop the old man off at his camp, and he thanks me formally for being his driver. While I'm collecting his walking frame from the back of the ute, he folds onto the ground like a collapsing camp chair. In front of his house is a low stretcher with a chewed-looking foam mattress, towards which he gestures when I return with the frame. Frail as he is, he's too heavy for me to lift, so he shuffles on his backside to the edge of the mattress, and I kneel behind him and grip him around the chest, lifting and heaving, the pair of us giggling at the undignified spectacle we present as I topple backwards, fending off the pack of scaly dogs that have rushed out to greet him. I pick myself up, retrieve his smart tan hat from where it has fallen and put it gently on his head, where he adjusts it to its proper, jaunty angle.

Over the next weeks, Jess and I work on the transcriptions of the stories and the editing of the video material, and Shirley and Evelyn set to work on the painted map. The map of the river is a blue snake on a red ground. It winds down the long strip of canvas, carrying with it the voices and stories of the people born along it who have lived and died there, or have been driven away to live somewhere else and remember it. It soon becomes clear that we need to go back, just a few us, to visit some of the places we couldn't get to last time because there were too many people and too many vehicles.

Wade agrees to use the IPA troopie, which is large enough to transport all of us from Mulan who want to make the trip. May Nungorrayi and Frank Clancy organise a contingent from Billiluna who have their own vehicle, and Jess and John bring Boxer out just for the day, as the big trip tired him out. We arrive at the river by lunchtime, and Boxer takes us to his conception site, the place where his father 'found' him in the form of a stone, which he put for safekeeping at the base of a big rivergum. We look for the stone, and the old man is distressed when we can't find it.

—Should be right here. Somebody bin takem.

—Maybe it got washed away in one of the big floods, John suggests, and the old man acknowledges that this may be so, although he's not convinced. But he is happy to sit there in the dappled shade of the river crossing, the bright grass flanking the long pools in which a cormorant dives and surfaces like a small submarine, its periscope head angling above the water, watching us with a beady, sceptical eye. Shirley's grandchildren play with Slippers, who they call Chlippet, tirelessly entertained by her obsession with tiny slivers of wood that she brings for them to throw.

At the dinner camp, kangaroo tails have been wrapped in foil and covered with coals. By the time we return they are cooked, dripping grease and giving off the pungent smell that permeates the cabin of a vehicle for months, and is difficult to explain to the mechanic who services my vehicle back in the city. 'Kangaroo tail', I say, when asked about the strange, greasy odour. I tell people not to eat it in the car, but they don't take any notice.

The community supermarkets stock frozen tails in bulk, although they have been banned on occasion after a spate of assaults in which they were used as clubs. The old man doesn't want kangaroo tail. He doesn't eat that bush-tucker rubbish, he says; he wants a tinned-meat sandwich with mustard pickle.

Another vehicle arrives, a freshly shot kangaroo bleeding on the roof rack. The occupants are relatives of blind May, and, like her, they harbour hopes of making a claim on the return of country. I spell out, very clearly, that the map is not part of any land claim, that I have no authority or skill in that arena, that the maps we make are a kind of document to gather up as much knowledge as possible, in an accessible form, before it is lost.

Jess and John and the old man leave in the late afternoon, in order to avoid too much driving in the dark. Wade and I take the troop carrier to get firewood, and I let Slippers out for a run on the way back. She dashes at the vehicle, a habit I have never been able to break her of, and goes under the wheel. Wade, who is driving very slowly, thinks she is just playing, but I have heard the small yip, and know that this time she has misjudged the vehicle, which is differently proportioned from my ute. Sick, I tell Wade to stop. The dog is curled like a shell, whorled into herself, alive, her eyes never leaving me as I go down on my knees and gather her up, fold myself over her. Oh Slips, you silly girl, you silly girl. I have no breath, only the tears streaming out of me, the hard ache at the back of the throat that makes it impossible to speak.

Frank ambles down the track in his flash shirt and bandanna and bare feet. I knew him as a young stockman, a fearless rider of buckjumpers, and a dandy larrikin, when he worked for my family. He takes Slippers from me and runs strong fingers up and down her neck. I am ready to invest knowledge and healing power in him, for there is nothing else to be done. The nearest vet is six hundred kilometres away, and something in me knows already she is done for.

Stretched out on the floor of the troop carrier with my hand on Slippers' chest, I feel the beat of her heart and listen to the rasp of her breathing. All through the night I lie awake, keeping vigil over my dying dog.

People are running on the grassy plain, ridden down by men on horseback, who shoot them one by one.

People are huddled and afraid in the goat-yard on a bright day like the day we visited, the sound of the wind coming up off the river and flickering through the trees with the smell of water, stirring the man in the corner to lift his head and observe that the kartiya with the gun has turned away to light a cigarette, protecting the lit match from that same wind with a cupped hand, inhaling while a shadow slips over the wall in a flicker of movement that might have been a lizard scampering, or the shadow of a hawk dropping low to see what kind of creatures are clustered in the stone enclosure.

The man goes down the slope, a shadow among shadows, to the bend in the river, and slips into the green, milky water that will hide him from the white men. His feet grip the stony bottom of the river as he moves among the perch and the rainbow fish that flick away in flashes of broken light from this creature passing through their domain. When he reaches the far side of the river, he stands up in full view of the kartiya so they will know he has tricked them, and disappears, and reappears, so they are no longer sure if he is real. Trickster, shape-shifter, he taunts them from the riverbank until two white men mount their horses and gallop south to the place where the river is shallow enough to cross.

The sound of singing unfurls like smoke across the water. It scatters the skeins of spray that loop from the horses' hooves, rises around them like a swarm of bees, and the horses rear and baulk as the singing beats them back. The white men feel the dark rhythm coiling out from the trees and swimming towards them like snakes cresting the ripples.

The trees breathe the voice of the singer.

The trickster moves by the river, there and not there, protected by the Snake. The child watches from the stinking carcass as his family are shot and burned.

The survivors flee to the protection of a neighbouring station.

The long silence falls.

Slippers doesn't die in the night, nor on the long drive back to the community. Several times her heart falters, stops, starts again. She is paralysed, but does not seem to be in pain. Her eyes never leave my face. Shirley's granddaughter Dani cries for the poor *kunyarr*, and for me. Shortly after we arrive in Mulan, when I have carried her to Wade's verandah and laid her on her own bed, when everyone has left us, her heart stops for the last time.

On the day my dog died she was running full tilt, the way she loved to do

Slippers' death changes the way people behave towards me. My sadness at the loss of my dog is proof that, in spite of being a *kartiya*, I feel pain. I am offered a choice of camp-dog puppies, offspring of a genetically dominant local breed with fruit-bat ears, pointed snouts, long narrow bodies and truncated flipper legs.

But I'm not ready to replace Slippers. She has been my constant companion for eight years — a mad, clever, loyal creature born on my birthday on the family cattle station in Queensland, part of a good-natured, self-regulating dog tribe ruled by my brother Bob, named by my nieces and nephew, and parted with reluctantly on the expectation that I would visit often so that they could see her growing up.

Wade and Lockyer help me to bury her at the edge of a red dune on the way to the lake, in a deep grave under a layer of mesh to stop the dingoes digging her up. It's a beautiful spot, from which you can see the lake to the west and the Walakarri Hills to the east, and it feels like a trace of myself is laid into the country with her.

+ + +

Jess, who is having difficulties with her boss and missing John, comes over from Balgo often and stays for several days at a time, editing the video and translating the audio transcripts into subtitles. She brings Suzy, the red-speckled bitch whose successful campaign to be adopted by *kartiya* has not cured her of her scavenging camp-dog ways. Her most recent escapade, which she barely survived, was to eat ten packs of frozen sausages, plastic and all, that Jess had put out to defrost. Only her long narrow head, now attached to a gargantuan body, recalls the lean and hungry animal she used to be. She is a charming and comical creature, and I appreciate having her dog presence around.

I work with Shirley and Evelyn to complete the map. There is a calm, easy pleasure in it, a camaraderie that leaves us all space to do the things we do best. In writing the placenames, Shirley rediscovers the literacy she learned as a child when she was sent to the mission school. While we work, she tells me about those days.

—They took us away from the station and put us in dormitories. When we got there they cut off our hair. Mine was really long, like my daughters'.

Shirley's daughters have miraculous hair, long and straight and glossy black.

—They changed our names, gave us new names. My name was Julie, but there was already someone called Julie, so they called me Shirley.

So strange to think of it, the clutch of girls mustered up by the Mission, shorn and re-named. Shirley is philosophical about it; she harbours no grudges. She laughs at the memory of their arrival at the Mission.

—The nuns was good to us, but I missed my family. My two sisters came with me, and my brothers. There was too many of us.

—What about you, Evelyn? Didn't they catch you?

—Nothing. I had my husband. They bin give me to him when I was young girl. I called him brother, I thought he was big brother for me.

They show no curiosity about my life. It's the here and now that interests them. It is enough that I return every year, and this project is evidence that they and the country are important to me. This map we are making together is a statement of identity.

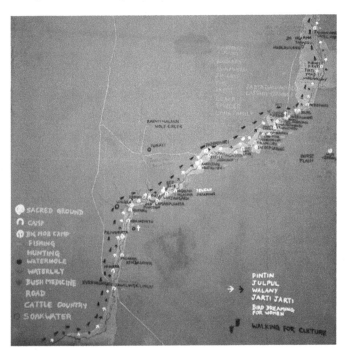

We devise a legend to indicate the nature of each site: a cross where people were killed by white men; a spiral for sacred places and a U-shape for camp sites; footprints to show the routes people travelled in the old days; bird prints to indicate *pirntiny*, the black-fronted dotterel, one of the many dreaming tracks that follow the river, a story that is danced by women. We make a stylised bullock's head to show where the cattle graze, and a waterlily for the places on the river where this prized food is found. We draw symbols for fishing and hunting and bush medicine, and for permanent waterholes. The story of the river emerges — the patterns of use, the resources it provides, the events that have taken place on it. Everywhere along its length are the names of individuals — where they were born or died, their totems and the country for which they are responsible.

Lockyer and his team have just completed a set of rooms attached to the basketball court, so we organise a joint celebration of the Sturt Creek mapping story and the completion of the building project. The map is hung in one of the rooms, along with paintings of the river, photographs of people and places, and the stories and testimonies collected on the trip. The ceremonial element is organised by the Sturt Creek mob, who burn green branches to fill the rooms with aromatic smoke, and paint up the kids and teenagers in preparation for dancing. The three old men have been brought down from Billiluna to sing. Jess and I stand at the back of the gathering. I have lost my dog, and Jess is about to quit her job, and we have forged one of those lifelong friendships made in adversity. Astonished to have brought this thing to fruition, we watch the dancing boys and listen to the voices of the old men rising and falling away and rising again.

ERASURE

The story of the massacre continues to tease my mind. I have heard it told several times since the old man's account by the river, and it accumulates layers and details with each telling, developing the weight and structure of a parable. Around the germ of the event weave the interventions of ancestral beings, the formal repetitions of oral storytelling, the naming of names, the outwitting of villains, the rise and fall of heroes. The number of white men involved shifts between four and five. I know that the oral testimony would not withstand the scrutiny of a historical investigation. It morphs with every re-telling, occupying real time and mythic time. In the slippage between fact and memory, a different truth emerges.

It is only now, through Aboriginal voices, that the story is being told, after a silence in which a generation of people, white and black, grew up without knowledge of the event. Of the Aboriginal people caught up in the massacre, only the names of the survivors are spoken — the child who witnessed it, and the trickster hero who escaped. When the silences that had settled over such incidents began to lift, and the child was a middle-aged man, he told his family what he had seen, and how his father had outwitted the white men and escaped, coming back later to find him.

Contemporary versions of the massacre are contradictory and confusing, and likely to obscure any attempt to tease out the historical facts. Even the story of the boy witness hiding in the rotting carcass of a bullock — a detail that I found convincing the first time I heard it — turned up in an account of a massacre further to the north. In one version, the four white men came with horses from Melbourne, rounded up all the Aboriginal people and drove them down towards the lake, where they shot them. A great-niece of Boxer Milner painted the story after he died, and said she had been told the killers were Germans. The tale morphs and flickers, absorbing whatever image of evil is current in the local imagination.

There is no doubt in my mind that a significant massacre occurred on the river, and most likely more than one. Historical accounts of the settlement of the river country describe a culture of periodic acts of reprisal by white settlers throughout the 1920s. There is also hearsay testimony of people fleeing Sturt Creek and taking refuge on neighbouring stations under the protection of the white managers.

I was told by someone who has lived a long time in the country that the place now associated with the massacre was not where it happened, the real location having been deemed too saturated with the dark event to be revealed. Given the tradition of secrecy and restricted locations in Aboriginal culture, I think this is possible. The implications this has for the marshalling of evidence that massacres took place is far-reaching.

Prohibitions organise the Aboriginal landscape — certain places are forbidden to the uninitiated, or to women, or to men; certain knowledge can only be passed on to the initiated. If a topography already dangerous with the capriciousness of ancestral beings is further haunted by the ghosts of murdered relatives, it is likely that there are many such locations that have never been revealed. If the Sturt Creek massacre did not happen in the place where it is memorialised, the authority to reveal its true location died with the old man who witnessed it; and if there are people still living who know it, they are bound to keep silent.

It's easy enough to imagine how the events could have been transferred to the site of the old homestead: the stone ruins with their evocation of time past; the detritus, including bullet casings and tin matchboxes, that gathers around settlements; the goat-yard; the 'well' hacked into the sandstone high above the waterline, most likely for the disposal of rubbish. We construct stories out of the fragments that the past offers up.

Among the white men whose names are associated with the massacre is Wason Byers, a man whose rogue status continues to live on in the stories told about him by those who knew him: 'If he didn't like you, he'd take a bull whip to you, and if he really didn't like you, he'd shoot you.' Another, Jack Barry, is described as 'cruel, a cunt of a thing', and Clarrie Wilkinson as 'one of the greatest of them all ... wonderful marksman, superb horseman, and outstanding cattleman'.

These descriptions of Byers, Barry, and Wilkinson come from an idiosyncratic unpublished document by historian Darrell Lewis, which he calls 'The Victoria River Doomsday Book', and in which he has recorded the names and whatever information he can garner about the managers of many of the Top End and East

Kimberley cattle stations. Compiled from newspapers, police and other government records, personal diaries and unpublished memoirs, and the recollections of people, the accounts are colourful and particular. Among the extensive references to Wason Byers is this quote from my mother, Marie Mahood:

> He told Joe and me in 1954 (at Beswick) about how, as a young man, he had 'trouble' with the police and wanted to disappear for a time, so he went south from Gordon Downs into the desert and lived off the land for two years, in what he described as 'wonderful grassy plains — great cattle country, but nobody will ever take it up because it is just too far from anywhere and surrounded by rubbish desert country'. (We remembered this later when we took up Mongrel Downs — exactly fitted his descriptions). He met there a small tribe of very tall (7 foot men) blacks, who pointed with their lips to the west as their country (Canning Stock Route — I have two other mentions of these tall blacks, and we employed 'Long Johnny' at Mongrel Downs — who was one of them). They were friendly to Wason, and he said they 'cracked their knuckles' when speaking, but he could not understand any of their language.

The route between Halls Creek and Katherine followed the upper Sturt through Gordon Downs into the Northern Territory, and continued through Wave Hill to Katherine. According to Lewis's records, between 1916 and the 1950s, Wason Byers, Jack Barry, and Clarrie Wilkinson moved up and down this route as, at various times, station managers, drovers, head stockmen, prospectors and cattle thieves.

When Wason Byers told my parents about hiding out in the Tanami grasslands, he didn't describe the details of his 'trouble with the police', but Darrell Lewis's 'Doomsday Book' offers some possibilities:

> While managing Sturt Creek station in the 1920s or 1930s he (Byers) was attacked one night by desert blacks. He escaped unscathed and in the morning he tracked the blacks into the desert. He caught up with them and, in his own words, '*evened the score*'. This story was confirmed and expanded during the Tanami land claim when elderly Aboriginal men told the hearing that several of their named relations had been shot by *'Western File'*.
>
> An old Territory cattleman, Dick Scobie, former owner of Hidden Valley station and friend of Byers, claims that Byers told him he had shot twenty-six blacks at Sturt Creek.

One of the stories that has become conflated with the Sturt Creek massacre is the well-documented killing of two white men, Joseph Condren and Timothy O'Sullivan, on Billiluna Station in September 1922. The first Billiluna homestead, initially established as an outstation of Sturt Creek, was about twenty kilometres north of the present-day community of Mulan. The bare facts of the story are that Condren and O'Sullivan were building a set of cattle yards with a team of Aboriginal workers when one of them, Banjo, shot both white men, handed out the station guns and ammunition to the remaining workers, and went on the run with his wife. The Halls Creek police were alerted, and a mounted patrol, accompanied by tracker Jack Bohemia, made their way to Billiluna. Banjo was tracked down, shot, and killed, but the local settlers, including Jack Barry, who was managing Sturt Creek at the time, were concerned that guns and ammunitions were missing. Discrepancies in the police records of the time indicate that there are several days in which the whereabouts of the patrol are not accounted for. Around the same time, rumours emerged of a massacre at Kanningarra, near Well 48 on the Canning Stock Route.

Like the Sturt Creek massacre, the modern versions of this event are various and contradictory. Some accounts say that a large number of people were killed near Kanningarra in reprisal for the killing of Condren and O'Sullivan. A painting by Daisy Kungah describes people being captured and chained at Kanningarra, and made to walk back to Sturt Creek, where they are killed by being thrown down the well and burned.

Although Condren and O'Sullivan were killed in 1922, and the Sturt Creek massacre (or massacres) occurred around 1929 or 1930, narrative logic has stitched together the surviving fragments, both hearsay and historic, into a single epic.

The story of the Sturt Creek massacre belongs to the ancient narrative tradition of the oral poem. It takes on the tropes and conventions of the epic tradition, wresting agency from the murderers and giving it to the trickster hero. While the epic poem may not pass muster as history, it speaks to the truth of the times, and throws a long shadow across the well-lit pioneer myths.

SONGLINES AND FAULTLINES

Tanami Downs, 2007

The Tanami is a secretive desert, subtle, unspectacular, repetitive. To the passing traveller it appears nondescript, its spinifex and wattle scrub plains punctuated by low blue escarpments that materialise on the horizon, only to disappear as the country drops into one of its shallow declivities. An observant eye might notice that this low-lying country has particular features — clustered eucalypts or massive termite mounds — which are indicators of the prehistoric waterways that once channelled broad, slow-moving bodies of water. And unless one deviates from the unsealed road that provides access through it, the Tanami seems to be a place almost devoid of people. Among the few markers of inhabitation are a roadhouse and an occasional sign indicating a homestead, a mining settlement, or an Aboriginal community. Since the federal government intervention in Aboriginal communities in 2006, there are signs that forbid travellers to bring alcohol or pornography onto Aboriginal land.

It has always been a kind of lacuna, from the days when it

represented the last blank on the map of white settlement to its present-day identification as the most direct and most boring route from Central Australia to the Kimberley. Lacking the glamour of the true desert, neither does it have the mountain ranges and dry rivers that give Central Australia its singular beauty. Great tracts of the Tanami are identified on topographical maps as 'spinifex sand plain'. Flying over some sections of it, it's possible to look down from the aircraft window and see not a single identifying feature.

In reality, it's a place dense with overlapping stories.

Unlike the more fertile regions of remote Australia, where the grazing of stock was the primary factor in the relationship between settlers and indigenous people, the Tanami encounter has always been about gold. While the country around its perimeter was absorbed into cattle stations, the Tanami concealed itself in non-entity. Its indigenous population, predominantly Ngardi, Ngalia, and Warlpiri, was not forcibly displaced by settlement, but extreme drought in the 1920s drove many people to cluster around the mining camps near Tanami Rockhole and the Granites.

From the first traces of colour found by the surveyor Allan Arthur Davidson in 1900, the story of gold has run like a seam of myth through the strata of the country. Allan Davidson was contracted in 1897 by the Central Australian Exploration Syndicate to survey the country west and south-west of Tennant Creek as far as the West Australian border. In 1900 he explored the region that is now called the Tanami, so named after one of the permanent rock holes identified by the local Aborigines.

Davidson is my favourite little-known Australian explorer. At the age of twenty-four, he headed an expedition into a part of the country that was still one of the blanks on the map. He was neither flamboyant nor incompetent; in fact, the only member of his expedition that did not survive was a small dog called Dodger, which 'rushed barking into the night' and was never seen again. His father, who he refers to as 'the pater', accompanied him on the expedition in the capacity of a prospector, and appears to have been comfortable under his son's leadership. The party explored some 30,000 square miles, mostly on foot, as the camels carried supplies rather than riders. The country was in a state of extreme drought, and the efficiency with which Davidson found water and feed for the camels, took readings and samples, surveyed and mapped their route, and wrote a detailed journal by campfire light is a measure of his unassuming intelligence. This 'Journal of the Western Expedition' was later published, along with accounts of his other expeditions, as a book, *Journal of Explorations in Central Australia by the Central Australian Exploration Syndicate, Limited, under the leadership of Allan A. Davidson, 1898 to 1900*.

Although Davidson identified a number of locations as having high gold-bearing potential, the finds were disappointing, and his report to the syndicate suggested that the returns at the fields he identified at Tanami and the Granites would not justify the costs involved in extracting the gold. He was proven right on both counts, until revolutionary changes in gold-extraction technology in the 1970s made previously unviable sites worth revisiting.

The hunger for gold being what it was, Davidson's warning was ignored, and the first mine was established at Tanami in 1902.

Lack of water, lack of suitable timber to reinforce the shafts, extreme summer temperatures and remoteness from resources made the gold-mining operations of that era difficult in the extreme. The Granites 'goldrush' of 1932 is a hair-raising episode of ill-equipped and ignorant novices from the south setting out in their hundreds to struggle and sometimes die along the track. The story is recorded in a first-hand account by journalist F.E. Baume, which was later published as *Tragedy Track*. I keep a copy in my travelling library for the sheer entertainment of its prose style, and to remind me of how the country was perceived by Baume and represented to an urban populace avid for stories from the 'dead heart'. And it is history of a kind, of which there's little enough about these parts. Baume arrived at the Granites on 30 October 1932, and described it thus:

Away to the west as a traveller approaches, a low ridge of cruelly red stone rises a few feet from the open spinifex plain, for here no tree has being and the spear-point grass is monarch of a fiery domain ... Even in South Africa, where distances are great, the most remote field is but a stone's throw from civilisation compared with this horrible place in a horrible desert.

... the Granite hill ... dominates the settlement like some evil genius, and as the day goes on and men grow restless with desert nerve strain, it seems to live and jeer and laugh at those who seek gold in its very entrails.

He is equally appalled by the conditions of the prospectors:

Desert cafard, irritation and nerve storm rush on even the hardiest when the sun sneers from a brazen furnace of the sky and the hot winds grip the gullet and fill the panting lungs with red dust.

When the dust of rumour settled and those opportunists who had survived the brazen sun faded back into the mirage, a handful of tough, experienced prospectors continued to eke out a living until the 1950s, when even they gave up and moved on.

In the late 1970s, using new technology and equipment capable of developing the open-cut pits that have come to mark the Tanami goldfields, North Flinders Mines, which owned the mining leases at that time, re-opened the fields at both the Granites and Tanami. Eight years of negotiations with the traditional owners ensued, during which exhaustive native title research identified the family groups entitled to claim royalties from what was to prove an astonishing resurgence of gold production. These days the Tanami region is gridded with exploration tracks, and the story of gold is re-calibrating the traditional patterns of ownership.

In Baume's time the notion of Aboriginal people having any entitlement to royalties accrued from gold mining would have been unthinkable:

> The desert black is cruel and treacherous and unstable. Even the missionaries, who may take exception to this statement, cannot deny the cruel murders committed in this part of the Northern Territory during the past few years — murders not committed because of a criminal instinct in the myall, but because he coveted things which the white man had and his tribal laws say 'What thou want, then if thou art a warrior, fight for and take ...' So the black tries to get what he wants, tries to get something he knew nothing about before the white civilisation burst into his hunting grounds.

In his thesis, *Golden Dreams*, Derek Elias discusses the evolution of the Warlpiri conception of country, under pressure from mining companies to define the hierarchies and boundaries of sacred sites. He suggests that establishing boundaries for the purposes of mining exploration has created a new way of identifying and commodifying country that places specific value on levels of relationship. He goes on to describe how the fixing of boundaries is conceptually different from the ways in which the Warlpiri define place. Site-clearance mapping, which had to be carried out before mining could begin, involved identifying sacred and sensitive sites, and consulting with the Aboriginal custodians about how the sites should be managed. The process was designed to lock down information about place in a permanent form — for example, 'that rock hole is sacred, we won't mine near there' — whereas in the Warlpiri cognitive framework of layering, mutability, and time, knowledge could be revealed over a long period by different people who had different degrees of knowledge. As a further complication, the more sacred a place to Aboriginal people, the less that could be said about it.

An equivalent redefining has occurred with regard to people's connection to country, and therefore to any benefits from that connection. Where once the location of an individual's conception and birth conferred certain rights, and father's country was the significant lineage, the displacements and diaspora caused by white settlement has created a broader set of criteria through which to claim rights, including mother's country and the extent of time lived in a certain place. This suggests a willingness among traditional custodians to extend the rights of more people to share in the bounty of royalties, or to benefit from the recognition of native title. The network of obligations through which Aboriginal life is mediated is visible here, but this flexibility of boundaries has also created a climate of suspicion and jealousy, and the fear that someone else is gaining an undeserved advantage.

There is an underlying tension that attaches to 'ownership', a term that seems to have displaced the older concept of custodianship. It would be interesting to trace that shift, to discover the point at which the subtleties of meaning were transferred from the emphasis on looking after and being responsible for country, to the more Western inflection of owning and gaining benefit from it.

+ + +

Between 2002 and 2008, when the Napier family manages the station, Tanami Downs becomes my second home. I become a kind of adoptive aunt, a seasonal nomad who brings along an eccentric collection of people and preoccupations, for which space is made and hospitality offered. As well as providing the base for my regular artist trips with Pam, it is the period when my friends and family visit, and for a time it feels as if my life is a coherent whole.

Over a three-day period in late January 2006, 550 millimetres of rain falls in the Tanami mine and Granites area. Based on geological data held by the mines, it is a rainfall event that could be expected to occur once every nine hundred years. The palaeo-drainage channels, following the barely distinguishable gradients of that ancient topography, become active river systems. Gerry Waugh, the mill manager at the Tanami mine, sends me a series of satellite images of the water moving across the country like an ink stain spreading through blotting paper. As the fossil waterways connect and diverge, and the water pressure lifts and falls, Jim Napier observes that the water in the palaeo-channel north of the station flows eastwards for a time before reversing and flowing west.

When I visit in May 2006, Jim suggests we drive out to look at the western lakes. The satellite maps indicate that Bullock's Head Lake, Lake Sarah and Lake Alec have joined to create a single body of water that extends across the border and cuts the bottom road to Ngulupi and Balgo. Before the wet, Jim had been grading the station roads in preparation for setting up the stock camp, and had left the grader several kilometres east of Lake Sarah.

—I reckon the water might be up to the tyres, Jim says. We probably won't be moving it for a while.

We crest the ridge from which Lake Sarah is usually visible as a distant blur of blue when full, or a clay-coloured smear when dry. Twenty metres beyond the ridge, the road disappears under water. To the north and west there is only water, a deep ultramarine blue. To the south a line of trees stand above the crowns of their submerged companions. Margaret had told me years earlier that the western lakes were on the track of the Rainbow snake, the ancient embodiment of water. At the time I filed away her remark without giving it too much thought. Now that phantom track is an inland sea.

Of the grader, a piece of equipment two-and-a-half metres high, there is no sign. Jim looks baffled.

—I know I left it here, he said.

—I guess you won't be moving it for a while, I say.

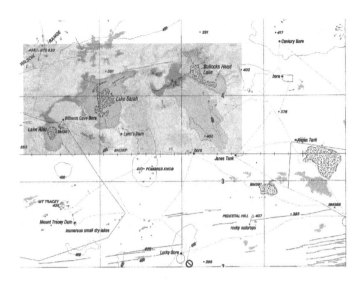

One of the reasons for this visit is to attend a meeting of the Tanami Downs directors, most of whom are senior custodians of the station and surrounding country, to consult with them about making a painted map. Since Patricia's death I've felt impelled to honour her dream of travelling with family to visit the significant sites on the station, and I've recently learned that both Margaret and Dora have diabetes. Margaret's condition is more advanced than Dora's, and she self-injects insulin, which she carries with her in a small Esky. Although the disease seems to be under control, it's an indicator that the time may be approaching when she can no longer travel.

Whenever there's an opportunity I collect Margaret, Dora, various grandchildren and interested others from Balgo, and bring them to the station to go hunting for snakes and goannas, digging for yams, burning country, visiting sites and telling stories. My journal is filled with diagrams of genealogies and dreaming tracks, lists of placenames and vocabulary. I have a number of maps of the station and surrounding country, including a copy of Davidson's exploration route, a composite satellite and topographical map, a geological chart, an aeronautical map, my father's hand-drawn map of Mongrel Downs, and several more recent station maps given to me by various managers. Apart from a couple of place-names, there is no Aboriginal information on any of them. The Aboriginal material has been recorded exhaustively through the native title process, but is not accessible to anyone outside that process. It seems fitting that I should apply the map-making prototype I've developed with the Paruku and Sturt Creek custodians to the place where I grew up.

Confident that people will be keen, I've already primed and gridded a length of canvas and outlined the key features, and when I roll out the map on the homestead lawn it attracts immediate interest. Within minutes I am directed to write the traditional names of the lakes and hills, and to mark the approximate locations of dozens of sites, along with the names of people associated with them. In the space of an hour the map is scribbled with chalk, and I have filled several pages of my notebook with cryptic notations. We agree to continue the mapping project the following year.

By this time I have given up my teaching job at the art school, deciding to take my chances on generating an income from my work in the desert.

+ + +

In May 2007 I ring the station to see if they need me to bring anything.

—Yeah, good, Jim says. Can you pick up a couple of cartons of bread and two packets of .22 Magnum bullets? The TOs have used all my bullets shooting bush tucker. And, yeah, that old Jakamarra says he's going to shoot you when you get here.

—Why would he want to do that?

—He's got some idea in his head that you're coming back with a company to make a land claim and take his country away from him.

—Where did he get that idea from?

—You know these fellas, someone gets in their ear and winds them up. I told him it was just you coming out to do stories with them. But the old man's adamant. 'I'll shoot that woman when she gets here,' he reckons.

—As a matter of interest, I ask Jim, if they've used all the bullets, what's he going to shoot me with?

—Probably one of them you're bringing with you, unless he's saved one specially.

I tell him no one is getting any bullets, or bread either, until they convince the old man I am no threat to him or his country.

The old man belongs to a family line I've not had much to do with, though he'd been present the previous year when we had all discussed the project. The confusion about maps and stories stems from the association with land claims and royalties accruing from the goldmines in the region. Every year when the royalties are handed out a frenzy ensues, with endless arguments over who is or is not entitled by birth or tenure to claim traditional ownership to the gold-bearing deposits of the region. Light-skinned distant relatives turn up and are welcomed with open arms, until their claim of kinship entitles them to a chunk of royalty money, when relations turn sour and they beat a retreat with their booty.

In the old man's mind I might well turn out to be one of these long-lost relatives, given my childhood connection to the country, and he is taking no chances. His threat is not to be shrugged off. The story goes that when he was little more than a boy, he killed his brother with an axe.

When I arrive at the station, Stacey tells me that she showed the old man the large-format picture book I had made with the Mulan mob about our mapping trip with Jim Bowler, and this has gone some way to placating him. I drive down to the cluster of community houses a few kilometres from the homestead and introduce myself.

—G'day, old man, I say. I'm the one you want to shoot.

He laughs, but his heart isn't in it.

The following day I travel with him and his family to Manyjurungu, a site on the stone-curlew dreaming track and part of the old man's songline where he'd walked as a boy, before he came in to the mines and had his first encounter with white people. He is in pain, and grumpy, and continues to refer to me as 'that woman'. To him I am merely a vehicle to drive him back to his country and give him the opportunity to sing some of the songs he'd been taught, and to claim emphatically as his own a section of the sacred dreaming track that intersects with what I later learned was a possible site for a new goldmine.

The old man is short and frog-like, and has a young wife who keeps him on the hop. She is a tall, glossy, confident girl, and expensive to keep. She is not impressed with the discomfort of the slow drive through almost impenetrable wattle and over broken sandstone rubble; she wants to be back home in her own community, watching DVDs and hanging out with friends of her own age.

I feel sorry for the old man, and I am moved when he speaks and sings of his country. We try to find a rock hole he remembers, but it isn't quite where he thought it was, and his pain and exhaustion defeat him. A wattle stake punctures a tyre on my vehicle, and while I change it the old man and his young wife sit, passive and indifferent, in the fine winter sunlight. Later, when he has recovered, we sit by the freshwater claypan that marked the northern boundary of his track and I record his reedy voice reiterating his claim to that piece of country.

—Mine! he says, over and over. Only mine, and that other one Jakamarra. We two for this country, that's all.

He lists all the names of people who might dispute his claim, or make their own bid, and outlines the evidence against them.

—That old man Bumblebee, grandfather for that mob, he sat down here only once. That's a liar story they telling for this country. When I was young boy, anybody stranger came into our country we spear 'em, same like kangaroo.

He sounds regretful that things have changed.

When we sit down together with the painted map, the old man is keen to unpack all that he remembers of the places he walked as a boy, and oversees with satisfaction their names chalked onto the map. I always find this part of the process thrilling, having learned enough by now to understand how things fit into the larger story. The old station template is embedded in me, along with the names that belong to that era, so to learn the original names and ancestral routes is to see the country come into focus with binocular vision.

By this time the old man and I are getting along so well that when he announces that his next royalty payment will be a million dollars, I joke that, since he is Jakamarra and I am Napurrula, his skin daughter, he should be looking after me. His face turns a sort of puce colour, and his deep-set narrow eyes send out a red flare. I assure him that I was joking — I am a *kartiya*, he is not responsible for me, where is his sense of humour? He hoots with laughter and relief as I back-pedal in several directions simultaneously, covering all possible reasons why he does not and will never have a reason to owe me anything. But after that I catch him watching me from time to time with a look that suggests he isn't completely convinced. I'm not sorry when he and his retinue leave for more civilised parts, where they have access to hot showers and television.

After the old man and his family have gone, I make a quick trip to Balgo to pick up Dora and Margaret, wife of the Bumblebee so emphatically dispossessed by the old Jakamarra. In fact Margaret's husband made no claim to belong to the country, and had died some years earlier. It was his widow, Margaret Yinjuru Napurrula Bumblebee, who had unimpeachable traditional claims to the country through her mother, Dora Mungkina Napaltjarri. Their friend Maudie comes along, and Margaret brings her grandson, Julian. The slow drive through the dark taxes my endurance, and I have to stop every half-hour, get out of the car and do some bends and jumps in the headlights in order to stay awake.

—You stop when you need to, Napurrula, my passengers tell me. We not in a hurry.

Margaret has developed an ulcer on her leg that won't heal. Because of her diabetes the risk of it turning gangrenous is always present, and the next morning I dress it for her, feeling a little sick. Neither Margaret nor Dora fits the profile of the typical diabetes victim. They are not obese, have never been drinkers, and supplement their diets regularly with bush tucker that they hunt and gather themselves. Dora, now bent and shrunken with age, must have been close to Margaret's height in her youth. She is still wiry and powerful. To have grown so tall and strong in the tough austerity of the desert suggests a metabolism honed to extreme efficiency by generations of adaptation. It's a cruel irony that flourishing in one environment may have rendered them more than usually suscepti-ble to the hazards of another.

Meanwhile, various other people are converging on the Tanami Downs homestead. Pam is coming out from Alice, bringing Jess, who is doing some work with Warlpiri Media for Reconciliation Australia. Coming down from Lajamanu in the north is a busload of American Baptists, accompanied by a contingent of Warlpiri Baptists who have invited the Americans to visit their community and their traditional country. Jim has warned the Baptists that the station does not have the facilities to accommodate them, apart from a shower block, a pit toilet, and some basic demountables without bedding. I wish I could see their reaction when, after a two-hundred-and-fifty-kilometre drive over one of the roughest and remotest roads in the country, they are offloaded among the recycled mining dongas and sheds and old tyres and mulga trees, to make the best of it with a group of desert Warlpiri and the fresh-ly slaughtered bullock and kangaroos provided by Jim. Among the visiting Warlpiri Baptists are several important traditional owners, and I am too busy persuading them to contribute to the map to pay attention to the baffled Americans wandering about the home-stead environs.

The group that gathers around the map includes Margaret and Dora, and Dora's youngest sister, Peggy. There is also gentle Mary Rockman, Margaret's niece, an ordained Baptist minister who preaches powerfully against holding on to Aboriginal culture. On this day she gives no indication of those beliefs, but helps to ex-plain the information offered by the older people. As always it is mostly women who are involved, but there is a moment when they call on Mary's brother, an intense, bearded fellow called Daniel who makes me think of John the Baptist, with his wild prophet's eyes and passionate advocacy of the spiritual realm. He knows the details of the fire-dreaming story, and might be persuaded to tell it. At first he agrees, but when old Dora makes a muttered remark and flicks her fingers with peremptory authority, he explains that he is *kirda*, an owner for that story, and it must be told by someone who is *kurdungurlu*, or worker. The traditional delegation of responsibilities requires workers to carry out the ceremonial activities under the supervision of owners. Margaret's sons could do it, but they aren't here. Instead, Daniel gives a tightly constructed genealogy of his clan, taking the line of descent through the men, and criticises the wandering web of connections Margaret had drawn the previous day.

The map is laid out in the shade near the Lajamanu bus where one of the American women has taken refuge. At intervals her voice squawks peevishly from the bowels of the bus.

—Is it time to eat yet?

Later, Pam gives a pitch-perfect rendering of the Southern vowels and disconsolate whine. 'Is it tarm t'eat yet?' becomes the catch-cry of the following days, and enters the vocabulary of the trips to come.

The Baptists stay only one night, the conditions proving too challenging for most of the international visitors. No doubt the adventure will give them stories to dine out on for years to come. Once the bus has departed with its passengers, the rest of us regroup. Having learned of my recent trip to Manyjurungu with the old Jakamarra, Margaret and Dora are keen to go there.

—My mother bin born down there, Margaret tells me. She was walking round that country when she was young girl.

Manyjurungu is one of a series of quartz and sandstone hills near the southern boundary of the station, beyond which the country stretches away into sand dunes and salt lakes. We make an expedition of it, Margaret and Dora and Maudie, Pam and Jess and I, the Napiers, the governess, and two station workers. Beyond the well-used station road, the first part of the track is overgrown with wattle and old spinifex — or 'finifex', as the women call it, a lovely sibilant that echoes the sound of its whispering stalks. In the passenger seat beside me, Margaret mutters.

—Too much rubbish, nobody looking after this country.

Further south the ground has been torched the previous summer by bushfires, and is clean and green with new growth. The young plants of *Triodia pungens* resemble fluorescent-green porcupines, the oxidised red of the soil lending the green a surreal intensity. There are pockets of soft annual grasses and the dark-green vines and pink convolvulus flowers of *yarla*, the bush yam. A few blackened corkwoods and the ubiquitous termite mounds are stunted verticals in the horizontal landscape.

It's old, flat, eroded country, the isolated outcroppings of granite and quartz and sandstone like the backbones of buried creatures, distance creating the illusion of mass and height, so that you are surprised to discover when you reach them that the high blue ranges on the horizon have shrunk to low red hills. They are the signposts through this part of the country, named in the mnemonic litany that teaches people to remember and survive. Every hill traps and channels water, so that when the moisture in the rock holes and clefts has evaporated, water can be found underground, if you know how to look for it. Every pile of stones is named, if only to indicate that it's where an ancestral being stopped to defecate.

—This place named Papakuna, Margaret chortles as we pass one such outcrop. That old man bin make a big shit here.

When I describe to Jim the general location of the rock hole we had failed to find with the old Jakamarra, he says he reckons he knows where it is. He takes us to a hole fifty centimetres deep and twenty centimetres in diameter in a plate of sandstone at the base of an outcrop of hills. A flat stone lid lies nearby.

—You wouldn't want to be the second bloke to arrive after a dry stage, Jim says.

On the perimeter of the group Dora stalks about, gathering the country back into herself.

—She says there's soak-water, other side, Margaret says.

We pile back into the vehicles and circle southward around the rocks until the old woman indicates that we should stop. Margaret and Dora and half-blind Maudie set off on their stork legs, eyes scanning the ground, hands clasped behind their backs like a trio of clerics pondering some point of theology. At fifty metres Dora makes a sharp turn, angles off to the south and sends Margaret ahead. It is obvious enough, when you know what you are looking for. Around a shallow depression, the red sand gives way to a moist, loamy soil, on which spindly, tall plants grow in profusion. Jim sends the station workers back to the vehicle for shovels, and they take turns to dig. A metre down they come upon a mottled, water-logged frog as big as a fist, and shortly afterwards another one. The loam turns muddy, and at two metres the slow seepage of water fills the bottom of the hole. It smells like rain on dry ground. I find a pannikin and hand it down to Jim, who fills it with the brown mud-filtered water and passes it up to the old woman. When she tastes the water her face splits into a smile of astonishing proportions, revealing rows of worn yellow teeth.

—Did your mother ever come back to this place after her mob walked to the mines? I ask Margaret, who shakes her head.

Given Dora's age, somewhere in her eighties, more than sixty years must have passed since she had drunk water from the soak. It lubricates her usually silent tongue, and she points out the line of stones that represent the yam dreaming: a diminishing sequence of standing stones, the largest of which is split vertically, its two parts leaning into each other like lovers. At the southern end of the outcrop there are flakes of worked stone and incisions in the surface of the rock face, where Jim discovers a second soak-water, more extensive than the first.

—Jim wins, Margaret announces. He's the winner for finding soak-water.

Tracking the sound and flight of birds, I climb to the other side of the ridge, and find a small cleft filled with water, protected by a jut of rock. Around the water it is all activity — chattering of zebra finches, soft glottals and whirring flurries of doves. From the spine of the ridge the country stretches away in all directions, the line of the yam dreaming running east-west, the path of the stone-curlews travelling from the south-west and encountering the fire dreaming that raced before the wind towards the west.

I've heard the story many times, how the curlew men saw a great bushfire burning in the north-east on the route they had chosen to travel, and decided, in spite of the danger, to keep flying. At the lake called Mangkurrurpa the fire caught them; some died and some were badly burned. An old *maparn*, a healer whose spirit occupies a sacred tree near Mangkurrurpa, covered the survivors with mud and ochre to heal their burns, and when they recovered they flew on to the north-east.

The cry of the stone-curlew seems to come from some other dimension, in which all the world's sorrow is lamented by the fugitive bird. By day they are silent and secretive, turning sidelong on their spindle legs as if to say, *I am invisible, you haven't seen me.* In the Dreamtime they would have been more robust, singing and dancing, creating the rock holes and soak-waters, flying from one stony ridge to the next. I imagine them, half-man, half-bird, dipping and leaping and making their strange, wild cries, falling on burning wings into the black plumes of smoke.

It's moments like this that shake me loose from my own filtered consciousness into the vibrating strangeness of a world in which there are none of the contemporary reference points I take for granted. They are the moments I wait for, because they offer a glimpse of some other kind of framework for knowing this country, this place we live in and belong to.

The next day we have a recording session. I've long wanted to get Margaret's story on record, and she tells it with gusto: being born somewhere to the north on Gordon Downs, travelling as a child with the droving mobs, and how the drovers put piglets in the packsaddles when they were too small to walk. Later she was a cook, and married a Walmajarri man and had five children, but all this time her mother and aunties taught her the stories and songs of her country — her mother's country, over which we had so recently travelled.

I proffer the microphone to Dora, jokingly, because she isn't one to say much, and to my surprise she begins to speak in English. When it becomes clear that she has plenty to say, I give the microphone to Margaret to hold before the old woman, and Dora lapses into her own language. The drink yesterday from the spring near her birthplace has acted on her like a magic potion.

Poet and linguist Lee Cataldi translated Dora's story for me from Ngardi high language, in a voice full of poetic resonance and pragmatic detail. The fragments I have reproduced have been altered only in the structure of line lengths and by some excisions to make them more accessible:

> We two went to Kuyurru, from Kuyurru to Warlu, at Warlu we
>   stopped.
> We camped, father was present, he made the camp.
>
> At dawn we set off again together, on foot, with the half-caste.
> He said, 'Wait until morning.'

We went together and he brought us to the white woman.
He said to us she would not be hostile.
She was there. We stayed there.
Later we went on to a creek, to the other side.
From there we set off.
We went east, we collected rations,
we went on, and in the west we stopped ...

Then we set off again to Wiripirn. At Wiripirn we slept.
From Wiripirn we went east from Munjawuny,
then south to Gordon Downs.
We stopped there at Gordon Downs. We ate what was nearby.
My brother attacked the halfcaste with an axe.
From there we took him upwards to Gordon Downs and I stayed.

We went to Ngawirdi, to Purluyantirni,
At that place we waited and waited for those other two,
from there we went on towards water, to Miriny.
We left Miriny where we had slept
and went to another place with water, to Jakunta,
and from the south to Yalungurra and there we stayed,
the place suited us.

We set out again.
At Majuny we stopped, my sister, my daughter and myself.
Thus we set off, we went on, at Warlu we stopped and slept.
There we collected yams and ate them,
we ate until we were full then set out again.
We travelled on until we were ready to sleep.

From there, having slept, we went to Puka, not far to the west.

We dug for water. This was a good place to camp.
This was a place for finding wallabies.
And here also we found edible grass seeds, two kinds,
and the seed-bearing wattle tree.
We slept there, and while we stayed the brother-in-law went.
Then he came back. 'Let's go,' he said,
and we set off to the south, to Wardiyawu.
Soon they went down for water. We got water and brought it
    down.
Further south we stopped to sleep.

Our time in the north finished, and I did not stay.
We went on to Mikin, which was not too good,
so we turned off a long way east.
We had to go a long way to find a spring.
From there we went to Mantirripu, from Mantirripu inside to
    Kipiki,
then to Kanapi, to the rock hole, from there to Ngipiri, a long trip.
We climbed up from there in a very bad wind.
We ate a big perentie, rain fell on us, we came back under a dark
    sky.

While they waited for the aunt we went hunting to Muwurlpari.
We hunted a snake, found and caught it,
then we returned to the camp where we stayed.

'Aeroplane, aeroplane!
At the camp, up above us, a plane, a plane above us! Look!'
We went and hid in the bush.
Then we came out of the bush and looked around above us.
'*Waraa*! Where has it gone?'

We all went to sleep, we placed the child between us and lay down.
At sunrise we left and went to Yantirripuru.
From the east, it may have come down.
The old man Nyunku-nyunku came from that direction.
'From there where it came down, now it is there.'

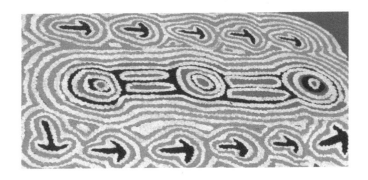

Only Margaret can follow the story, but Pam, Jess, and I are enthralled by the rhythms and gestures of the old woman's delivery, her hands speaking with as much authority as her voice. And there are words we all recognise — *kakarra, karlarra, kulirra, kayili* — east, west, south, north. These are the cardinal directions, the words for which are consistent across the languages spoken in the region because all the stories for this country involve travelling.

Early in the morning we came out and lined up.
There were two old women, a visit.
He came out now, the young man.
They brought the young man to us
and there they initiated him.
When that was finished we went,
we stopped at Wara for vegetable food.
We stopped and camped and slept. Then we went back.

'Policeman there!'
The policeman came up to us.
'Stop! Hold the dogs!'
He shot at them.
He tied up the man. My brother.

Then we went a long way south to Mount River,
and at Mount River we lost the old woman.
We went up and down through the hills to Tarrku,
to Mount River, to Kampiny, to Kiliki, inside.

'A group of armed men are coming!'
A group of men came from Balgo, from the east
and at sunrise they fought.
We stayed there and waited for the bullock meat.
Then we went west.
A long way north we ate and slept, at Pijan-pijan.
Then we went to Jupkarra,
 to Kunyarrjarra, to Linji,
from Linji west, to Gordon Downs.
At Linji a man came with a horse, just one.
'He's going to speak to us!'
'What for you coming?'
'Auntie.'
'Might be trouble.'
'Let's go north.
A long way north.'

She talks for almost an hour, until her voice rasps to a standstill.
—Did you hear all that before? Pam asks Margaret.
—Nothing, she says.

+ + +

It is common now to treat the journey as a metaphor, but there was a time when the journey and the traveller and the story were the same thing. Just as the journey and the ground it traversed were the same, so too was the person who made the journey and described it. Place lodged in the body, as essential to its proper functioning as the circulation of the blood and the apprehension of thoughts. There was a time when we walked into consciousness through our journeys, when our awareness was brand-new, so that the shape and texture and sound and smell of the journey remained in us, a real and vivid part of our substance.

Maybe it was this that forced a burgeoning in language. Maybe the small human ancestor, the one whose descendants found their way out of Africa, maybe that little brain grew to the task of naming all it saw, describing all it experienced, on her way into destiny. Maybe this is how language began, as a journey and a poem.

+ + +

It's been some time since Margaret has been back to her mother's country, and she's itching to burn the areas where the buck spinifex and turpentine wattle has taken over.

—You tell Jim we gotta clean this country, she tells me, and I pass on the message.

Jim looks dubious. The last time the traditional owners cleaned the country, the only thing left standing was the anthills. But that was a November fire, a 'mistake' that the hot wind got behind and swept down through the spinifex until it reached the salt lakes and ran out of vegetation to burn. This is June, already proving to be a cold winter, and there's a lot of moisture in the country after the big wet season. Although the country Margaret wants to clean is part of the station lease, it's fringe grazing land, and the cattle rarely travel far into it. It's safer to burn in the cool and moderately calm conditions than risk the summer lightning setting off a holocaust. Jim agrees with this, and a few days later I find myself enlisted as chief driver for the cleaning operation.

Margaret's housekeeping technique is to sit in the passenger seat of my utility with a skirt full of matches, which she strikes and throws out the window at short intervals. I keep my eyes on the wheel tracks, twin orange lines barely visible under the leaning swathes of spinifex. In the rear-vision mirror I can see the nibble and flare of flame, and the boil of black smoke as the resinous heart of the spinifex ignites.

—If we get a flat tyre, I'm going to keep driving.

—*Yuwayi*, otherwise we cook the motorcar.

Margaret thinks this is hilarious, but I'm not amused.

The flames of Margaret's fire are visible through the night. Waking before sunrise at our camp site near Mangkurrurpa, I can see the glow to the south-west, mirroring the dawn that is still only a glimmer to the east. The hills of Manyjurungu are dark shapes on the horizon. It feels close, intimate, familiar.

It's as if we just swept out the kitchen, I think.

STOCK ROUTE DREAMING

2007

The river is a highway, the names along its length the signposts of deep time. In spite of being moved off their country, the river people still hold a wealth of detail in their knowledge of this particular homeland. Where the river breaks and diffuses into a mosaic of claypans and swamps, memory also diffuses, and ownership becomes contested. Satellite imagery shows a landscape as pockmarked as the surface of the moon. In this ephemeral topography only the names of a few places survive — of the soak-waters and permanent pools, and of the semi-saline claypans that grow the samphire *Tecticornia verrucosa*, prized for its edible small black seeds that are harvested when the plant dries out. Otherwise, this landscape is defined by evidence of white settlement — the yards where cattle were held and branded, the fence-lines and paddocks of the station days. Where the water gathers again into the broad flat reaches of the lake country, memory clarifies, but with less detail than along the river.

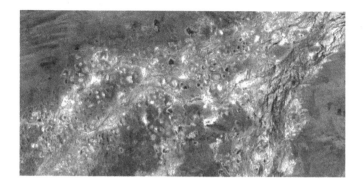

The waterhole where the Tanami track crosses the river, near Billiluna community, is called Jawilingkilingki. It is the last permanent waterhole before the river forks, and marks the end of old man Boxer Milner's country. Beyond it, the twin channels weave their way down to the Paruku wetlands, the eastern channel feeding into the lake that Augustus Gregory named Gregory Salt Sea in 1856, the western channel dividing its waters between half-a-dozen shallow freshwater lakes that are marked on early maps as plains, indicating that they are often dry. A vast flood-out of claypans fills the delta between the two arms of the river, and an elevational map of the region reveals that this low-lying country was at one time part of the inland sea of which the current lake basins are a remnant. These floodplains and permanent waterholes provided the grazing country that became Billiluna Station, later divided into two stations, Billiluna and Lake Gregory.

Beyond the lakes, to the south-west, a chain of wells that came to be called the Canning Stock Route follow the course of ancient channels buried beneath the sands of the Great Sandy Desert. Passing through country occupied by some of the last people to leave their desert way of life, the Canning Stock Route is an incomparable storyline, an almost perfect example of a narrative that occupies two simultaneous realities. The one best known to white Australians until recently is the story of establishing the stock route in order to bring beef on the hoof from the Kimberley to the West Australian goldfields. In 1906, the job of finding water and sinking wells was given to the West Australian government surveyor, Alfred Canning, and, by his own lights and those of the time in which he lived, he fulfilled his brief admirably. That the wells his party established were on the sites of Aboriginal waterholes and soaks, and that the structure of the wells often made the water inaccessible to the desert people who depended on them, was not factored into the original assessment, although it was the reason for the subsequent destruction of many of the wells and the hostility of the people whose country had been transgressed.

When Alfred Canning set out to survey the stock route, it was generally assumed that the Aboriginal denizens of the desert were a primitive people with primitive conceptual systems. Whether Canning was familiar with the work of his contemporaries Spencer and Gillen is something I don't know, but there is no evidence that he took on board the emerging knowledge of a complex cosmology and culture.

Within a decade of its establishment, the Canning Stock Route was considered too dangerous, and the water supplies too unreliable, for travelling stock, and it was almost another decade before the wells were refurbished in a way that made them usable for both stock and humans. The stock route was in regular use between 1931 and 1959, when a thousand bullocks would be mustered every year from Billiluna and sent in two mobs down the stock route.

It is this period that is still within living memory of the Kukatja, Pintupi and Martu people for whom the desert was home. It is also a time that is significant to the Walmajarri lake people and Jaru river people, since by then their homelands had been turned into

cattle country. While their relatives in the deep desert watched with
bemusement as the bullock mobs walked south, the Walmajarri
travelled with them as cooks and stockmen and camel boys.

Harry Hall, who was the mainstay of the Mongrel Downs stock
camp in the years we lived there, told my mother the story of making one of the last trips down the Canning as a twelve-year-old
boy. My mother transcribed it for publication as 'On the Track',
a chapter in a collection called *The Stockman*, which also contains
chapters by Mary Durack and R.M. Williams. As far as I know,
it is the first published account of the Canning by an Aboriginal
stockman. I notice in a recent travellers' guide to the Canning
Stock Route that the transcription is wrongly attributed to Mary
Durack. So much for history.

Harry made the trip in the winter of 1956 with Wally Dowling,
who was taking the second mob down the Canning that year. Mal
Brown, brother of Billiluna manager Len Brown, had taken the
first mob a month earlier, it being the practice to split the bullocks
into two mobs of five hundred head each. It was not practicable to
travel with larger numbers, since the water had to be bucketed up
from the wells and tipped into a trough, and it took all night to
water a mob of five hundred. On the trip Harry made, they were
carrying a recent advance on mule power — an engine and fuel to
pump the water, which took about six hours.

There are several elements of his tale that have stayed with me,
as they clearly stayed with him. At Well 43 they encountered an old
man and his two sons, a teenage boy and a little boy, and gave them
some beef. On the return trip, they found the teenager at Well 44,
with a half-healed spear wound in his side. He told them that, soon
after they had passed through, a Kukatja man had come into their
camp. He seemed friendly, and they had shared their food with
him. Sometime in the night he had leapt up and speared the old

man, and then bashed in the head of the little boy. The older boy had run for his life, sustaining a serious spear wound. Knowing the drovers would be returning, he had gone north and waited near the next well. Wally Dowling took the teenager back to Billiluna, and he grew up to be the stockman called Pluto. Another event that frightened the young Harry was his sighting of a corpse — an old woman lying dead in the spinifex. It was the custom of the desert people to leave their dead for the animals and crows, once the spirit had left them. The Walmajarri buried their dead, and Harry thought the desert people very primitive.

Harry also told my mother a story told to him by his auntie, who had been a cook on a droving trip ten years earlier. She had woken in the night to the sounds of an attack, and had run for the night-horse tethered nearby. The boy on night watch had escaped with her, but they were the only survivors, making their way by stages back to the station.

These were the stories the Walmajarri told. For the thirty years during which the stock route was a corridor through the desert, they had been cattle people. A droving trip was as much a part of the annual cycle of events as their initiation ceremonies, which now took place during the months that were not dedicated to cattle work. The Martu and Kukatja watched the mobs passing south, and eventually came to depend on them for some of their winter supplies, once they had learned how to differentiate and use the food. Freda Tjama describes one small party of people devouring each kind of food separately — one person ate all the flour, someone else ate the tea-leaves, a woman ate several pounds of salt and had a headache for days. Meanwhile the Walmajarri lived in the porous zone of the borderlands, making their accommodations with the settlers who had taken up their country for cattle, in an uneasy and sometimes volatile relationship.

The Canning always hummed in the background as one of those half-mythical stories I grew up with. In 1962, Billiluna Station included Lake Gregory, which did not become a separate lease until 1965. At that time, the station was owned by the Doman sisters, Margaret and Lorna. Lorna was married to Bill Wilson, who owned pastoral properties in South Australia. Margaret ran Carnegie Station, near Wiluna at the southern end of the route, where the Billiluna droving plant was spelled before making the return trip after the bullocks were delivered. The Aboriginal people who remembered her spoke of her with respect and affection. Rumour had it that she was more than just the employer of boss drover Mal Brown — and while I have no proof, I hope it's true. I met her when I was twelve years old, when she rescued me from the Perth boarding school in which I was incarcerated, and took me to her farm for the Easter break. She was a tall, big-boned, no-nonsense woman, and I spent several happy days throwing out fodder for the stock, feeding the poddy calves and driving around the paddocks. The old drover sat in a chair by the wood stove in the kitchen, sipping rum and making occasional gravel-voiced remarks.

The closure of the Canning Stock Route in 1959 contributed in part to my family settling in the Tanami for long enough to establish the links that still hold me, the better part of a lifetime later. In 1962, the search was underway for a route to take cattle from Billiluna to Central Australia and the southern markets. For cattle to travel north to the ports at Derby or Wyndham, they had to pass through country infested with cattle tick, restricting access to certain markets and significantly lowering their value. The tick-free status of Billiluna stock, along with their freedom from pleuro-pneumonia, meant they could travel into the Northern Territory and southern Australia without restrictions, and could be purchased as breeding stock by Central Australian cattlemen whose herds had been depleted by drought.

The exploration party included Bill Wilson, two Central Australian pastoralists interested in purchasing cattle from Billiluna, the Alice Springs manager of Elder Smith stock and station agency, and my father, who was a field stock inspector attached to the Animal Industry Branch of the Northern Territory administration, based in Alice Springs. The party crossed the Tanami to the north of what would become the stock route without finding suitable surface water for travelling stock, and it was on the more southerly return journey that they discovered the ephemeral lakes and the grasslands that had been described to my parents by Wason Byers a decade earlier. It was excellent pastoral country, and Bill Wilson, the two cattlemen, Bill Waudby and Milton Willick, and my father, Joe Mahood, applied for a pastoral lease. Willick and Waudby withdrew from the partnership within the first year, for reasons I don't know, and my parents entered a joint partnership with Bill and Lorna Wilson. My father took on the management of the new station, which would function both as a breeding property and as a staging point on the route to market for the Billiluna bullocks. Billiluna Station was without a manager for a few months around the time that some basic infrastructure was being installed on Mongrel Downs, so my father took over as interim manager until the new one arrived.

I imagine this is when he acquired the map of Billiluna Station that I found among his papers after his death, the excision for the Canning Stock Route showing as a strip through the middle of the lease. The map was a beautiful object, foxed and stained. I had a copy of it made before laminating the original onto a piece of canvas, along with several other maps, and incorporating it into a painting. In retrospect I'm horrified that I treated it in such a cavalier way, especially as I later cut the painting into several vertical panels that

I used as the basis for a series of drawings. The map is just visible, spanning two panels, obscured by the pigments and charcoal of the superimposed drawings. I've lately begun to peel away the surface layer of laminated paper, along with the drawing, to expose the map beneath. It's a painstaking process, and only partly successful.

I love this map. It is two things at once — an artefact designed for practical use, and a document on which time has wrought another topography. It is full of hidden stories, secrets, lost histories. On the black-and-white copy of the original, the stains that have seeped through the folds show up like Rorschach inkblots along the fold lines. The inkblots mirror each other in diminishing layers of saturation, the modulated grey tones and ragged edges creating a shadow topography, the contours of a secret country. Their almost-symmetry hints at an organising principle more fundamental than the grid on which the map is based.

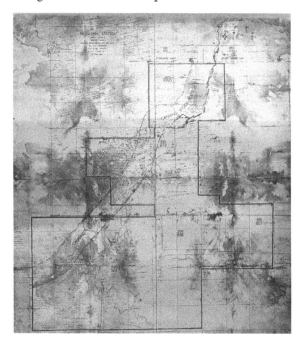

The date on the map is 30 July 1963, and the scale is marked as two miles to one inch. According to this measure, the stock route is approximately three miles wide, encompassing the eastern arm of Sturt Creek and a swathe of claypans and anabranches across the flood delta. It was in October 1963 that my father took over as temporary manager of Billiluna, and I have a photograph of him at Well 51, or Weriaddo, the last of the Canning Stock Route wells. It's a few kilometres inside the station boundary, close to Delivery Camp, where the big mobs that travelled down the Canning were delivered to the drovers.

Alfred Canning, sinking that final well at a brackish soak-water west of Paruku, transcribed the name he heard as Weriaddo, which in the current orthography is written as Wirriyarra, and is almost interchangeable with Riwiyarra, the name of the man who escaped the Sturt Creek massacre. His descendants say that the names are different, but they agree that Riwiyarra was adopted by lake people from this area, and their own association with the lake is based on this. He had two wives and fathered seven children, whose descendants identify as river people with a traditional connection to the lake. Riwiyarra evaded the massacre and fled south to the lake. His family told me that he was shot some time later — whether months or years is not clear, nor who shot him.

—Some *kartiya*. Murderers, was all that my questioning elicited.

As the trickster hero of the morphing massacre narrative, Riwiyarra lives on in the imprecise contours of the shadow country. His last surviving son, who might have been able to say who he was and where he came from, died recently in the Halls Creek frail-aged facility.

Well 51 has been disused for many years, and the windmill that was erected to replace the hand windlass of the droving days no longer functions, though its blades still turn when there's a wind. Among the earliest entries in my father's diary is a reference to equipping Weriaddo, so the windmill was installed in 1963. By 2005, when I first saw it, it was one more piece of broken infrastructure from the station days.

+ + +

The Canning Stock Route Art Project is an ambitious attempt to tell the story of the stock route through Aboriginal voices. Conceived in 2006 by my friend Tim Acker from Balgo days, and taken up by his partner, Carly Davenport, who pitched it to the Perth-based cultural organisation FORM where she worked, the plan was to travel the length of the stock route with the traditional owners of each section, painting the country and recording the Aboriginal stories and memories of the stock-route era. The paintings, photographs, and documentary films produced during the trip would provide the material for an exhibition at the National Museum of Australia, to coincide with the 2010 centenary of the opening of the stock route, and to bring into focus the untold dimension of this pioneer myth. A network of existing art centres — Martumili in Newman, Mangkaja in Fitzroy Crossing, Warlayirti in Balgo — served as communication nodes to draw together the Aboriginal people best placed to provide structure and direction to the project, and Tim's position advising art centres on management practices gave him access to all the main players.

By 2007, the Paruku mob have already made painted maps of Lake Gregory and Sturt Creek, and my role as co-ordinator of map-making projects has been incorporated into the annual work plan of the Paruku Indigenous Protected Area. As our contribution to the Canning Stock Route project, we are invited to paint a map of the section of the Canning that falls under the jurisdiction of the eastern Walmajarri. It is my fourth consecutive year of spending several months in the community.

For the first time, I have access to a data projector to prepare the map, so I rig a primitive pulley system in my quarters, which I am now sharing with the IPA equipment, and project the stock-route section onto it. This is more difficult than it sounds, and less accurate than the hand-drawn grid-and-transfer method, but it is faster, and the scatter of hundreds of claypans that comprise the flood-out delta are more easily traced with projection. Once I have the template drawn in chalk, I enlist the help of Lulu and Anna Johns to paint the base map, which we will carry with us, rolled in a length of sewer pipe.

The section of the stock route that the Paruku mob is entitled to claim and map is the excision through the Billiluna lease, still in existence today. To travel it means following the original road, the dry-season track from Billiluna that skirts the western edge of the flood-out country. We have among our party old Frank Gordon, who made the trip three times as a young stockman. As for the rest, most of them have participated in mustering the bullocks and taking them to Delivery Camp, to be handed over to the drovers. Bill Doonday worked as a stockman on Billiluna, and Bessie cooked for the stock camp as a young woman.

South of Billiluna we pass through an extended belt of desert-oak country, the grand, mysterious trees whispering their ancient conversations, and then turn east to Nelly Yard, an old set of stockyards located near a deep, permanent pool called Kurrumpajartu on the western branch of the lower Sturt. An elegiac mood takes hold of the travellers, and they wander about, patting the timber rails of the stockyards, pointing out where the bough shed used to be, where the stockmen used to camp, where the women used to fish in the afternoons before the men came back from mustering.

On our first night out we camp at C25, so named for one of Canning's marked trees, carved with his initial and a number to indicate the route taken by his party. The traditional name of the place is Nyarnajarra, which translates as two deep waterholes, and we set up camp on the banks of one of them. In the morning I bring out the painted map and chalk the names of the sites we have visited so far, and any details people think should be added. They want to put down the names of all the Aboriginal cooks and stockmen who made droving trips, but most of the names can't be spoken aloud because the people are dead.

—You can writem down later, quiet one, Charmia instructs me.

We are a small party — Wade driving the troop carrier and me driving my ute, ten passengers between us, and Pirate, my new dog. Wade is towing a heavily loaded trailer, and the shattering corrugations break its springs on the second morning, about ten kilometres out from C25 in the grasslands north of Delivery Camp. Wade calls Mulan on the satellite phone for someone to bring a replacement trailer and pick up the broken one. The weather is good and there is bush tucker to be had, so it is no hardship to wander and explore until the trailer arrives, and the equipment and supplies are transferred.

I am happy. There is nothing I like better than exploring new country, especially in the company of people who have stories about it and connections to it. Although they are mostly elderly and need looking after — wedging Bessie's portable toilet seat between the swags on the roof-rack of my ute is a daily challenge — they know me well enough now not to order me about. Among the party is Daisy Kungah, whose father came from Kanningarra near Well 48. Younger and more robust than the others, Daisy proves

to be an asset, gathering firewood, washing dishes and making and
distributing cups of tea.

While we wait for the trailer I take some of the party to the
outer-western lake of Kilangkilang, and then on past Werriaddo
to Delivery Camp, where Bill Doonday and Frank Gordon become animated, talking about the stock camp days. Both Frank's
parents travelled the stock route, his mother as a cook and his
father as chief camel man. I write down pertinent bits of information and take GPS readings of the locations people say belong on
the map. The replacement trailer doesn't arrive at the breakdown
camp until after dark, so we settle in for another night, and move
on the next morning.

When it is discovered at the Well 49 lunch stop that the tobacco supply has run out, the heavy smokers in the party want to
turn back, but Daisy delivers them a blast of invective that carries a
stronger charge than nicotine withdrawal. She is impressively fero-
cious, with her thick grey hair recently shorn for sorry business,
and a rolling eye that most of the time is only a little off-centre,
but becomes wild and wandering when she is angry. Her fury dis-
patches the opposition, and although I don't understand what she
has said I get the gist, which is that they are not going to sabotage
her opportunity to visit her father's country, which she had not
seen for many years.

Later that day, we come out of the sand-dune country into
grassy plains dominated by a spectacular range of flat-topped
sandstone hills. Daisy directs us to the foot of one of these, capped
by two jutting, westward-angled ridges. These are her sisters, she
tells us, two Nangalas who stopped here to groom each other's hair
for lice. I take a photograph of Daisy grinning proudly beneath
the majestic nit-picking Nangalas, glowing red-gold in the light
of the lowering sun.

This makes me think of an earnest young art student at the university where I taught until recently. She was visiting from Canada, and was critiquing the dictionary of an Aboriginal language (she didn't specify which language — I'm not sure if she was aware that there was more than one) because it had been brought to her attention that there were no words in it for 'beauty', and she interpreted this oversight as a covert form of racism, reinforcing the assumption that Aboriginal people lacked aesthetic appreciation. I didn't take her to task — the crit session was almost over — but there were many things I might have said. For instance, that words like 'fat', and 'shiny', and 'healthy' all meant 'beautiful'. And that beauty may be inferred in the bond between two ancestral sisters picking the nits out of each other's hair.

There was no question that Daisy found them beautiful, her body bursting with the joy of being back in her father's country. Earlier, when we had crested the last sandhill, and the gold and silver and sage and crimson of the plains and ranges had come suddenly into view, I yelled aloud at the sight. In the passenger seat beside me, Charmia also yelled, *Karnti*! In the eyes of an elderly desert woman, wild potato was as beautiful a sight as the shining hills were to me. She insisted we stop while she investigated the nearest plants, and scampered across the desert terrain like an elderly elf.

We set up camp within a protective arc of the range, and it feels as if we are tucked between the paws of a great beast. Someone remarks that the landscape looks like the cowboy-and-Indian country in the movies. In the morning a butcherbird calls from the cliffs, a liquid double note that spills and echoes in the sandstone amphitheatre. It sings on, while Daisy scouts for firewood and I fan last night's coals to life and set the billies to boil. It is cool, what the Walmajarri and thin-blooded Wade call cold, and Daisy and I are the only two humans moving in the shadow of the range. When I look up to try to spot the bird, I see that its song is coming from the point where the sunrise touches the northern side of the range. As the sun rises higher, the shadow slips down the side of the hill, draining away as the hill fills with light.

—I'd sing too, I say to the bird, if this is what I woke up to every morning.

After breakfast we pack up and drive as close to the Kanningarra rock hole as we can get, and then walk the half-kilometre of stony track to reach the permanent rock pool that is tucked under an overhang of cliffs. At the rock hole, Wade films Daisy speaking about her father and what she knows of the place, while Charmia stands by. Later, Lulu tells Charmia off for allowing herself to be filmed on someone else's country, and Charmia begs Wade to make sure to cut her out of the film before it is shown to anyone.

Well 48 is near the turnoff to Kanningarra, and we stop there while Frank recounts his memories of walking ahead of the cattle, pulling out poison weed. We have travelled beyond the jurisdiction of our painted map, which people agree ends at Well 50 in the south and Jawilingkilingki in the north, where the Tanami road crosses the Sturt. The core party of Martu and Kukatja artists and the support team, which includes my friends Tim Acker and John Carty and Danny Glasby, are travelling up the stock route from the south, but there is no sign of them. The nicotine-deprived members of the party are beginning to implode, so the decision is made to go back and to only make camp if it is too late to make it to Billiluna before midnight. I would have preferred to stay and reconnoitre with the northbound travellers, but everyone other than Daisy is out of their comfort zone, and we are out-voted. There are too many ghosts out here, too many untold stories — and no tobacco.

—I need a shower, Bessie says on the drive home.

—I need a shower too, I say. I stink!

—Yeah, me, I really stink, Bessie says.

—Us too! they call from the back seat. We all stink!

Back in Mulan, we regroup and prepare for a final gathering of the artists and support team at Lake Stretch, also called Nyarna, which means 'deep water', the permanent waterhole and campground south of Billiluna. Word comes through that the party travelling up the stock route has arrived, and that groups coming in from Fitzroy Crossing and further afield are on their way. I collect my troops, tents, bedding, dog, and the painted map, and we set off again.

It's a slow trip, towing a trailer on the track through the floodout country of the lower Sturt. We cross the two red sandhills where Bessie was born, driving for a time through soft red country with scattered desert oaks and eucalypts, until we reach the first of the claypans, a perfect circle surrounded by thick, low ti-tree, and this year full of water. It's one of my favourite spots, and I always stop here if I'm travelling alone. There are scatterings of mussel shells on the sandy banks, and grinding stones and flakes of quartz that indicate old camp sites. From here the vegetation changes as we enter the zone that would once have been part of the ancient lake basin. This is the heart of the country on the painted map, the eastern edge of the stock-route excision that follows the eastern channel of the Sturt. On the satellite image it looks like a spray of foam.

Whenever we drive through this part of the country, the women test my knowledge of the different trees and their Walmajarri names and uses. *Wakila* is an important medicine tree, *Eremophila bignoniiflora*, which I have no difficulty recognising because of its bright-green drooping leaves. It is used to make infusions, and the leaves are burned for smoking women who have recently given birth, and for smoking babies to make them strong. I have more difficulty with the two wattles, *parrayari* and *pukurlpirri* — not in telling them apart, which is easy enough, but in remembering which is which. Eventually I realise that *parrayari* is *Acacia pachycarpa*, the same tree that grows along the edges of the plains on Tanami Downs, and which botanist Peter Latz has identified as one of the rare wattles of the Tanami region. Here it grows along the drainage lines of the Sturt as well as on the plains. *Pukurlpirri* is *Acacia stenophylla,* prized for the sweet gum it exudes at certain times of the year, which is edible and was also used in traditional times to bond spearheads and woomera pegs. In these motorised days, it's used to mend holes in car radiators.

Today my passengers are Bessie and Lulu, Monica, Wendy Wise, and Anna. Wade will bring the rest of the Mulan mob in the troop carrier. The camp is in full swing when we arrive, with groundsheets spread in the shade, and painters working on half-finished canvases. I stake out a spot and put up the tents under the supervision of my passengers, who wait until the last tent peg has been driven in before saying that there are too many trees in this location and they want to move up to the open country near the cattle yards. I tell them they are welcome to move under their own steam.

—You should listen to us, Napurrula, Lulu says.

I think of a number of answers to this, but say none of them.

The project is a rolling media event, and there are clusters of people operating various kinds of recording equipment — still cameras, video cameras, buffered microphones. A contingent of newspaper reporters is expected to arrive sometime during the

186

day. The camp kitchen is a functional arrangement of benches and condiments and stacked boxes of foodstuffs. Two cooking fires support a multitude of blackened pots, and a large laundry sink has been set up for washing dishes. A dismembered bullock lies in a pile of gum leaves on an open trailer.

I recognise Tim Acker's hand in this orderly and practical arrangement, and find him at a table under the shade of a big river red gum, doling out paint from plastic containers. Since the Balgo days I have encountered Tim at various places along the network of tracks that service our semi-itinerant work practices. It might be in Perth or Alice Springs or Canberra — or, just as likely, Balgo or Koonawarriji or Newman. Today it happens to be the last watering hole on the Canning Stock Route. With the toughest part of the journey behind him, he's relaxed and cheerful. If I were ever faced with a desert-island survival scenario, Tim would be at the top of the list of companions I'd want on the island.

John and Danny would come a close second, not for their survival skills but for their always-entertaining conversation. They are at the fire drinking tea, and I spend a pleasant half-hour catching up with them, ignoring the pointed mutterings coming from those at the Mulan camp, who are hanging out for a cup of tea and lunch. Anna has identified a nephew among the Fitzroy mob and is organising some personalised service, and Monica has gone off to find brothers and cousins and aunties from the desert branch of her family, but Bessie and Lulu sit in state, waiting for the acknowledgement owed them as traditional owners of the country. I take them a cup of tea and a sandwich, and observe the shifting dynamics of the camp as people come to pay their respects, share sorry business, and gossip. Appeased, the sisters become cheerful and talkative, and Bessie waves her cup at me to indicate that she wants more tea.

Space to work is at a premium, so I scout the area for a suitable spot to lay out our big canvas. There's a shaded grassy area not far from the water, and I throw down a groundsheet and unroll the map, weighting the corners with stones. People drift over to look, and the Billiluna contingent gathers to discuss the protocols of who will paint where.

Most of the canvases painted by this gathering of artists reflect the conventions of Western Desert art — the routes people travelled in the bushman days, the songlines of the ancestors and the circuitry of embodied knowledge. The stock route was one track among many through their homelands. There are a number of highly acclaimed artists in the group. Observing the works in progress is like entering a force field in which the gesture of laying paint on canvas completes a circuit that begins and ends with country, the body of the painter serving as a transformer to direct some of that perpetual current into a visible expression of the charge it carries.

What the Paruku mob are doing is mapping the double sensibility that has held sway over this part of the country since the first white settlers followed Sturt Creek down to Lake Gregory and laid claim to the remotest pastoral country in the Kimberley. The lake people had to contend with *kartiya* and their cattle a generation before the desert people. By the time the cattle were travelling down the Canning on a regular basis, the Paruku Walmajarri were displaced or enlisted into the cattle culture. But the story didn't end there. One hundred years after the first white men brought their stock down onto the floodplains and coolibah flats of the lake country, the native title rights of the Walmajarri were acknowledged at a formal handover, and the cattle stations of Billiluna and Lake Gregory were declared the first Indigenous Protected Area in the Kimberley.

To replicate the formal topography of the *kartiya* map is just a starting point. This is both a map and a painting — it needs to hold up aesthetically in the company of the vibrant works being produced by the other artists. I suggest that since we have recently visited most of the country on the map, we should use different-coloured dots to indicate the different types of vegetation. It's agreed that this is a good idea, and we mark out rough boundaries to indicate shifts in country types and vegetation. Between the two arms of Sturt Creek are the grasslands — pale creams and bleached ochres. Just south of Billiluna the country has been recently burned, and is covered in bright new growth, so lime green over red ochre is the colour code of choice for that area. Beyond it, the stretch of desert oak is yellow ochre and black. And so we paint according to what is growing and flowering at this time of the year. The yellow of wattle bloom marks much of the east, and on the south-west corner of the map Charmia stipples in a section of fine black dots to show that there's been a fire.

The newspaper journalists have arrived, and I am asked several times to move so that the photographer can get a picture with no whitefellas in it to disturb the integrity of the image. The third time it happens, Anna suggests we tell the photographer I'm a little bit half-caste. Shirley Brown is cross on my behalf.

—We wouldn't have this map without her, she says.

I'm half amused, half irritated. While I have no interest in being included in the photographs, this desire to keep the whitefellas out of the picture distorts the reality that our stories are enmeshed, and can't be separated. Which is what our map is all about.

In the late afternoon, the paintings are laid out side by side along the bank of the lagoon, the corners held down by cans of beetroot and pineapple and baked beans from the expedition supplies. It's a remarkable sight, a route through the desert represented and conceptualised in so many different ways.

The next day Tim distributes the surplus supplies, and the camp resembles a refugee food drop. Anna, who minutes before has been telling me she feels too weak to roll her swag, scurries about filling an enormous garbage bag with Weeties and toilet paper and tinned food, and anything else she can lay her hands on. Monica stows the best part of a bullock's hindquarter under a mattress on the trailer. In the boom-and-bust economy of the desert, it's boom time, and no one is about to miss out on this opportunity. I snaffle a box of anchovies from a passing child, who can't possibly want it.

Once the supplies have been handed out, the various groups pack up in preparation for departure. I dismantle and fold the tents, roll swags, and pack cups and plates and cooking utensils.

—Hey, Napuru, you forgot this, Lulu complains, brandishing her cooking pot.

—I didn't forget it, I just haven't got to it yet. How come it's always about what I should do, or haven't done, or forgot? What about, *Hey, Napuru, you doing a really good job!*

Several times during the next hour, as I load the gear onto the ute and trailer, Lulu tells me I'm doing a really good job. I can't tell whether she's being ironic, but I don't think so.

Although we blocked in large areas of the map while we were at the Lake Stretch camp, there are a lot of details to complete before it is ready to send off for the National Museum exhibition. Wade agrees to let me use the concrete slab behind his demountable as a painting space, and Lulu is the painter who turns up day after day to work on the map until it is finished. Sometimes she enlists a group of young women to help, but most days it is just her and me. The painting attracts a flow of visitors to comment on and admire it.

Lulu is in her element. She can paint dots for hours, mixing the paint to a particular consistency and then working with a rhythm of dip, dot-dot, dip, dot-dot that fills sections of canvas with surprising speed. That rhythmic energy transfers itself to the canvas, animating the surface into fields of shimmering colour. I learn to dot, sitting beside her, but I never achieve the loose, intuitive pattern that flows off the end of her dotting stick. It is like working on the mosaic with Lucy. My sections are too consciously plotted, the mind rather than the body controlling the process. But I teach Lulu about mixing colour, which she takes on with enthusiasm. Visitors come and go, the life of the community flows around us, and I begin to understand that for Lulu the painting is not only a source of status and income, it is a meditation practice that keeps her anchored and calm amidst the pressures and demands made on her by her family. Although only in her late fifties, she is a great-grandmother several times over, the centrifugal force around which the clan turns.

+ + +

Until it was destroyed in a fire that burnt down the kitchen and the staff dining room of the Billiluna homestead sometime in the 1960s, a hand-drawn map of the stock route graced a wall of the dining room. It was described to me by Bruce Farrands, of Rabbit Flat Roadhouse fame, who worked at Billiluna as a stockman in the early sixties. Annotated over the years by the hands of different drovers, it was as much a record of the seasons and events that occurred along the desert corridor as it was a description of a route. I can only imagine it, thirty years of stories inscribed on it, a desert scroll documenting the seasonal passage of herdsmen travelling south through the winter pasture with the cattle, returning north, much faster, with their camels and horses and mules, living mostly off the land. Harry Hall said galahs were good eating if you were hungry enough. Without mishap, the trip down and back took five months.

It would be interesting to compare the drovers' map with Canning's map. While there would be many differences, there would also be much in common. Canning noted the types of fodder along the route. I imagine the drovers' map described areas of poison bush and the places where feed was reliable. Encounters with the desert people would be recorded, and whether they were hostile or friendly. Both maps are journeys, scrolls on which the day past is inscribed, and the day to come, for Canning at least, a blank to be inscribed.

A map produced for *Ngurra Kuju Walyja — One Country One People: stories from the Canning Stock Route*, shows the northern section of Canning's map overlaid with an edited version of the dreaming tracks that traverse that area. Based on a map compiled over many years by the anthropologist Kim Akerman, it is an intricate web of routes — some short and looping and turning back on themselves, some passing through on long, wandering itineraries. Canning's corridor through an empty landscape is put into context as one track among many through the desert. While it does not have the ancient authority of the Dreaming, the Canning Stock Route shares certain characteristics with these itineraries — the violence and ruthlessness, the hard work of making and changing the landscape, the encounters in which trickery and trust are bartered, the accidents and misfortunes and achievements. And it is the stock route that has brought together the custodians of all the jurisdictions it passes through, mapping them into a shared contemporary narrative that reconfigures the desert as a web of stories and journeys told in many voices.

But the definitive conception of how the Canning Stock Route intersects with the dreaming tracks was made by a senior Martu man called Billy Patch, who took part in the expedition for the Canning Stock Route Art Project. He drew a grid in the sand to represent the songlines — establishing them as the fundamental co-ordinates of the desert — and superimposed the stock route on the grid like the transient track of a snake.

MAPPING COMMON GROUND

Far from being purely practical documents — surrogates of space or the mind's miniatures of real distribution — maps have played an important role in stimulating the human imagination to reach for the very meaning of life on earth.

—J.B. Harley, *A History of Cartography*

The first time I read these words, I experienced the rush of excitement that accompanies a 'yes' moment, when somebody articulates something you have always felt but have not experienced as a clear thought.

There's something about the cognitive territory that maps occupy which links place to memory and emotion, short-circuiting language and taking us into realms of abstraction and metaphor. And it may be that the origins of language are in there, too. The need for early humans to communicate information on the dangers and resources of their environment would have seen the development of language closely aligned to the ability to interpret and describe place. The mapping impulse was likely one of the first drivers of human cultural evolution; and maps, the physical expression of that impulse, come to us freighted with the wonder of burgeoning human consciousness.

I have always loved maps: the way they sit between drawing and writing, incorporating both; the particularity of detail; the way place is rendered both accessible and mysterious; the suggestion of stories and journeys. A true map doesn't take you to where you imagine it will. It's a starting point into the unknown, a nod towards having a plan. It allows you to step out and make it up as you go. A good map is a work in progress. You can create a dialogue between language and place, you can move things around until some fortuitous arrangement detonates a run of associations that takes you somewhere you didn't know you could go.

Imagine a detailed topographical map that also defines the fluid borders of Aboriginal language groups. There's a map of the posited language borders taped to the wall of my donga in Mulan, and the boundaries marked on it bear little relation to the porous and complicated linguistic terrain of the region with which I am familiar. Warlpiri, Ngardi, Ngalia, Kurinji, Walmajarri, Jaru, Kukatja. What shapes the geographic edges of something as definitive as language? What kind of topography creates a barrier that language doesn't cross?

Language speaks place; place shapes language. Humans organise themselves through a framework of sounds that describe their relationship to those places, and storytelling evolves. The mapping of thoughts and ideas, the creation of stories to carry the meanings of place, becomes a vehicle to carry the meanings of being human.

There is a distilled, mythic elegance to the shape of it.

Map-making was the common ground on which my Aboriginal companions and I put together our different conceptions of the country, and it allowed me to drop in and out of that world, thus avoiding the attrition and disillusionment that afflicts most *kartiya*. It also gave a sense of agency to the people who collaborated with me — an involvement in work that had real meaning for them, as well as payment and daily routine. I provided the format and the structure, and managed the technology. The women, for it was generally women who worked with me on the maps, provided the knowledge and did the painting.

The maps captured the imagination of the local mob. They were concrete evidence of the knowledge that existed in the country, and they represented country in a way that everyone could understand, including the *kartiya* upon whom so much of the negotiations about land depended. Their scale and robustness gave the maps authority as objects, and the fact that the people themselves had painted them, albeit under my supervision, gave everyone a sense of ownership and investment. But the maps also aggravated the simmering arguments about who came from where, who owned which place.

The use of dotting to represent types of vegetation on the Canning Stock Route map had opened up the prospect for using mapping as a tool that could take land-management practices beyond the fraught zone of ownership, and anchor them to the monitoring of changing land conditions, especially the impact of fire. I hoped this might help to bridge the gap between environmental-management pressures and traditional management practices.

A satellite image of any part of the remote desert in Australia will reveal a landscape on which some mysterious geometry has been wrought. I don't mean the geometry of the dunes, although that is dramatic and beautiful. I mean the shadow trace of fire, which in places appears to have been achieved with random scissor cuts, straight-edged and sharp-cornered, strips slicing across the dunes, sections where the land seems to have been folded like paper and chopped symmetrically into peaks and valleys and spread flat again. The country over which the most recent fires have passed is stripped of all but the raw colour of the earth itself, which varies from pale gold to deep red. Regrowth softens the scars, shadowing them with a bloom of green or bluish grey that darkens as the vegetation takes hold, so that in places the country looks as though someone has pasted dressmaker's offcuts from half-a-dozen fabrics onto its topography.

While the knowledge of indigenous land management still exists, the practices themselves are no longer exercised with any consistency. Those practices were contingent on people moving around the country and harvesting what it provided. Since people have settled in communities of one sort or another, and get their supplies from the local store, hunting and gathering has become recreational rather than necessary, with the result that easily accessible country is over-utilised, and vast tracts of less accessible country are not utilised at all. While some places are burned too frequently, others are left to natural forces — usually to lightning strikes in high summer that produce savage and destructive fires rather than the moderate fires which occurred in the traditional mosaic burning regimes.

But it's likely that in certain conditions those vast, destructive fires occurred regardless of local burning practices, when unprecedented amounts of vegetation built up after heavy wet seasons, and early storms coincided with unseasonably high temperatures.

There are fire-dreaming tracks in many parts of the desert. *Warlu* is one of the great ancestral pathways across the Tanami, which suggests that fire has always been a violent and unpredictable force. These days, the tract of grazing country that occupies the grasslands directs the fire to the south or north of its ancient route, but from time to time it roars up out of the Dreaming and puts the Tanami to the torch. I've driven south on the Tanami track through a November night, with flames eating at the roadside and flaring up the branches of hakea and wattle.

The North Australian Fire Information website recorded fire activity across the Kimberley as colour-coded monthly and annual fire scars. It was a laborious process, using the dial-up network in Wade's office, but I eventually managed to download all the fire scars for 2006 and 2007. After I had projected and traced the outline of the scars onto the canvas base map, Lulu, Anna and others would fill the outlined sections with dots colour-coded for a particular year.

The games room became our permanent work room, and as long as Wade remained the IPA co-ordinator I was able to pursue the evolving nature of the project, responding to what people told me about the sort of maps they wanted. Apart from producing the fire map, which was updated every year and became Lulu's particular project, we mapped the changing water levels of the lake from its ancient dimensions to its current reduced size. But the maps that engaged people most were what we called the family maps — the detailed sections of country for which particular families were responsible. These became statements of identity, and defused the tensions about who should work on which map.

+ + +

In Russell Hoban's fable, *The Lion of Boaz-Jachin and Jachin-Boaz*, the father, Jachin-Boaz, a trader in maps, makes a map for his son, Boaz-Jachin.

'It was to be nothing less than a master map that would show him where to find whatever he might wish to look for, and so would assure him of a proper start in life as a man.'

In the time in which the story is set, lions have become extinct, and when Jachin-Boaz shows the map to Boaz-Jachin and challenges him to name something the map will not help him to find, the boy replies, 'a lion'. Shaken by the truth of his son's response, and troubled by the lack of meaning in his own life, it is the father who leaves home, taking the master map with him and leaving a note to say that he has gone to look for a lion.

Boaz-Jachin works on a map of his own, but it is a poor thing in comparison with the marvellous map made by Jachin-Boaz. Angry at his desertion, the son goes in search of his father and the map that had been promised to him. At the beginning of his journey the boy visits the site of an ancient temple, where a relief carving depicts a lion hunt in which a wounded lion bites the wheel of a chariot. Boaz-Jachin feels his own rage and pain through the stone lion, and in an act of sympathetic magic he draws a perfect replica of the lion and sets it loose.

The lion is an elemental force, a psychic expression of Boaz-Jachin's anger that finds Jachin-Boaz long before his son does. Hoban treats the metaphoric lion as a physical albeit invisible reality, which attacks and injures the man in scenes that are both comic and alarming.

The master map provides the impetus for Jachin-Boaz and then Boaz-Jachin to leave home, but it is the unfinished business in Jachin-Boaz's life, and Boaz-Jachin's poorly executed and unfinished map, that bring the lion into being. Father and son are searching for an emotional truth that nearly kills them both.

The metaphoric implications of this story captivated me. The authority and limitations of the master map, the clumsy attempt to formulate a personal map, the fertile, dangerous space between them — all these spoke to me of the task I had taken on.

Aboriginal people hold their master map in the stories and songs and embodied memories of places and journeys. Mine is the unfinished map, the search for a moral compass with which to travel the same ground. From time to time, a lion takes shape — a tawny glimpse on the daylight horizon, a set of prints on the lake shore. Lions are dangerous beasts, and I work in constant trepidation of being eaten.

KARTIYA DAYS

The hothouse environment of remote Aboriginal communities brings out the worst and the best in the *kartiya* who work in them. During my time in Balgo and Mulan, I've seen irrational hatreds, petty power struggles, physical and verbal assaults, incompetence, sabotage, and abuses of power. I've also seen people achieve remarkable outcomes under extraordinarily challenging conditions, and I've made lifelong friendships based on bonds forged under pressure, when the raw material of personality and character is exposed.

Because of the size and nature of Balgo's population — around 400 people, approximately seventy of them *kartiya* — there is always friction somewhere, spot-fires of tension that can flare into conflagrations. Mulan, with 150 people, and only a dozen or so permanent *kartiya*, is much less volatile; during the first four years that I work there, it is, for the most part, a relaxed and pleasant little community. Lockyer's visits generally coincide with mine, May to September being the optimum time for projects, and Sandra,

Kate, Phil, and various configurations of their children visit for shorter or longer periods.

Sandra and Lockyer live on a block of land in rural Victoria not far from the collective, Common Ground, that Kate and Phil set up in the 1970s with several other couples. Based on idealistic principles that have been thrashed out and recalibrated over the ensuing decades, Common Ground is now a self-sustaining property and conference centre dedicated to environmental and social-justice principles.

Encouraged by Lockyer, and motivated by the desire to experience the reality of remote community life, Kate and Phil take on the job of community administrators in Mulan from May to November 2005. They are tall, lean people, and a couple of months into the job they are moving like flighty racehorses, showing a lot of white around the eyes and laughing hysterically at little provocation. They come to dinner one night looking more wild-eyed than usual, and recount the experience they have just had on the back road to Mulan. Some locals had killed a large kangaroo by hitting it with a car — their sedan showing bloody evidence of the slaughter — and wanted to gut and dismember the animal in order to fit it into the boot. Lacking the right tools for the job, they borrowed a shovel and a pocketknife from Kate and Phil, who had to witness the process, later described to us in grisly detail by vegetarian Kate.

Tanya Vernes visits regularly, having embarked on a study exploring traditional Aboriginal land-management practices. She enlists my help with the ongoing research for the Walmajarri dictionary, a project I'm naturally inclined towards because of my interest in plants and language. It's through Tanya that Wade Freeman is head-hunted for the job of IPA co-ordinator, which he takes up in 2006.

Wade transforms the bachelor slum of the IPA demountable by creating a cool, shaded living space on the front deck, growing tomatoes and pawpaws and salad greens, and planting native trees and bougainvillea around the chain-link fence that surrounds the compound. The IPA compound becomes the centre of Mulan whitefella social activity, with mahjong evenings and Sunday pancake brunches, film nights and pizza nights — the pizzas cooked in an oven that Wade builds from termite-mound adobe.

The long-time permanent nurse — a tall, dry, droll woman with the wonderful name of Manon Dupree — is Wade's closest neighbour. She smokes menthol cigarettes and drinks Diet Coke, and is a mean mahjong player. Jess visits often during the year she spends in Balgo without John, and we call ourselves the Ruby Champions after the Champion Ruby tobacco we both smoke, and achieve the distinction of losing at mahjong by astronomical margins.

Lockyer and Phil play in a band back home in Victoria, and Lockyer is always ready to entertain us with his mandolin and his own songs. He sports a goatee and a haircut that makes him look like he's been electrocuted, and belts out his signature song, 'The Back Road to Mulan', with the energy and panache that inflects everything he does. When Phil is in town he accompanies Lockyer on drums.

Lockyer is an extrovert, and in the hours when the rest of us are hunkered down in our boltholes trying to recoup the energy that has been sucked out during the day, he is on his verandah surrounded by kids, teaching them to play the mandolin and making up songs about their world. In a bid to persuade the locals to eat horses — which would solve the growing brumby problem — Lockyer butchers a horse shot by Wade, and hangs its quarters in the sitting room of his donga, there being nowhere else safe from dogs and other predators. The horse had knocked down the fence around Wade's exclusion zone, and paid the price. People eat the meat — no Walmajarri is going to turn down a free feed — but they aren't much taken with the flavour, which lacks the lubricant of fat they prefer.

Wade's environmental position is hardline. He cut his teeth as an activist in the forests of south-west Western Australia, and if he had his way every hoofed animal in the south-east Kimberley would be removed. I tell him he will never persuade the local people to get rid of the cattle; too much of their identity is embedded in the cattle station and, besides, beef is a major part of their diet. But Wade is not a man to relinquish his principles. Or his hair. When he arrives in Mulan, he has a mass of hennaed curls tied back in a ponytail. The radical hairstyles and colours that would later become popular among the young men haven't yet reached Mulan, and Wade's hair draws much derisive comment from the local mob, who have strong and conservative opinions on what is gender appropriate. Lockyer and I, who suffer from hair envy, make remarks to the effect that when Wade gets cold he can crawl into his hair and curl up like a marsupial. In the years Wade spends in Mulan he never cuts his hair, which becomes a wild grey tangle as the job of keeping it hennaed becomes too difficult. It must be horribly uncomfortable in the long, hot summers, when the temperature tops fifty degrees Celsius for weeks on end.

The population is enlivened for a time by the activities of two brumby hunters, who the locals call 'the horsemen'. They have been contracted to capture some brumbies for the Sheik of Dubai, who wants to try them out as endurance horses. The brumbies, generations away from the domesticated Arab and thoroughbred working horses of their origins, although still showing evidence of their bloodlines, prove impossible to trap, and the horsemen resort to sitting in gum trees and shooting passing animals with dart guns.

The back road to Mulan continues to provide encounters, anecdotes and entertainment. One of the horsemen, returning from Halls Creek with a carton of XXXX beer on the tray of his LandCruiser, came upon a car bogged at a sandy crossing. The travellers were local Walmajarri men heading for Mulan, and the horseman towed them out of the bog and up the steep bank of the crossing onto hard ground. During this process the carton of beer was noticed, and an offer made to purchase it. The horseman refused, having bought the beer for himself, but the men were insistent. They had a whip-round, and a spokesman offered the horseman eighty dollars, twice what the carton had cost. At this point the horseman gave in, and said if they wanted it that badly they could have the beer for forty dollars. The spokesman gave the horseman forty dollars, winked, and pocketed the rest.

—They won't know the difference, he said, and took the carton back to the car.

They wasted no time getting stuck into the beer, and the horseman, having offered to stay behind the travellers to make sure they got through, followed a trail of XXXX cans all the way to the community.

The worst of it, he says, when he tells us about the encounter, is that he is the only person in Mulan who drinks XXXX by choice, so people will think he's drunk his way through an entire carton on the back road and thrown the cans out the window. And all the drinkers, except the spokesman, believe he took the eighty dollars.

Romance blossoms between Wade and one of the teachers, Gillian, and he is happy, though with Wade it is sometimes hard to tell. The headmistress takes exception to the relationship, although they are consenting adults in their thirties, and bans Wade and anyone associated with the IPA from entering the school premises. This is the first intimation of the toxic regime to come. Gillian's position in the school becomes intolerable, and at the end of the year she resigns and takes a job as project manager with the IPA.

Gillian's only friend and ally in the school, Kylie, is a feisty Brisbane girl on her first year's teaching post. With Gillian's resignation, Kylie inherits the role of scapegoat, which she exacerbates by continuing to fraternise with the IPA. Refusing to submit to the bullying, Kylie sets in motion a formal complaint, which ultimately succeeds, but which makes her second year in the school hard to bear.

In 2008 a group of us, including Lockyer, Kate and Phil, Jim Bowler, John Carty, and me, representing an expanded network of *kartiya* with connections to Mulan, hold consultations with the local mob to discuss their long-term aspirations, and how we might contribute our various skills in a practical way. The timing coincides with the archaeological dig instigated by Jim, and with a change of community administration. The management model preferred by the Mulan council is to employ a couple, one of whom takes on the position of CEO, and the other the job of managing the community work force. In the new configuration the woman is the CEO, and her husband is the works manager.

Lockyer is the first to flag that there might be difficulties. He has been challenged by the new administrators about the grant structure of his community-building project, which includes money to pay his salary as project manager. It seems that earning an income from the work you contribute to the community marks you as a parasite on the indigenous economy.

Kate and Phil, who have made the trip from Victoria for the specific purpose of the consultations, come away from a meeting with the CEO and her husband in a state of shock.

—They said that we were exploiting Aboriginal people, Phil says.

Phil, who wears his very big heart on his sleeve, is almost incoherent with the injustice of the accusation. In an attempt at damage control, I talk to the CEO, and meet a wall of suspicion concerning the motives of Jim Bowler and the archaeological team that is about to commence the dig, the value of the Indigenous Protected Area program, the credentials of the Paruku network, and the ethics of Lockyer's building project — anything, in fact, that doesn't fall under the direct control of the new management.

We back off and do our best to get on with our various projects, but it's clear that a new order has arrived.

DOTTING THE GRID

Mulan, 2008

As a result of his reconnaissance trips to Paruku/Lake Gregory in 2006 and 2007, Jim Bowler identified a promising site for archaeological exploration. Located on Parnkupirti Creek — called Salt Pan Creek on topographical maps — a cliff face revealed layers of sedimentation that represented 200,000 years of lake levels and monsoonal activity. Twenty or so metres to the west, a gully disgorged stone flakes and tools from its eroding banks before it joined the creek.

There's a lot of serendipity in Jim's choice of site. It is the traditional territory of Boxer Bililuna and Kilampi Pye, brothers whom Jim met on his earlier visits in the seventies, and is close to the waterhole where the ancestral dingoes went into the ground for the last time. Jim owns a painting by Kilampi Pye that depicts this final chapter of the dingoes' journey.

Jim has enlisted the expertise of two eminent archaeologists, Mike Smith and Peter Veth, who bring a team with them — including John Carty as a consulting anthropologist — to assist on the excavation. There is some excitement at the beginning of the dig when partially exposed bones are investigated near the base camp. While Mike and Peter dig and dust carefully around the protruding knobs, Bill Doonday pronounces it the site of an ancient murder. As the emerging shape of the bone reveals a socket, Peter, of a more excitable temperament than Mike, says that it might be a pelvis, and suggests that the surrounding hard soil might be a fireplace. Is it a kangaroo pelvis, the remains of a prehistoric meal? Mike doubts that it's a kangaroo, and unearths a large tooth, which he hands to Doonday to identify.

—*Puntu*, Bill says, meaning human.

—I don't think so, Mike says. It's too big.

—*Puntu*, Bill says again, although it is clear that the tooth belongs to a creature much larger than a man.

But there is a story Bill wants to tell, and he is prepared to marshal all the available evidence to support its telling. That there has been a murder here is the grit of the story. We never learn whether it was white against black, black against white, or any of the other possible permutations. The bone emerging from the hard clay soil takes on the shape of a horse skull, which may have lain here for fifty years, or five. Bill lapses back into his habitual silence, and whatever dark events he has struggled to reveal go back into the silence.

We regroup at the dig site, a kilometre from the base camp. All the Mulan elders are present, and a fair representation of the middle generation, including Julianne Johns and her husband, Stephen Yoomarie. The archaeological team and the Mulan mob assemble in the creek bed at the foot of the cliff, and Jim Bowler explains the timeline written on the cliff face, pointing out the bands of cobblestones and silt and clay that indicate alternating eras of high rainfall and long drought. These correspond to the cycles of the ice ages, which peaked at approximate intervals of 100,000 years and produced the droughts that laid in the dune fields of the big deserts, blocking the channel that had once flowed to the sea, and creating the lakes in the whitefella version of the Two Dingoes story.

Julianne and Stephen are enthralled.

—I thought this was just a swimming hole we used to visit when we were kids, Julianne says.

The weather in August 2008 is bitter. It is very cold, and a filthy wind blows every morning and sometimes all day. Up on the ridge above the cliff, the archaeological team are doing it hard. They have to work for every inch of ground hewn out of the baked clay and layered cobblestones. When we visit, bringing the schoolkids and local adults, we encounter dusty red people coated in the fine ferrous earth that blows out of the trenches with every chip of the mattock or crowbar. The first trenches have yielded little, and the nature of the digging calls for extreme measures. Stephen Yoomarie is called on to operate the community backhoe, which chews a two-metre trench out of the side of the erosion gully.

Embedded in the back wall near the bottom of the trench is a silcrete cobblestone core from which flakes of stone have been struck. It is not possible to date it accurately without testing, but it is clear that it is very old. The cobblestone lies in a thick layer of similar silcrete cobbles that could only have been laid down by roiling torrents of water during periods of intense monsoonal activity. From its location near the middle of the layer, the scientists deduce that it was picked up, flaked, and discarded in situ, where it was covered by similar stones brought down by subsequent torrential flows. Above the band of cobbles, a skin of limestone indicates a time of high lake levels and still water, before several thousand years of windy drought shrank the lakes and covered the limestone with a deep sediment of fine red clay.

The scientists take soil samples from the various levels in the trench and from corresponding levels on the cliff face. These will be subjected to thermoluminescence testing, a dating technique that is more precise than carbon-dating. Based on his previous explorations of the region, Jim makes a confident assertion that the core stone is from the late Pleistocene era, somewhere between 30,000 and 50,000 years ago. In spite of his scientific caution, it is clear that he is excited.

Mike maps the minutiae of the excavation site, drawing it to scale on A4 pages of graph paper, noting the smallest details with the kind of intent observation common to scientists and artists and Aboriginal people. Reading the country is a skill that can be brought to bear in different ways for different purposes. He allows me to make copies of his precise and elegant diagrams, which I tell him I want to use as the basis for paintings. The diagrams map both the horizontal layout of the site and the vertical faces of the excavation trenches, and employ a language particular to its scientific purpose — dumpy levels, termite voids, pisoliths, poorly sorted sub-rounded cobbles. Pisoliths, I'm delighted to learn, are very small stones.

With the discovery of the core stone, the dig has achieved its purpose, and the scientists pack up camp and depart for their various research institutions. The antiquity of human occupation on the shores of Paruku has been established. Just how far back that occupation goes will be revealed by the results of the core-sample tests.

John stays on, dropping his anthropological gravitas and reverting to Jakamarra, and Jess arrives with their six-month-old baby,

Maggie. In lieu of a christening, Maggie is to undergo a formal smoking ceremony, and John and Jess have asked me to be her godmother. We make a trip to Balgo, where the baby is approved by friends and family. The old women who represent the hardcore cultural authority take us to the outskirts of the community, where they make a fire beside the road and collect branches of *marnukuji*, the conkerberry bush used for ceremonial smoking purposes. Laid on the fire, the green branches produce a fragrant white smoke, and Maggie is stripped naked and passed through it. She wails with fright, a little pale-skinned creature held firm in the dark hands of the old ladies. As a daughter of Jakamarra and Napaltjarri, she is Napurrula, which makes her my little sister as well as my god-daughter.

After John, Jess, and Maggie leave, I begin a series of paintings for an exhibition to be held in Canberra later in the year. Using watercolour for its convenience and portability, and working on a small scale to avoid failing on a large scale, I struggle to process the impact of constant exposure to a landscape mediated through Aboriginal eyes and minds.

The experience of the archaeological dig has raised more questions and tensions about how to resolve the conceptual conundrum I find myself in. I've been using the grid for some time as an intermediary between map-making and the ground-based imagery of Aboriginal painting. Mike's gridded, information-filled diagrams have given me a formal tool to apply to the making of this new body of work. Just how to do this is not yet clear.

In 1993 I saw an astonishing exhibition of Aboriginal paintings from the Holmes à Court collection, and knew that it was the first time I had seen my country represented in a way that spoke directly of its essence. There were other artists who had come close — Fred Williams, John Olsen at his best — but they didn't give off the visual shimmer of the desert, the breathing energy of these works. I understood two things simultaneously — that here was an iconography and an organising principle that perfectly expressed my experience of the country in which I had grown up, and that I could not use it.

Finding an iconography and an organising principle that was embedded in my own hybrid European-Antipodean culture became my driving preoccupation. The ancestral imprint that gave the desert paintings such authority and power was not available to me. Nor were the domestic and ceremonial elements of women's paintings. I needed to find an equivalent that belonged to my own culture.

The horizon and the grid have been central to representing three dimensions on a two-dimensional surface, producing the perspective we take for granted in traditional western painting. Renaissance artists used a device called Alberti's Veil, a transparent vertical grid, through which a landscape, figure, or object could be observed and reproduced with great accuracy on a gridded canvas or sheet of paper. Buildings and roads were drawn in perspective by establishing a vanishing point on the horizon and having all sets of horizontal lines converge on that point. Grids and horizons carry a long European pedigree as tools to organise and distort reality in order to reproduce what the human eye sees.

The grid has had a bad press as a colonial tool, especially when applied to mapping, but that is only part of the story. The mapping grid that is based on latitude and longitude distorts the shape of continents when it is used as the basis for a two-dimensional map. But the co-ordinates it represents, north/south and east/west, are embedded in the natural world: the rising and setting of the sun and moon; the axis on which the planet spins. Our bodies are oriented to these co-ordinates, or used to be until we became an indoor-dwelling species.

There's a powerful aesthetic element in the grid, especially when it is hand-drawn so that the perfect symmetry is lost. And Billy Patch had represented the Western Desert songlines as a grid. The contradictions, the doubleness, was where the charge lay.

+ + +

When I revisit the archaeological site, the raw cuts of the trenches and the conical piles of displaced earth make a stark geometry among the natural patterns of erosion. Sitting in the stippled shade of the ti-tree, I imagine this place when the monsoon brought rains powerful enough to strip rocks larger than a man's fist from the high ground and bring them thundering down onto the flatlands: a cobbled shoreline a stone's throw from the water's edge; a camp set among whatever shrubs and trees grew in those wetter times. A man picks up a stone, feels its weight and contours, discards it, and selects another. Yes, this one will do. The toolmaker strikes the stone several times, knapping six razor-sharp flakes from the surface. He collects the flakes and leaves the cobble, knapped face down, where it is buried under similar stones brought down by the next monsoonal torrents, and lies undisturbed for 50,000 years.

Although a creek runs through it, this is hard country. The main vegetation is spinifex and *kupartu*, a drab, leathery, fire-tolerant shrub that produces tough brown nuts that are used, when nothing more interesting is available, to make necklaces. Stunted ti-tree grows at the junction of the creek and the erosion gully, and the river red gums that cling to the southern bank are slender and undersized. Since the archaeological team departed the wind has dropped, which makes painting possible, though not comfortable. The cessation of wind has brought out the ants and bush flies, which crawl and bite and drown in the painting water.

Among the stones in the creek bed are ochres of every colour, although deep red is uncommon, and occurs only in hard little discs of liver-coloured stone. I have long since been given permission to use the ochres, and have spent hours sorting and grading colours — pink, white, cream, sienna, umber, yellow, mauve, orange, light red, purple, lilac — beguiled by their range and subtlety. The local painters prefer store-bought acrylics, and only use the ochres for body painting and occasional school cultural activities.

But the ochres won't serve my current purpose, which requires the brilliant transparency of watercolour. I draw the east face of the erosion gully on watercolour paper ruled into a barely visible grid, and paint what I see, one square at a time. Completed, the work spans three small sheets, the third panel consisting of a painted grid of feathery brush marks and dots. They're not dots, I tell myself, they're pisoliths. But there's no question that I'm dotting the grid, a transgression I contemplate with alarm. As long as I keep the paintings small and unostentatious, maybe I'll get away with it.

I scale up sections of Mike's diagrams — a profile of the edge of the erosion gully, details of the trench faces that include the termite voids and poorly sorted cobbles. I paint an aerial view of the location — the round hummocks of spinifex, the red circles of termite mounds, the speckled banks of the creek — superimposed on a grid of subtle earth tones. I paint the edge of twilight through the *malarn* trees, the horizon dissolving into an effervescence of dots. I paint a gridded landscape of the *kupartu* and termite mounds, and scrawl a line of text along the bottom: *In the gap between two ways of seeing, the risk is that you see nothing clearly.*

I drive to Alice Springs, and fly south with the work as carry-on luggage. The exhibition is called *Edge of the Visible.* No one seems to notice that I've crossed a line.

HIATUS

Mulan, 2009

In March 2009, my mother dies suddenly and without fuss, two months short of her eighty-third birthday. She dies at home in the house my father built, with my brother Bob at hand. It is a good death, if there's such a thing, but it leaves us startled with grief. We had thought her indestructible.

When I arrive in Mulan later that year to continue with the mapping project, I receive the customary sorry acknowledgement of hugging and wailing from those who know me well, and a handshake with downcast eyes from others. Bessie embraces me with real emotion, and Anna tells me she cried when she heard of Mum's death. I have brought some of my mother's possessions — including clothes, handbags, and shoes — to distribute, which makes Anna happy, as she is one of the few people small enough for the clothing to fit.

The Napiers have gone from Tanami Downs, six years crumbling at the last into bad feelings and unfinished business, and the station is in caretaker mode when I travel through. In Mulan, an expedient alliance between the white community managers and one of the powerful local families has succeeded in having the IPA base, and Wade and Gillian, relocated to Billiluna. Lockyer's project has been scuttled by the same managers, who brook no challenge to their grip on the community, and he will not be back in the foreseeable future.

It's disorienting to find the IPA compound deserted. I have been forewarned to expect a fishy stink in my donga, which has recently been used as a dissecting laboratory by a group of scientists examining a worm infestation that has exploded in the local fish population. The smell is discernible, but faint. While I'm unpacking my car, Rebecca Johns and her husband, Joe, drop in for a cup of tea and to check their recently applied hair colour in my mirror. They are on a health kick, and have just been on a long walk. They regale me with descriptions of the bad dietary habits of Aboriginal people.

Someone has used my demountable to store the useless, expensive, broken things that no one has the heart to throw out: a scanner for which all the cables and power leads have been lost; a fax machine whose internal workings have been displaced in some irremediable way; and a computer screen the kids threw paint over in the summer they broke into the compound and ransacked the co-ordinator's house.

I realise, when I face the annual chore of stamping my own private order on this provisional home, that I have held in my mind the expectation that it will be as I left it — clean, orderly, undefiled. In the time it takes to restore it to something resembling the place I left, I think about nothing much beyond the decision to take all the electronic gear to the tip this year, as an act of moral fortitude. They are like damaged friends, familiar and dysfunctional, but with a right to occupy the world as I do. To dispose of them is a kind of murder. If they had not been dumped in the tiny space that must now function as a kitchen I would let them be, but this year it's a choice between me and them.

In the months I've been away, a number of keys have gone missing. The main gate to the compound is chained shut, secured by interlocking padlocks for which the keys have been lost. Some of the padlocks are of the heavy-duty type, forty or fifty dollars each. I estimate the value of the chain of padlocks holding the gate shut to be about two hundred dollars. There's a logic of decreasing efficiency in the system, the final and functioning padlock a flimsy piece of equipment that could be sawn through with a nail file.

Once settled in, I drive to Billiluna to visit Wade and Gillian, and to meet the crew working on the fish project. The team of scientists are red-eyed with exhaustion, having dissected hundreds of fish and counted thousands of worms in the past week. The most revolting of the worms burrow from the gut into the muscle of the fish, and resemble bloody strings of dental floss. The worm infestation has had a serious impact on both a summer food staple and an important form of recreation for the locals, and the research, resourced by the West Australian Department of Water and supported by scientists from the University of Canberra, is an attempt to identify its cause.

The house that Wade and Gillian have been allocated in Billiluna is much more salubrious than the Mulan donga, but it lacks the character that Wade's industrious building and gardening and adapting had lent to that humble building. Wade's three-year contract is almost up, and he has applied for a job in East Timor, which he seems likely to get. Gillian will continue in her role as project officer until the IPA ten-year management plan, still in draft form, is completed. Years in the making, the document is marked with the fingerprints of so much consultation it's becoming illegible.

Evelyn Clancy and Shirley Yoomarie are in Billiluna, and when they spot my vehicle they ask for a lift back to Mulan. Shirley is ready and waiting with two grandchildren when I drive around to pick her up early the next morning. She has a computer, wrapped in a blanket, that she is taking back to Mulan for the kids. Evelyn is at Daisy's place, still asleep. Her baggage, when she gets herself organised, includes a pair of enormous hi-fi speakers and a bucket of cooked emu.

Back in Mulan, Lulu is in a fury because her family have not been included in payments for the fish project.

—Did they do any work on the project? I ask.

—Nothing, nobody told them, she says. Maybe I can't work for you with the mapping.

—When did I ever do the wrong thing with you?

—No, you don't do wrong, but I can't work for you anyway.

—Okay, you don't want me around, I'm out of here.

Of course she will do the work. She couldn't bear not to be involved.

Money is at the heart of many of the tensions between black and white, and between black and black. I would never claim to understand the root of these conflicts, or what the money represents, apart from its purchasing power. What I do know is that someone will pursue twenty dollars with the same fierce commitment as they will pursue two hundred dollars, and that any perceived inequity or favouritism results in a serious fallout. Since my projects all involve payments, I have learned to keep clear records, available for anyone to see, and to insist that people sign when they receive payment. As long as there is consistency and transparency, and I can show a direct correlation between hours worked and money received, things run smoothly. I've also learned to follow up any complaint of a mistake — because it is usually legitimate — and to apologise and put it right. Over the years these simple principles have taken the grief out of money business, though the potential for grief is always there.

A trudging stick figure is making its way along the dusty road. It's Anna, wearing several layers of my mother's clothes. Someone has plaited her bush of hair into neat ridges, so she appears to be wearing a basket on her head, the loose ends fraying out in a nicotine-coloured nimbus.

She hails me, opens the passenger door, and climbs in.

—What now? she says.

—I don't know, Nakarra. What do you want to do?

—Shop. I need Weet-Bix and washing powder. And cigarettes. You'll buy it for me?

—What do I get for it? I say.

—Love, she says.

—I'm not sure that's enough, I say.

—We can go out and get some bark?

—Okay. I need to get out of here for a while.

—You not wrong.

Anna has chosen me as her protégé and personal driver.

—I love you, Napuru, she says. This is true, for sure.

I believe her. Anna was born during the long trek her people made to the Mission from the Canning Stock Route, and her mother died soon afterwards. She was raised by the Catholic nuns who, it seems, were kind enough to the thin, clever girl. Anna took to heart the church teachings and the desire to be good. I sense the need in her for white companionship — her emotional sensibilities shaped in childhood by something orderly and undemonstrative. She is the intellectual of Mulan, and keeps abreast of social and political developments in the indigenous world through

NITV, the National Indigenous Television network. I have taken to watching it, in the absence of the ABC, to try to make sense of some of her gnomic pronouncements.

—I hate that word 'half-caste', Anna says, apropos of nothing in particular.

I squint sideways at her.

—You don't look half-caste to me. You been hiding something?

—Nothing!

When Anna laughs, it's as if a series of small percussions occur in the region of her bony shoulder blades.

—They used to call me half-caste because I could speak really good English. English is my first language. I was really smart. I used to help the teachers in the classroom.

It is only on pension day that Anna deserts me for the pleasures of the gambling circle.

—How can you gamble? You don't have any spare money.

—I save it up.

—You save up so you can gamble?

Anna's face screws up in amusement, like a child caught out in some harmless naughtiness.

—Only little bit, she says.

At night I succumb to a trickling sorrow, partly related to my mother's death, but also to do with seeing Margaret in Balgo with her leg amputated after the diabetic ulcer turned gangrenous, and knowing that it can only be a matter of time before the disease kills her. And I am saddened by the departure of friends and the knowledge that an era is over.

I drive out to visit Slippers' grave, my little dog now three years dead. The hills of Walakarri to the east are very clear in the winter light. It's a beautiful time of year, but there's too much grief in me to feel it properly. Pirate dashes about on the red sandhill, chasing lizards and dancing with his shadow.

My mapping team are ready and eager to work. They arrive at eight o'clock and work through until four, sometimes longer. Lulu turns up and works longest of all. We make a trip to the lake to measure current water levels, accompanied by an elderly visiting relative of Lulu's, who speaks to me in the bullying tone that a lot of the old ladies use towards *kartiya*. Lulu leans in and says to her in an undertone, 'Napurrula doesn't take orders.' Later, I overhear her saying to the old lady, 'I like working with Napurrula. She finishes things.' It's her way of letting me know the relationship is intact.

The others won't let Evelyn near the maps because she's too messy, so I give her the job of washing the brushes and changing the painting water, and she turns into a brush-cleaning fascist. Kids drop in to see what's going on, and are tolerated until they begin to whine or fight and are sent on their way. When we embark on the family maps that consist of detailed sections of country around the lake edges, the daughters of the senior women are enlisted to help with the painting, and there are days when between a dozen and fifteen women of all ages are deployed in a highly structured pattern, each working on the map of her own family jurisdiction. A large map of the lake system, depicting its various dimensions from palaeo-lake and flood levels to the shrunken shoreline of drought years, is delegated to Shirley Yoomarie and her sister Mabel. They are capable of astonishing periods of concentration — up to five hours of dotting without a break.

Lulu has taken ownership of the fire map.

One morning there's an edgy energy among the women.

—What's going on? I ask. Did something happen?

—Monica's niece trashed her house, someone says.

Monica's niece is also Anna's daughter-in-law. I can't work out what led to the assault on Monica's yellow house, but Anna is afraid that Monica will go looking for the girl in Anna's house, and wreak havoc in return.

—But Monica's your friend, I say. She won't do anything to hurt you or break your house.

—Take me to my place, she says. I need to lock up.

There's a tone of voice I've learned to recognise that means, You don't have a clue, just do what I say, so I grab my keys and we drive to Anna's house, passing Monica stalking along the road with a crowbar, making a low growling noise that is a concentrated form of her usual asthmatic breathing. Her brilliant white hair has been recently dyed stark black, and, combined with the pair of wraparound mirror sunglasses she's wearing, she looks like an elderly indigenous goth. She ignores us as we drive past.

—Hurry, Anna says.

The verandah of the house is enclosed in a solid weldmesh cage, and the gate has a padlock and chain looped through the mesh. In her haste to lock it, Anna drops her cluster of keys. Her tiny wrists look fragile and ineffectual as she struggles with the heavy padlock and the coarse loops of chain. I see that she is afraid, and I'm jolted into the knowledge that I have no idea what goes on at this other level of people's lives. I take the keys from her, secure the chain, and lock the padlock.

—It's okay. Calm down.

I put my hands on the small shoulders, the delicate bones, and she leans against me. Anna has various medical conditions, including intolerance to gluten and something that causes large, warty protrusions on her face and body, and is responsible for her diminutive size. Her youngest granddaughter has inherited this condition, and I have been party to the process of convincing the medical team monitoring the child that she is not neglected, not suffering malnutrition; that she is, in fact, cosseted, indulged and spoiled, because she is a precious only child, and her bird bones and luminous eyes and high intelligence are a direct legacy from her grandmother, along with the condition that inhibits her growth.

Monica arrives as we are about to leave, and does a circuit of the house, continuing to growl.

—She's not here, Monica, I say. Do you want a lift home?
Anna hisses at me under her breath.

—What? says Monica, who is deaf.

—There's nobody here, I shout. I'll give you a lift home.

—Shop! she says, and gets into the back seat. Anna hops in the front, and I drive to the shop.

During the week that a visiting hip-hop dance team works with the kids in the community school, class attendance is 100 per cent. The energy spills over into the rest of the community, because people are freed from the general anxiety about what the kids are up to, especially in that dead space in the afternoons when the desert ennui is at its strongest and even the conscientious students usually don't bother to go back to the classroom.

Outside school hours they flock around the dancers, aping their every move, strutting their interpretation of cool. The group leader of the team of four is Aboriginal, a sturdy, confident young man with a fine delivery in motivational hyperbole. The kids flourish under the physical challenge and discipline. It makes me believe that it should be possible to link the teaching of literacy and numeracy to the physical intelligence that is shining out of every child. Surely it would be possible to dance numbers, to choreograph addition and subtraction, to design a rhythm and pattern for the learning of letters.

At the end of the week the kids perform what they have learned — an event attended by the entire community. There's clear talent in many of the kids, and even the clumsy ones perform to applause and encouragement. But I feel uneasy watching the sexual pelvic-grinding moves that all the girls, including the youngest, have mastered.

One Saturday, when I'm preparing a projection for the

following week, a procession of children weaves through the community centre. The children range in age from four to seven or eight, and they are acting out a funeral. Several of them brush the air in front of them with clumps of gum-leaves, and hum the low, keening note that is the sound of sorry business. The child chosen to play the corpse is laid out on the concrete block that has been built to stop vehicles from driving into the basketball courts, his arms folded on his narrow chest, the black swatch of his eyelashes trembling with suppressed glee while the others chant and bend around him.

Blind May Nungorrayi has died as a result of her diabetes, and her daughters ask me for photographs of her from the Sturt Creek trip we made several years ago. I print and copy a selection, and agree to help them make a booklet for the funeral, on the proviso that they bring me the material they want to put in it. When they don't follow it up I'm relieved, because it's another job I don't have time to do.

Anna lines me up for a lift to the funeral, which is to be held at Balgo. I pick her up early, and we sneak out on the back road so no one sees us. Having several times taken a carload of people to Balgo for a funeral — a gruelling event that can take the best part of a day — and then driving all over the community looking for my passengers when the ceremony is over, I've chosen discretion, which is less exhausting than valour.

When we arrive, Anna directs me to the parish house to see Father Eugene, who is trying to locate the body, lost in transit somewhere along the two hundred and fifty kilometres of road between Halls Creek and the community. The funeral, due to start at nine, has been put back to midday. I discover that I've forgotten to bring any money to buy lunch. I rarely carry cash, so that I can answer honestly that I don't have any when people want to borrow some.

—Don't worry, Napuru, Anna says. I can get pensioner's lunch for free, and you can share.

She buys me a bottle of water from the store.

There's a flatness, a lostness to the days — a feeling of missing something you've never had, remembering something you've never known. I feel myself slipping down into that place where everything is too much effort. It's been a long time since I did anything for my own creative needs. I crave the time to write and paint, to begin to marshal whatever it is this split life has taught me.

—This year has been really hard, I tell the mapping team. I'll only come back to work next year if you invite me.

—We invite you, they say.

On the morning I plan to leave Mulan, I rise early to pack the car. A warm wind, precursor of the hot weather to come, blows from the north, and the sound of crows and country music comes from the visitors' quarters next door, where a solitary plumber has set up a makeshift kitchen on the deck. He leaves the radio playing day and night, its melancholy tunes mourning the hapless lives of cowboys. The crows quarrel over a loaf of sliced bread pillaged from his supplies, scattering crusts and torn shreds of plastic around the dusty gums.

When I make my rounds to say goodbye, I find a community meeting under way, called by Shirley Brown to settle the problem that has been escalating between the office and store managers. Apparently the CEO's husband has assaulted Mr Storekeeper, and Mrs Storekeeper has threatened the CEO. I drive out of town to the spectacle of *kartiya* making idiots of themselves.

IMPROVISATIONS II

There's a sequence of several years that has become one continuous span of time in my memory, in which the mapping work is the only constant amidst a cascade of changes that are mostly negative. Wade's job remains vacant for two years, and whenever I return to Mulan I find myself acting as an interim co-ordinator of the Indigenous Protected Area program, doing the sort of administrative work I hate and for which I am least suited.

As the *kartiya* relationships in Mulan imploded, my relationships with the Aboriginal people become paramount. In the past, when the ambient tensions of this work-in-progress world became too intense, good *kartiya* company provided a haven where we could debrief and regroup. My friendships with the Aboriginal people are of a different order. Because of my history, I can be fitted into the highly mapped ontologies of the Aboriginal world in a way that most *kartiya* cannot. This carries with it both privileges and expectations. It is often assumed that I know much more than I do, and understand more.

—You should know that, Napurrula, people say to me, taking for granted that my childhood has imbued me with the same skills of observation and way-finding as Aboriginal children, and there are times when I'm not above sneaking a look at my GPS to save face.

My collaborators on the map-making are mostly women of a certain age — widows and grandmothers who have a degree of autonomy the younger women don't have. Although I also work with the rangers, who are predominantly young men, my natural milieu is among the older women who grew up, like me, in the station days. Most of them are only a few years older than I am, but the differences in our diets and life experiences make them seem much older. Before we begin any sort of bush trip, I check that they have their various medications for blood pressure, diabetes, asthma and other chronic illnesses, and pack a basic travelling kit of Panadol, Betadine, runny tummy treatment and rubbing liniment. They are all grandmothers, and some of them are great-grandmothers many times over. Most of them are the primary carers for grandchildren whose parents are absent or unpredictable.

They have long ceased to question me about my single and childless state, although in my first year I was taken to visit the women's fertility site — a stone representing *lungkurta,* the blue-tongue lizard. If I wanted a baby I should rub the stone, the women told me, but I declined. Tanya, however, with her biological clock running and a strong desire for children, rubbed the stone. It seems to have worked, because when she next visits Mulan to work on the dictionary, which is nearing completion, she tells me that she is pregnant with twins.

By the time I began working in Mulan it was a matriarchy, with all but two of the older men gone, and the cultural knowledge hived into the women elders, who guarded it well. The foremost of these is Bessie who is, along with Charmia in Billiluna, among the last of the speakers of eastern Walmajarri, the language of the lake people. Bessie and Charmia are old enough to have avoided being sent to the Mission and schooled in Kukatja, the dominant language among the half-dozen or so languages of the people gathered in Balgo. Kukatja was the language learned by the priests and nuns in order to translate and teach the Bible, and has become the lingua franca of the region. The demise of her language causes Bessie much grief, because when the language goes, much that is unique to the eastern Walmajarri culture will disappear.

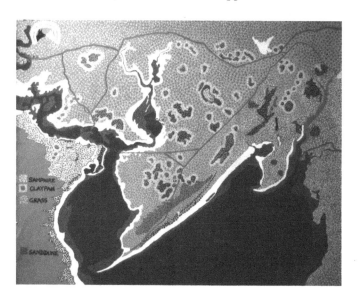

One afternoon we make a trip to Kilwa, and Bessie calls out her customary greeting to the lake serpent, the forceful cadences ringing out over the water and bringing the swans to see what is going on.

—When I dead there'll be no one to talk to the lake in its own language, she says later. This statement still haunts me. It encapsulates the significance of language loss across the continent as conversations with the ancestors fall silent.

Bessie is a relentless campaigner for the things she believes in, driven by frustration that others don't share the urgency she feels. She has passed on some of this drive to her daughter Shirley, and many of the projects I am involved in began with conversations with the two of them about ways to record and preserve knowledge. In Bessie's presence I always felt I had a job to do, until she received a health scare that required a blood test, and there was a week of anxiety waiting for the results.

When I call in to see her, I find a scared old woman taking stock of her circumstances.

—I not frightened for dying, she says. But there's too many things I know that we didn't write down yet.

I sit beside her on the verandah, which faces the small, round grassy hill in the centre of the community, and she takes my hand and holds it for a long time. There's not much to say, so I don't say much. When the results come back they are clear, and within a few days Bessie is as fiery and demanding as usual, but something has shifted between us.

Bessie rarely paints, so her main role in the map-making is as a consultant — her mind is a memory bank of placenames, and the stories attached to those places. Lulu is the painter. Ten years younger than her sister, and with good literacy, she has made a niche for herself working with *kartiya* as a cultural adviser, which sometimes creates tension between the sisters. Lulu is on every steering committee and advisory board in the region, and often double-books herself.

While I feel a sense of privilege that it has been possible to reach this place, along with the deepening of ties and understanding comes a concomitant awareness of my own ineffectuality. With the ever-broadening scope of the work I do comes a stretching of my capacity to understand what it is we are really doing together. I'm making it up as I go, reliant on the advice of the people I work with, aware that there are hidden agendas all around me. And there's the fundamental contradiction that as soon as you become attached to outcomes, things begin to unravel. Once the *kartiya* attachment to identifiable results forces its own formal structures onto the process, it upsets the delicate calibrations, the continual adjustments necessary to keep people engaged.

There are days when I wonder whether the imbalance between the roles we inhabit has skewed any possibility of real friendship, real respect. It's the tiredness that does me in, the impossibility of achieving anything of lasting value, the limited resources, the lack of support, the negotiating around mad and tricky white people, the contradictory, pointless bureaucratic pressures, the vast gulf that separates this world from the one that finances and tries to fix it.

But mostly what I feel is a comfort in the presence of Aboriginal people, a familiarity from the beginning of my life coming full circle, an absence filled. It is possible to touch people out here, to be continuous with the skin of others, to take on something of the meaning of skin in its inclusiveness. People lean into one another, touch and take hold as an extended form of conversation. I wonder if I'm becoming one of those sad misfits who can't function in their own culture, and who hang out with Aboriginal people because they are more tolerant and accepting than whitefellas.

Get a grip, I think.

When Charmia's brother, Ned Cox, visits Mulan, he asks to see the big Paruku map about which he has heard so much, in order to check the information recorded on it and to contribute what he knows, which is encyclopaedic. I bring the map and lay it out on the stage in the community centre. Ned sits down in the centre of the canvas and removes his prosthetic leg, which he uses as a pointer. The leg wears a new sandshoe, and is coloured a deep chocolate-brown to match the colour of his skin. The red sedan that has brought him here is drawn up nearby, its bonnet raised. Since he's not using it for the moment, the old man's custom-made walking stick props the bonnet open while several young men rummage in the engine. A camp dog that ventures onto the map is belted with the leg, and bolts away screeching.

An animated conversation circulates among the people who have gathered around to listen to the old man while I write his instructions on the canvas in coloured chalk. In him is housed the knowledge of generations, the history of a place and its people, the creation stories of the region, the escapades and delinquencies of the ancestral beings, the complex genealogies of the regional clans, the politics of white occupation and Aboriginal reclamation. To have access to his knowledge is to have access to the many-layered story of the southern Kimberley. For a moment, the map comes to life. This is what it is for — to generate stories, to gather people together, to remain forever unfinished, its edges open, its voices continuing to speak.

LACUNA

2010

During one of my stints as interim IPA co-ordinator, Pam and Rachel drive out to visit me. Pam knows from previous experience how distracted I am likely to be if they stay in Mulan while I'm in work mode, so she suggests we spend the time in some of our familiar haunts. I don't need much persuading — swag and dog on the ute, and I'm out of there.

I meet Pam and Rachel at Rabbit Flat, and we drive back along the Tanami Highway to a turn-off south of the Granites — the beginning of a track I have been wanting to explore for years. My brother Jim had driven along it the previous year, so I know the track is in fair condition. Our destination is a salt lake called Lake Fidler in the sandy channel of ancient marshlands that bisects the old access road we used when we lived on Mongrel Downs. Heavy rains in the mid-seventies washed the track away, and an alternative access to the station via Rabbit Flat was established. The route that had linked the stock-route bores from Refrigerator Well in the Northern Territory to Pussycat Bore across the Western Australian border fell into disuse, and sections of it became a seed trap for the ubiquitous grey-leaved whipstick wattle, or eroded down to the gravels and laterite that lie beneath the sand.

The track takes us first to the old stock-route bore of Sangsters Well, dubbed 'Gangsters' back in the sixties as a tribute to the pair of desperadoes who built the tank and windmill, stealing quantities of equipment in the process. Approaching from the north, we cross a series of limestone ridges. Colonies of red cathedral termite mounds inhabit the low-lying country between the limestone seams, their anthropomorphic forms like vast fertility goddesses, holding the country in thrall to their brooding, sentient silence. The windmill is visible from a long way off — a spindly tower ending in a nub from which the blades have fallen, its single out-thrust arm signalling to us across the low scrub. A few scraggy bloodwoods festooned with woody galls grow around the bore, and we share a makeshift lunch in their thin shade.

The varied vegetation of solanums and cassias and wattles and pussytails is typical of the country we have just crossed, but when we angle south-east onto the old access track, the landscape turns spinifex monochrome, with the occasional stunted corkwood poking its burnt-stick fingers into the sky.

And then the silver disc of the salt lake appears, with the eerie suddenness of a negative space in a flat landscape. At the point where I swing my vehicle off the road towards the lake, I see my brother's tracks, and know that the place had grabbed him in the same moment by the same jolt of memory.

Our mother is driving, foot flat to the floor and teeth gritted, hitting the sandy stretch along the lake with everything the old Zephyr station wagon has got, and we are hanging on, four kids, no seatbelts, yelling in terror or excitement or both, at least one of

us howling from whacking head or face on some part of the car's
interior when it bounces over a washout, the lake a whisper of silver
light beyond the pink rim of the dune, a white promise that next
time, next time it will catch us, next time we won't get through.

I drive a hundred metres along the shoreline, Pam and Rachel following, to a place where we can park the two cars beside each other
and stretch a tarpaulin between the roof racks for shade. It is late
September, and hot — that time in the early afternoon when the
country stops breathing and the body's circadian rhythms hit zero.
Before us stretches the pale blank of the salt lake, with a slick blue
gleam of mirage blending the lake edge and the sky into a vanishing
horizon. Apart from a few varieties of grass and a prostrate purple
Swainson-pea recently identified as unique to the Tanami, the only
vegetation along the edge of the lake is the stunted regrowth of
ti-tree that must have burned in a fierce summer bushfire, leaving
nothing but charred stumps and a few scorched limbs half-buried
in sand.

A torpor settles over us, and we lie under the tarpaulin, dozing
and sipping Ribena until there is a shift in the light, when, as if
someone had flicked a switch, we all get up and walk off in different directions. Pam and Rachel head out onto the lake, while I go
with Pirate along the low shoreline dune, which I know from my
travels with Jim Bowler is a lunette formed by wind-driven waves
forcing lake sands into a crescent. To the north is a red sandhill
that appears to be covered in much denser vegetation than the surrounding landscape. It is separated from the lunette by a channel
of stinking black mud, which Pirate and I cross at the narrowest
point, unleashing a sulphurous reek as feet and paws sink into the
muck. Climbing the red sandhill is like entering a different country. Taller by several metres than the surrounding plain, and of a

colour indicating that it is considerably older than the lunette, it cuts between the large playa to the south and a chain of smaller salt pans on the northern side that must, when filled, decant into the main lake via the channel we have just traversed.

The sandhill has escaped the fires that destroyed the trees along the lunette, and hosts a flourishing, though stunted, colony of ti-tree, along with a microcosm of typical Tanami vegetation — spinifex, mulla-mullas, solanums, acacias, grevilleas, eremophilas, cassias, swainsonas, crotalarias. The tracks of a bustard appear so recent that the bird itself must be hiding in the ti-tree, alarmed by the sudden appearance of strange creatures in its domain. I wonder what could provide enough water to keep it alive, and whether there is a secret source of fresh water in this salty wilderness. The Granites mine, the nearest water source I know of, is about forty kilometres north as the crow flies, or in this instance possibly the bustard, which can fly, although it isn't built for the long haul.

What the red dune indicates is that a few hundred thousand years ago this lake was full, the marshlands were an active waterway, and the surrounding country supported quite different vegetation and animal life. These acidic desert soils are not conducive to the preservation of bone, so it's unlikely that megafauna fossils are lying buried under the lunette, although, in freak circumstances in the limestone country, bones can become opalised. Forty-five years ago two hundred bullocks bogged and perished here — the tail end of a drover's mob that got a smell of water and followed it to the point of no return. I wonder if any of their remains survive out there under the salt. We used to imagine we could hear their ghostly bellowing as we hurtled past in the airborne Zephyr.

I leave the red sandhill with reluctance, but the sun is dropping close to the horizon and I need to collect wood from the remains of burnt ti-tree along the lunette. While Pirate and I have been exploring the sandhill, Pam has cut the word SILENCE into the crystalline surface of the lake in perfect Times New Roman capitals.

We set up the folding table and chairs out on the lake, and drink champagne in the twilight, toasting the red flare of sunset and the reflection of the three-quarter moon in the film of moisture on the lake surface. Pam is pre-occupied, the edgy sparkle that animates her usual persona absent. She tells us she has been experiencing a peculiar sensation in her voice — a tiny thrum that is more notice-able when she is tired. She is going to see a specialist in Sydney on her next visit south.

We regroup at Lake Ruth, my beloved lake, Mangkurrurpa, green and pink and vivid with birds and wind. The stand of old, wild twisted ti-tree where we set up camp is as familiar as the walls of houses I've lived in. For three days we wander and draw and talk and read and swim. It's good to be here with these friends to whom nothing needs to be explained.

I visit this place year after year, and every time it is different. It is difficult to imagine what new aspect it will present. I've seen it bone dry, crisp and brittle with a crust of silver weed. I've seen it spilling out from its basin to waterlog the surrounding spinifex and grasslands. Once it was a still blue dish on which a dozen swans arched their question-mark necks, and another time a grey mud flat giving off the stink of vegetable decay. One year, a colony of rufous flying foxes, travelling far outside the usual limits of their territory, had taken up residence in the strip of ti-tree where we are camping, and laid it waste. When I was young I saw it newly filled, the colour of milky tea.

Today it is dense with weed, green on the verge of a red shift, rimmed and banded with sky-blue water, its sandy edges pink with mats of prostrate flowering sea heath. Beyond the flowers are clumps of blue-green samphire and orange tiny purslane. A flock of glossy ibis stalks in the shallows like a coven of small black witches.

A magpie lark has built its beautifully constructed cup of mud on a high branch of the ti-tree under which I've rolled out my swag, and the nestlings make a sound like rattlesnakes whenever they detect movement. Far out on the weedy surface, black swans graze and doze, and a pair of brolgas pose like effigies. A spoonbill feeds alongside the glossy ibis, sieving water through its bill.

This evening the resident dingo is white and cautious, sipping from the edge of the lake in the late afternoon.

Among the birds clustering and scurrying in the shallows are dotterels, stilts, sandpipers, avocets and plovers, and some small, busy brown birds I can't identify. Five stately brolgas arrange themselves in cuneiform, and two more spoonbills stake out a patch of shoreline from which to skim and sieve. A baldy-faced stallion comes to investigate whether we pose a threat to his mares, and Pirate rushes at him, and retreats when the stallion stands its ground. I check on the cache of grinding-stone fragments I laid at the base of a ti-tree several years ago. Sand has covered the broken pieces, but they are still there. They have been underwater for much of the time since I left them there for safekeeping, and will be again, no doubt.

Pam and Rachel are keen to spend some time at Lake Gregory, and work waits for me in Mulan. We leave Lake Ruth with reluctance and drive west, crossing into Western Australia in the late afternoon and deciding on a whim to turn south to Ngulupi. It's a couple of years since I visited the outstation, and the place has lost the last animating traces of human inhabitants. It is peculiarly silent, with no Major Mitchell cockatoos sounding the alarm, no owl flapping from its roost in the rafters of the shed — no longer any roosting place for the owl, since the last strips of roofing iron have peeled away. None of us feels inclined to linger. There's something beyond sadness here, an existential void in which time and nature are stalled. We retreat to the mulga several kilometres back along the track, and set up camp among the soft yellow grasses and the dwarf anthills that have long ago shed their red wool caps.

At Pussycat Bore, where we stop for morning tea, the long-tail mulla-mullas are out in profusion, twitching and jostling like crowds of green-tailed cats. I haven't seen them here before, but it occurs to me that this may be how the bore got its name, rather than from the presence of the feral four-legged variety. They demand to be gathered, and between us we collect armfuls. Mine will grace my spartan quarters in Mulan, and hold their shape and colour for several years.

In the few days left to Pam and Rachel before they have to return to Alice, we camp near Parnkupirti Creek at the edge of the coolibahs, and then head out to Lirra for a barbecue with Bessie and Shirley and Lauren, a visiting Kimberley Land Council staffer. Bessie calls out to the lake to let it know who we are, and the rest of us walk to the top of the sand spit that divides Lirra Lagoon from the vast body of water the explorer Warburton named Gregory Salt Sea in 1856. This is where Pam and I camped on our first visit to Lake Gregory fourteen years ago. Waves break in a lacy froth on the hard white sand, and multitudes of waterbirds strut and float in the shallows. It smells and sounds like the sea. As we watch, hundreds of small black ducks lift off the southern lake and cross the spit in long, low formations that go on and on, barely clearing the surface of the lagoon, on into the twilight until they become invisible.

Pam and Rachel and Lauren are mudded by Shirley and Bessie while I gather firewood for the barbecue. As Shirley cooks steak — a chunk of tough Lake Gregory rump — purple clouds boil up out of the west, with an eye-shaped vortex in the centre that Bessie commands to 'Go round! Go round!' It works for a while, but in the end she can't hold it back, and the wind belts sand into the steak and blows the folding chairs along the shore. Shirley, Bessie and Lauren pack up and hightail it out before the rain hits, expecting us to follow. Shirley tells me later that they drove up the hill at Mulan to look for our lights, and when they couldn't see them, Shirley said, 'She's a mad old bushman. They'll stay out there in the storm.'

Which is what we do. We sit in Pam's car eating our sandy steak, leaving an alarmed Pirate to sit out the storm in my car. The wind drives the rain almost horizontal, and we imagine all those ducks piled up on the eastern shore of the lagoon, flailing and swearing.

So whose bloody idea was it to fly over here?

Duncan, get your effing foot out of my mouth.

A smouldering log cartwheels along the beach in a shower of burning embers. Flares of sheet lightning illuminate the place like a photo negative, detailing the frilled waterline and the corrugated chop of the waves. Horizontal zigzags catapult across the western sky like the snakes in the willy-wagtail story, in a cloud of dust and rain! After an hour the storm passes over and the sky clears, and I return to my own vehicle to sleep.

At 2.00 a.m. the rain wakes me — a steady downpour out of a low, starless sky. I wake the others.

—We have to go, I say. The road will be running in places, and it'll look bad, but there's nothing that will stop us before it soaks in. If it rains till morning, we'll have trouble getting out.

It takes us more than an hour to drive the twenty-five kilometres back to Mulan.

—You sure do a good send-off party, Rachel says next morning.

+ + +

A couple of months later, when I am back in Canberra, Pam contacts me. We arrange to meet at the small writing studio I rent in the Gorman House Arts Centre. In the last year she has shed the weight she had accumulated during recent years, recapturing the damaged beauty she had in the early years of our friendship. Her usual vivacity has been replaced by something more fragile. She sits in the armchair in my simply furnished room — desk, chair, armchair, bookcase. The walls are covered with the maps and diagrams and photographs that refer to the writing project I'm working on. Under the window I have Blu-Tacked a set of Violet Sunset prints Pam selected and sent me from the hundreds of slides she has taken on our trips together. We have talked intermittently about putting an exhibition together of Pam's photographs and my text.

—I've been diagnosed with a medical condition, she says, and stops. I can't say it.

I push a notepad and pencil towards her.

—Write it down.

She takes the pencil, and prints MOTOR NEURONE DISEASE on the notepad. I read the words, which I don't fully understand, but I do understand the look in her eyes, which contains a terrible acceptance, and loneliness, and fear.

—What does it mean?

—It means I have three years at the most. I have the quickest-acting kind, starting at the top and working down. I'll lose my voice, and it will get harder and harder to swallow.

She shows me her hands, where there is a discernible atrophy of the muscle between her thumb and forefinger.

—That's why I've been having trouble unscrewing jars and turning doorknobs, she says.

It's several years since she first mentioned that particular difficulty. This thing has been incubating for a long time. She tells me that when she began to experience the nerves jumping along her arms, she knew it was serious.

—I was terrified it was Parkinson's disease, she said, and I'd end up shaking and drooling in a wheelchair. Now I wish it was Parkinson's.

She nods at the Violet Sunset prints on the wall.

—That's one of the projects I want to finish.

—Yes, I say. Of course.

—I'm going to beat this disease, she says. I'm going to be a miracle of modern science.

In the next days and weeks, I do some research on MND. The more I learn about it, the more appalling it becomes. Trying to absorb the reality of the disease is like walking into a black, muffled, absorbent wall, over and over. Whenever I think about Pam, my mind goes blank.

MAPPING UNCOMMON GROUND

Mulan, 2011

The Paruku IPA continues through 2011 without a co-ordinator, and I'm once again persuaded to fill the position during my annual stint in Mulan. It turns out to be fortuitous timing, coinciding with a project I've agreed to co-ordinate with the artist Mandy Martin. Mandy has built an artistic oeuvre on painting the Australian landscape, depicting it in Romantic Sublime style as a threatened space and an aesthetic resource. This position has brought her inevitably to engage with environmental and indigenous issues, and Paruku is a site rich in both.

The aim of what becomes known as the Paruku project is to bring together Aboriginal and European interpretations of the history, culture, and physical environment of Paruku. This includes the production of paintings, prints, photography, and sculpture for an exhibition at the Araluen Cultural Precinct in Alice Springs; and a book of scientific and historical essays, indigenous oral histories and traditional stories, photographs, and reproductions of the artwork, to be published by CSIRO.

During a two-week field trip, Mandy brings a team of people to Mulan and supervises the production of paintings and prints by the local mob. Among Mandy's support team is the American writer and curator Bill Fox, who has recently become the director of the Center for Art + Environment at the Nevada Museum of Art. Bill writes about the effect particular landscapes have on human cognition, and is keen to further explore an indigenous perspective.

Since my energies are taken up with the day-to-day logistics of managing people, I persuade John Carty to keep tabs on the indigenous material and to record the oral histories and stories associated with the paintings. Among the Mulan participants is Hanson Pye, son of Kilampi Pye, and now the senior custodian of the Parnkupirti section of the Two Dingoes dreaming story. It's serendipitous that Hanson is in the community for an extended period. In all the years I've been coming to Mulan, he has rarely been here, but both he and his brother Kevin claim they are back in Mulan for good, and have joined the IPA ranger team for which I am now responsible.

The brothers have a seamless traditional genealogy and uncontested jurisdiction over the Parnkupirti dreaming track, and Hanson is rare among his generation for the depth of his cultural knowledge and his willingness to share it. Having missed the earlier archaeological dig, he is captivated by the story of the buried stone, which I explain to him, and by the layers of time inscribed on the cliff face.

While the rest of the Mulan painters work on figurative story paintings, Hanson produces a remarkable interpretation of the Parnkupirti archaeological site. The painting, which he calls 'Parnkupirti Layers', is divided into an upper section organised in a geometric pattern of green, yellow, and red oxide, and a lower section similarly constructed with black, grey, and sienna. He explains that the stone is located where the two sections meet. Above it is human time, up to and including the present. Below the stone is *Waljirri*, the Dreaming. As a seamless appropriation of science into an Aboriginal worldview, it is breathtaking.

Equally remarkable are the abstracted forms that represent time and place. A maze-like arrangement of angular shapes — red oxide in the upper section and black in the lower — divide grids of dotted colour into a formal geometry as precise in its way as Mike Smith's graph diagrams. At the centre of the painting, within the upper section and directly above the seam where the stone is located, Hanson has drawn a capital H in red oxide. Outlined in green and embedded in a square of the sienna-coloured dots that fill much of the *Waljirri* section, it is clearly a self-portrait, located at the crux of the world, embedded in the present and limned in the Dreaming.

Mandy is keen that there should be a painting on which everyone collaborates, and asks me to provide a suitable template, using the panoramic five-panel format she prefers. The Parnkupirti site seems an obvious subject for a collaborative work. Central to the story of Paruku, the creek is a topographical feature that lends itself to a painting composed of five panels. I consult Hanson, who approves the plan, and use a satellite projection to block in a bird's eye perspective of the creek, cliff, and erosion gully. Transferring satellite imagery is an imprecise craft, but familiarity with the location allows me to simplify and select, and I'm pleased with the painterly result.

The next morning we assemble on the flat near the dig site, armed with paint, water, food, and the expectation of spending the day painting. The ranger team, headed by Jamie Brown and inflated to an unusually large number with the addition of the Pye brothers, erects a canvas canopy for shade, and I lay out the painted template and explain, with Hanson's help, what we propose to do. There's some consultation among the senior women, led by Charmia and Evelyn. The site is too sacred, they say, too dangerous for women to paint. The rangers must do the work of painting, and the women will keep vigil. The *kartiya* men can watch, help mix paint, or do whatever useful tasks are delegated to them, but the women must not look. Our job is to hold a safe space for the men to work in.

It's the kind of occasion that can't be orchestrated, when *kartiya* plans lose traction and cultural authority takes over. The small matter of me having painted the underpinning layer seems not to matter — there's a pragmatism in what can be overlooked for the sake of a larger purpose. Watching the senior women take control fills me with quiet glee. Although we *kartiya* are responsible for setting up the event, we are peripheral to the deep levels of engagement that follow. John photographs the progress of the painting over the next two days, and fills me in later on the details. There are no restrictions on my knowing or talking about what happened, only on witnessing it at first hand.

Using a small reproduction of his father's painting as a guide, Hanson marked the ancestral sites on the prepared canvas — the waterhole where the dingoes went into the ground, the two hills representing the ancestral brothers with whom Hanson's father and uncle are identified, the tree and the stone that represent the brothers in earlier manifestations. Hanson's woolly yellow terrier, Sox, was enlisted to make the dingo tracks along the creek, but he refused to submit to having his feet painted and pressed onto the canvas. The various rangers, working independently on the different panels, painted their own version of paw prints.

After a couple of hours most of the *kartiya* drifted away, leaving only Bill Fox and John to witness the process through to completion. At some point the panels were laid together, and the different styles of painted prints noted. In John's photographs the variations look wonderful, but this did not fit the conservative aesthetic of the rangers, and the entire creek, which I had painted white, was painted over in black to obliterate the tracks. It was then repainted white to provide a pristine surface, and one ranger was delegated to paint the tracks in a consistent style across all the panels.

Bill Fox, observing this process, took the over-painting to be a deliberate erasing of the *kartiya* mark from the path of the ancestral dogs. John corrected this misinterpretation when it came to light, and confirmed that the reason for the repainting was aesthetic and practical rather than an assertion of cultural authority. Cultural authority was brought to bear in a different way when Hanson decreed that the painting was too significant to leave the community, and therefore could not be exhibited. In order to navigate this obstacle, I was asked to produce a second template, on which Hanson and Jamie Brown painted a replica of the original work. The replica, which did not carry the numinous significance of the original, was exhibited and purchased as part of the collection of Mulan paintings that travelled to Nevada. The original remains on the wall of the Paruku ranger office in Mulan.

+ + +

Since the left-of-field experience of painting with the rangers, I'm keen to do something more sustained in the way of collaboration. Apart from the maps, Lulu and I have worked together on paintings several times over the past few years.

During the fieldwork for the Paruku project, I had the opportunity to fly over the lake in a small plane, and I took a series of photographs before having to concentrate on not throwing up. Among the photographs are several fire scars, one of which looks like an ancestral being, a creature of scorched earth and shimmering edges stalking across the landscape. From the red and black of freshly burned ground to the green and yellow of new growth, the entire image is constructed of dots. It's an aerial view of a pointillist landscape, but there's a clear sense of perspective, a horizon line just outside the frame. I tweak the colours to a higher saturation level and print the image. Then I block in the broad outlines on a canvas under-painted in red oxide, and give Lulu the canvas and the print.

A couple of days later, she summons me to the building that serves as the Mulan art centre, and shows me what she has done. It's an astonishing minimalist rendition of black and green on red, a dance of energy between burning and growth. The burned ground is animated with a shifting scale of black dots on red ground. Green dots mark the new growth.

What Lulu has done is demarcate the boundaries. The edges are my ground, where nothing is fixed. I bring to bear my skills as a colourist, to make the edges shimmer in and out of focus, and tease out the perspectival tilt — a random snap from a light plane, or a hawk's-eye view.

OBSCURED BY LIGHT

April 2011

Pam and I spend a week camping and painting in the MacDonnell Ranges, revisiting many of the places where we worked together before the Tanami claimed all our time and energy. Pam had wanted to make a final trip to the Tanami, but her illness is progressing fast, and she's afraid to be far from medical attention. Although she can still drive, she is becoming increasingly frail, and it takes a fair degree of nerve to be a passenger in her car as we negotiate the tough terrain of back tracks in the western MacDonnells.

During the day we carry on as usual, going our separate ways to observe and absorb and draw, but the evenings by the campfire are difficult. Pam is too tired to make the effort to talk much. The sharp consonants are slipping out of her verbal repertoire, so that when she speaks she sounds drunk. Since she can no longer drink wine, it's an irony she could do without. And I struggle to sustain a one-sided conversation while two decades of past conversations hum behind the encroaching silence.

We have been offered two possible time slots in 2012 to exhibit the Violet Sunset work at the Araluen Cultural Precinct in Alice Springs. Pam favours the July slot, which allows more time to have the photographs printed to her exacting standards, but I say we should take the earlier option in February. What I don't say, but we both understand, is that the latter date may be too late.

+ + +

August 2011

En route to Mulan to prepare for the Paruku project, I call in to Balgo to see how Margaret is faring. I find her established in her granddaughter Beverley's house, surrounded by family and in good spirits, although it's clear that she has at most a few months to live. When a sore on her remaining leg turned gangrenous, she and her family decided to let the diabetes run its course without the interventions of another amputation, dialysis and hospitalisation thousands of miles away, and the likelihood of her dying away from her family and country.

In October she falls into a coma, and we assemble to pay our last respects, but she rallies and is more lucid than she has been in many months. She was called back, she tells us, so that she could have some more time with her family, and tell them all the things she needed to say. For three weeks she seems to exist in an illuminated other dimension. It can't last, but it's astonishing to witness.

+ + +

November 2011

The call we had been expecting and dreading comes on a Sunday morning.

—Come now. The grandmother is leaving us.

It was the eldest granddaughter, Beverley, who summoned us,

her grandmother's name already consigned to the realm of the unsayable.

I make a thermos of tea, and pack fruit and muesli bars in preparation for what I know will be a long and gruelling day. By the time I drive around to collect the people who are expecting me, they are ready and waiting.

Margaret Yinjuru Napurrula Bumblebee is in the last stages of her dying, a journey to which we have all been witness for many weeks. She has been surrounded by the care and love of her family, and the unobtrusive ministrations of the community nurses, as a steady parade of people have come to pay their respects to this woman of high degree. After the false alarm a few weeks earlier that brought us all rushing to her bedside, she has fallen into a final diabetic coma, her face distended and almost unrecognisable with oedema, her hands like inflated latex gloves. Beneath the blankets, the mass of her tall body tapers strangely, the missing leg more notable in its absence.

This death is taking place within the stream of lives for which she has been responsible, over which she has exercised authority and influence. Five generations of the family are here. Dora crouches like an effigy on the bunk alongside her dying daughter. Cynthia, the granddaughter Margaret raised from babyhood, cares for her with loving, slovenly attention. Her surviving children, all sons, lurk smoking in the shadowy corners of the enclosed verandah. The great-granddaughter, a lanky, boyish creature of an age with the youngest of the grandsons, bookends the generations with Dora, the ancient being whose attention never wavers from her only child.

Three of Margaret's children are dead: one killed by the same disease that is now killing his mother, two by violent misadventure. There is unfinished payback business, said to be leaching away at the health of those charged to carry it out. What I know of that story has the ingredients of a Greek tragedy. Two of the living sons are beginning to show evidence of diabetes.

We each take a turn at the bedside, sitting for a while holding one of the bloated hands, paying our respects to Dora, who barely responds. The Mulan contingent settle themselves at the edge of the verandah to gossip, play cards, catch up with people, and let the day unfold to its own rhythm. I am not expected to hang around with them, and don't.

—You should go and see your friends, Napuru, they say, but I don't have *kartiya* friends in Balgo any more. Instead I drive out to the edge of the pound, park the car in some shade, and read. Discoloured gusts of smoky wind flail at the sides of the vehicle. I eat my muesli bars, drink tea, doze, and read some more. When the wind drops I take Pirate for a walk. In the late afternoon I go back to check whether there has been any change, but Margaret lingers on. There is a consensus among the Mulan mob that we will go home and return in the morning.

Next morning, around seven, Beverley phones to tell me that Margaret has died in the night.

—Tell the others, she says.

Before we reach Balgo I am instructed to pull over, and everyone gets out of the car. Beside the road are slabs of the white ochre used to make the paste that people paint on their faces and bodies as a gesture of mourning. It's all very efficient. The stone is collected and ground, the paste mixed, each of us is smeared on the forehead and cheeks, and we continue into town to the sorry camp. I am directed to sit with Dora, who is stripped down to a skirt, her hair shorn, her face and body plastered white. When she sees me, she wails and grips me tightly.

The day ebbs and flows as new groups of mourners and family arrive from further afield. Fresh bursts of grief accompany the arrivals, and people gather in groupings that reflect particular relationships to the dead woman. Evelyn, who is also Napurrula, indicates that I should sit with her, and someone takes my place beside Dora. Unobtrusive directions are offered throughout the day, so there is no occasion when I find myself at a loss. Whatever choreographed order governs the occasion sweeps me up and carries me with it. It's been a strange privilege to have known this woman, and one I've never quite risen to.

Too late now, I think, as I sit on the concrete slab outside the sorry house, squeezed among the Napurrulas.

+ + +

February 2012

... only an absence, obscured by light
and a shell buried in red sand ...

Pam chooses a phrase from my poem 'Searching for the Inland Sea' as the title for the Violet Sunset show. We install *Obscured by Light* at Araluen in late February. Pam's voice is gone, and she is very thin, but her attention to the details of the installation is uncompromising. Until now I have had very little input, beyond providing the text to accompany the images and making some suggestions about the configuration of the photographs. The photographs are printed on aluminium panels that give the images a glowing, saturated colour. Fifty-or-so panels, each fifty by eighty centimetres, are arranged on the gallery walls to convey a loose, absurdist narrative. Violet struts across the salt lake with her suitcase; she attempts to scale the side of a water tank, one stiletto precariously balanced on a star picket; she peers into an empty freezer at Ngulupi. The skeleton of the dead camel looms under water. The blocks of text, printed on small perspex panels, are designed to play against the images as a roving story, shifting the meaning depending on where they are located. The plan is to move them around several times during the progress of the exhibition. I have to fight Pam for the initial placement of some of the texts, and only get my way when I point out that this is supposed to be a collaboration.

—For someone who can't talk, you're pretty efficient at making yourself heard, I say, and she smirks.

The texts in question stay where I put them for the opening night and the artist's talk, after which Pam moves them to where she thinks they should be, and where they remain until the show closes.

Along the dark wires of night come
the messages I hide from during the day.
I'm mad
I'm lost
I'm afraid

Each time she reaches the end
she finds she has forgotten the beginning.
She does not forget the endings.

Everyone is alone. It is
possible not to know this.

+ + +

July 2012
When Pam dies, I am at Well 33 in the Great Sandy Desert,

working with Martu people on a project called 'We Don't Need a Map'. It is 4 July 2012, barely four months since the opening of *Obscured by Light* at Araluen. It's pure chance that Fiona Walsh, a scientist in Alice Springs who is also a friend of Pam's, knows where I am and how to contact me. I'm glad I'm in the desert when I get the news. It's a day after the full moon, and I go out and sit on a sand dune until the moon rises.

If I had my own vehicle, I could drive east on the Gunbarrel Highway and be in Alice Springs in 24 hours. Instead it takes me three days, during which time I drive one of the hired troop carriers to Newman and catch a series of flights that involve hours and nights in airports bringing me at last to Alice a day before the funeral. I stay in Pam's house for the last time. It is haunted by her presence — the old Pam, before she got sick. I am one of several people who speak at her funeral. None of it seems real. The physical person is gone, but the space she occupies gets larger and larger.

+ + +

July 2013

Anna is the next to die. She lies down for a rest one afternoon and doesn't wake up, her tiny body giving up at last under the stresses it has borne for most of its life.

I can't bear this, I think, when Julianne rings to tell me of her mother's death. But I can, of course, because there's no alternative.

I set out on my annual pilgrimage across the continent with a burden of emotional baggage heavier than any I have carried since my father's death more than twenty years ago. The cascading losses of recent times are stamped into the landscape.

REQUIEM

Tanami, 2018

The sun drops over the horizon as I pass the homestead gate, so I turn east and drive directly to the lake in order to make camp before the light is gone. This year, both Lake Ruth and the country are dry. There's a dullness in the vegetation, a dusty weight to the air, a subtle edge of stress, even where there has been no impact from stock. The latest station manager left a week ago. He lasted three years, which is longer than most. Part of the challenge for me in returning is the need to re-establish my credentials with each new manager to retain my access to Tanami Downs. In practice, it's the traditional owners who have the last word, and they have mostly been happy to see me return, but the people with whom I've had the strongest bonds are dying now, and taking their knowledge with them.

It has been twenty-one years since I first started coming back to this country — long enough for a child to be born and grow to maturity. Instead of a child, some earth-born incubus has been hatched and nurtured on the austere geography of the place, giving rise to a stretching of my psyche to embrace ways of knowing and being that I struggle to translate. Partly it's about being exposed to minds wired during pre-contact childhoods. Partly it's about believing that we all had that capacity once, that the physical attributes of place were among the earliest factors to shape the human mind, and that the template is still in there among the tangled circuits of urban *Homo sapiens*. It's about wanting, as a white Australian, to find a vocabulary to tell as best I can the story of a place.

I am not thinking about any of this as I drive the familiar track along the edge of the airstrip, dog-legging south and east to cut through the stand of ti-tree on the western edge of the lake. In the last of the light, the eastern horizon has taken on the evening colour-shift of rose pink above duck-egg blue, the rest of the sky bleaching to lilac and the evening star just visible. I'm thinking about ghosts, and whether I'm ready to meet them.

I've long made my peace with the dog ghosts — old Sam who made the first pilgrimage back here with me has been dead for seventeen years, and his successor, Slippers, for seven. They shadow the incumbent dog, Pirate, as he makes a detailed examination of the camp site, sniffing and pissing, dashing out onto the lake surface to bark at imaginary predators. This annual journey has been a part of his life since he was born.

The human ghosts assemble as I set up camp: Patricia, who died violently, and whose spirit still stalks unappeased; her mother, Margaret, whose death, like her life, was exemplary; and Dora, Margaret's mother, who will join them soon, having lapsed into the final stages of diabetic collapse. There's a grim set of reversals here, when the youngest dies first. And there's the ghost I've yet to face. Pam died a year ago, less than two years after she was diagnosed. I have not yet been able to give proper acknowledgement to this churned thing inside me, grief masquerading as a kind of peevish anger.

I pull the swag off the Hilux and look for a flat spot from which I will be able to see the sunrise. I gather wood, and light a fire. It's a minimalist overnight camp, requiring little more than the barbecue grill, the billy, and a folding chair. My meal is a basic salad, lamb chops, and red wine in a metal beaker, which I raise to the memory of its previous owner. When Pam's belongings were being divided among her friends, I claimed the beakers that were part of her kit, and which we always used for the wine that lubricated hundreds of evening conversations in the fifteen years of field trips we shared.

She would never have tolerated such a spartan camp and basic supplies. While I'm a competent camp cook — and enjoy it more than conventional cooking — my basic method is to buy the food types that require minimum preparation while still providing a balanced diet, and eat them in the simplest possible combinations. It saves a lot of fuss, but it doesn't make for meals to linger over. Pam loved food, and spent a lot of time planning what we would eat. She supervised the food shopping for our trips, making sure we had treats and luxuries, and ate well even when our fresh supplies were gone. *The Two Fat Ladies* was popular at the time, and we used to joke about doing a cooking show called *The Two Thin Ladies*, producing fabulous food cooked on a campfire in exotic desert settings.

It's too warm to sit close to the fire, so I set my chair at the outer edge of the firelight. The waxing moon is bright enough to reveal the flat expanse of the lake with its dark rim of ti-tree, the pale surface giving off a faint light. The *wirntiki* are quiet and *Warlu* is asleep, while the old *maparn* stands sentinel.

This lake, where ancestral pathways cross and ancient waterways meet, is my point of entry and departure, the place where my two lives intersect before I step into whichever persona is needed for the task ahead. In the morning, I will walk across to the other camp site at the eagle tree and carry out my ritual of arrival. But for the moment I just sit, listening to whatever the silence has to say.

The years shift and flicker like a random slideshow. Pam took thousands of photographs of the country — colour-saturated, beautifully composed images that, if I'm not careful, could displace my own way of seeing and remembering.

+ + +

The mapping of a friendship is a delicate art. Pam had a vast constellation of friends, each with a particular place and part to play in her life. The bedrock of our friendship was the country and the trips we made together. It was where we both explored what mattered to us, and although I can't speak for Pam, I'm guessing that the differences between us were as important to her in teasing out what she believed as they have been to me.

I remember the details of the first trip we made together, and the last. Of the many in between, I have a clear recollection of places and events, but I couldn't tell without reference to my diaries what year things happened. And the diaries themselves aren't reliable, because I tend to leave out dates for months at a time. It's the places that hold firm in my memory.

The lakes are at the heart of the story: Lake Ruth, Bullock's Head Lake, Lake Sarah, Lake Gregory, the salt lake, Lake Fidler. These are the names by which I knew them first. Later I learned their traditional names — Mangkurrurpa, Yanypurru, Wanpirru, Paruku. When I asked Margaret what the salt lake was called, she said, 'That's cheeky snake country. We don't go there.' I never learned the Warlpiri name for Lake Fidler. Whether full of water or dry, they were our camp sites, as they had been camp sites since the country was first inhabited. Amphitheatres of the imagination, they allowed for the surfacing of the mythic strands from which we both sought to construct meanings of one sort or another.

The trajectory of our friendship followed the trajectory of these journeys, coming back again and again to the same places, to find them and ourselves familiar but subtly different from the last time. We were like migratory birds, driven to return year after year.

Although Pam loved the desert, she loved the beach equally, especially the long, windswept sands along the south coast of New South Wales, with their backdrops of white dunes and ancient banksia forests. While she was studying in Canberra, she went often to the coastal village of South Durras, and eventually bought a holiday cottage there with her friend Helen Maxwell. In the year after she was diagnosed with MND, Pam did a series of drawings of shearwaters that had washed up in their dozens on the beach at South Durras, exhausted by their long migration from the Bering Sea. She drew them, with their delicate skulls and angular, twisted necks, plunging blindly upwards, or falling.

She walks, weather permitting, to assuage loss,
treads out the measure of a day's anguish
along sand dunes and beaches,
plucking the small detritus of creature cast-offs,
the shells and husks of other lives,
feathered and reptile, mollusc and vegetable,
tide washed, wind-scoured, honed to a nub,
the whole shape imagined
in a fluted edge, a broken curve,
in half a hollow like
a cupped hand.

She collects, the days shortening into winter,
reading her wrack of scraps,
throws seed pods, and the bones of mice
to foretell the future,
in a blue shirt, bending to look, and look again,
the puzzle of fragments re-assembled
to frame the shape of absence.

Hand in a pocket, thumbing the worn edge of
a stone, or bone,
the afternoon's ballast thrown out
and the day tilting
towards some sort of ending.

The first thing the disease took from Pam was the ability to swallow. She persisted for as long as she could, struggling to get down the soft food and sauces and soups that a coterie of friends prepared, before finally submitting to the peg that allowed for nutrition to be taken directly into her stomach. As the muscles of her throat and mouth failed, she lost the ability to make the sounds that require a subtle range of muscle flexion to produce them. Her speech retracted month by month from the language of an adult to the mumblings of a baby. As with her determination to eat for as long as she could, she continued to speak long after her mouth and tongue could produce distinguishable words. She insisted on taking her friends along with her, forcing us to pay attention, to develop listening skills that drew on context and substitution and intuition — she would brook no pretence that we understood what she had said when we did not.

When Pam died in such a cruel and protracted way, she had the last word so definitively that I am left with a hum of unspoken responses, distracting and incoherent as tinnitus.

To explore Pam's work is a way for me to better understand my own motivations, which both differed from and resembled hers. Her thesis put forward the premise that it was only by coming and going, what she called 'a necessary nomadism', that one could establish and maintain a viable relationship with the country, but in fact she made a home in a particular part of it and then explored its immediate environs in an intimate and sustained way. I believe the nomadism made her anxious, in the same way that travelling into unfamiliar country makes desert Aboriginal people anxious, the range of their travels either limited to their own territory or negotiated with the custodians of neighbouring territory. After twenty years of living in Alice Springs, I think she felt very much at home in the surrounding landscape, and it was only when she travelled beyond its gravitational pull that she felt the anxiety of the stranger in a strange land.

No matter the irritations and disagreements, there was no one else I shared this world with so consistently over such a long period. She understood the consuming necessity of coming back, of being here. I think that the compulsion that sends me back to spend time in the communities, to challenge the boundaries and limitations I recognise in myself, is a mirror of the compulsion Pam felt to go back to university and do the Masters, to challenge herself where she felt most vulnerable.

+ + +

I wake before sunrise, and watch the horizon turn from the galah shades of pink and grey to bright orange, as if a fire is advancing over the rim of the world. So it did in the Dreaming, burning its way west through the heart of the grasslands, scorching, maiming, replenishing. But this morning it's just another sunrise, and with it comes a breeze that arrives with the warming of the air, and is welcome because the flies are plentiful and persistent. Pirate is sitting up in the back seat of the car, watching my swag for signs of movement. If I don't shut him in the car he spends the night on red alert, barking at dingoes and cattle and figments of dog imagination. I get up and let him out, and he circles me, leaping with excitement that the day has begun. It must be hard on dogs, having to wait on the whims of their owners.

I fan the campfire coals to life, put the billy on to boil, and make a few notes in my diary. There are no big projects pending this year, no urgent tasks, apart from the preparations for Anna's funeral.

There is vegetation on the lake edges that I've not seen before. Samphire is growing around the main basin, indicating that the lake is accumulating salts. Scattered clumps of *Senna notabilis*, cockroach bush — so-named for its profusion of flat, brown, segmented pods — punctuate the sandy littoral between the ti-tree and the samphire. Although it's a native plant, *kanpirr kanpirr*, the bush name of my other friend and collaborator Kanpirr Veronica Fatima Lulu, cockroach bush is an indicator of disturbed soils. This is the first time I've seen it here. And I've never seen as much damage caused by stock. So much for the decision several years ago to fence off the lake to protect it — the closed gate I came through is keeping the horses and cattle inside the fence, and the dry grasses have been chewed to a nub.

But the place still holds its healing power. It is something to do with its proportions — large enough to feel the lift of light and space, but contained within the low, white ti-tree-covered dunes. Mangkurrurpa feels, has always felt, safe. Its local spirits are benign, its energies calm. This doesn't change, regardless of whether the lake is filled to the brim, or is shallow, or dry. The old *maparn* custodian still stands as the tallest tree on the northern side. On the south side is the eagle tree, so named for the eagle's nest in its branches. It's an alternative site to the one where I'm currently camped — the configuration and size of the trees makes it easy to stretch a tarpaulin between them for shade in the hot weather, and you can see the sunset from there as well as the sunrise. When the lake is at its highest, both sites are under water, and camping is relegated to higher ground in the spindly new ti-tree.

Crossing the southern edge of the lake on my way to the eagle tree, I notice the prints of dingo and camel among the cattle and horse tracks. Fresh camel tracks suggest that the fence is down somewhere. The sand beneath the eagle tree has been invaded by some sort of straggling weed, and I can hear Margaret's voice in my head.

—*This place need cleaning.*

—*Yes, I know*, I say. *Next time, when I can stay longer.*

But now I have something to do, a half-serious ritual that has evolved as I've come to better understand both myself and the culture I'm about to enter. I sit down at the foot of the eagle tree and wait.

The last time I camped here, I saw a running dingo in a red lake. The lake was shallow, the light had almost gone, and the skin of water held the red of the sunset. The dog itself was not visible, only its inverted reflection trotting along the seam between light and dark — a horizon within a horizon, a pool of crimson light, and a black dog running upside down.

Today, sunlight shivers in the branches of the paperbarks, white on white, and throws nets of shadow on the white sand. A crested pigeon, silver-grey, whirrs off into the spinifex like a wind-up toy, ridiculous in its plump alarm.

—Hello, Napurrula, I say.

Napurrula is a sisterhood, a set of relationships and responsibilities. She is daughter of Napaltjarri and Jakamarra, sister of Jupurrula, wife of Japanangka, mother of Napangardi and Japangarti; she is echidna, wild potato, red and yellow flowers. She is generations of women connected through time and space. In a world where individual identity draws its conviction from collective identity, she is both one and many. At times, when I inhabit her, she is a clown, a mask, an evasion. In the fractured looking glass through which black and white regard each other, seeing shadows and reflections, she is indispensable.

Napurrula is the skin name I was given shortly after I was born, when my parents lived at Hooker Creek, now called Lajamanu, a couple of hundred kilometres north-east of here. Back then, skin names were rarely given to white people, only to very young white children who were born in the country. To have been so named has been a great advantage. It links me to the families who belong to this part of the country, and at the same time it circumvents the proprietorial naming that can happen in a working relationship, where a white person is given a skin name that identifies them as a resource. Bessie and Lulu, who are Napangarti, would never have given me the skin name of their mother, which would put me, theoretically at least, in a position of authority over them. I used to feel self-conscious about claiming my skin name, but in recent years I've more than earned my right to it.

When I'm not here, I imagine Napurrula living between Mangkurrurpa and the salt lake. The salt lake is on the edge of the wild country, a remnant palaeo-channel from the time of the inland seas, when giant snakes of water crawled across the continent, coupled and fought in slow convulsions that shaped the ancient geography of the country. I don't believe in the ancestral beings, but there's a space in my mind that registers their shimmering traces. The tremor of their passage moves like a ripple of light along a dune, leaving its trace in a rime of salt flushed into the samphire. It's impossible not to read the country this way, with the voices of its custodians in my ear:

Those two snakes flew from Jarluwangu to Granites, looking for wives. They saw two women but when they came down to look closer they saw they were too old.

That's the three dingo puppies. Their mother left them to go look for tucker, and she didn't come back yet.

The hummocks called The Puppies are eroding piles of sandstone sediment. I can never see that cluster of hills without feeling an existential anxiety for the abandoned puppies, waiting through the aeons for their mother to return. And I saw the two snakes flying east one morning, lit pink by the dawn. I woke up at

Mangkurrurpa and they were directly above me, two sinuous banners of cloud with broad, triangular heads pointing towards the sunrise. For a moment, before my rational mind took hold, I was awake to a world in which everything was animate, and felt my heart race with astonishment. When I recognised them as clouds, my sense of wonder was undiminished.

Napurrula frees me into becoming someone clearer and more simplified than the persona that carries me through my other life. I set aside my introspection, leaving it for safekeeping by the eagle tree, to be collected on my return. A more robust and unselfconscious being takes hold, with a sense of theatre and a willingness to play the fool, a skin both absorbent of cross-cultural nuance and resistant to manipulation.

The desert people I know have a powerful sense of entitlement. Their personalities are big, their lives unpredictable, provisional, and epic — full of tragedy, drama, violence, and humour. Their one immutable commitment is to family and country. Although they suffer the incremental effects of poverty, violence, and poor health, their ability to live one day at a time, their focus on having their immediate needs met, creates an astonishing capacity to recover and endure. They did not survive one of the harshest environments on the planet and the vicissitudes of colonisation through passivity and fatalism, but through a fierce and insistent determination to exploit every available resource. As a solitary *kartiya*, prone to self-doubt and without the support of friends and family, it's a struggle to hold onto my autonomy. To function effectively, it's necessary to define myself in brighter, broader outlines than I might otherwise choose.

+ + +

Mangkurrurpa, 2004
Place and memory together confer a kind of immortality. From my

spot under the eagle tree, I can see Margaret sitting cross-legged on a groundsheet, scrubbing her hands and forearms in preparation for making damper. She has assembled the necessities within easy reach — the large enamel mixing bowl, the drum of flour, a tin of baking powder, a billy of water.

—I bin cookie for droving camp when I was young, she says with pride.

Her two small grandsons, for whom she has fought and won a custody battle, race about naked on the dry lake surface.

—Puttem trouser, Margaret tells them.

The older boy climbs up to the eagle's nest and shits in it, to everyone's disgust.

—He's mad one, that one, Margaret says.

Her granddaughter Cynthia sits beside her, watching. A child of the first of Margaret's sons to die, she is eleven or twelve, still eager to learn, still happy to be part of these visits to the country that is part of her legacy. On subsequent visits, as she gets older, she will turn sulky and recalcitrant, before transforming into a warm and loving young woman. I have a photograph of her at the age of five, standing in this same place with a black-headed python, *muntuny*, the result of a successful hunting trip, draped around her shoulders. In the photograph, her aunt Patricia stands grinning beside her, along with Patricia's daughter Beverley, a shy teenager in a blue-flannel shirt. Margaret, always the tallest in any group, holds the head of the python, and Dora's gargoyle grin looms from the shadows of the ti-tree, where she hunkers by the campfire.

They share my solitude, each event occupying its own precise moment. In the moment in which Margaret is making damper, Dora crouches in the almost identical place and posture as she does in the earlier photograph, happy beyond measure to be here in this place that is part of the geography of her being.

In the evening, I sit beside Dora while she talks of her life in this country, a childhood in the bush with only rumours of *kartiya*, those pale-skinned beings that spent their time digging in the ground, making holes like monstrous bilby burrows. Her voice rasps into the night, and Cynthia's black eyes shine from the nest of blankets where she is curled beside the old woman. The two boys, children of another of Margaret's sons, have fallen asleep. Margaret herself sits listening, asking an occasional question, prodding her mother's memory. The old woman's English, rarely used, is easier to understand than her daughter's. Pam is in a camp chair by the fire, John Carty in another, listening to the old woman's voice as it weaves its tale of first encounters.

—I bin born south from Manytjurrungu, my dreaming is *ngatijirri*, budgerigar. It bin dry out here, no water, dry time, nothing to eat. My father bin take us to mine. I was *karntarr*, young one with little milks. First time I bin see *kartiya*. Same colour like tin meat. We bin see motorcar, we bin think he's a big animal running on his knees. We didn't stay there that time.

When her mother falls silent, Margaret speaks.

—My dreaming is *wirntiki*, curlew bird. *Wirntiki* got burnt at this place, Mangkurrurpa.

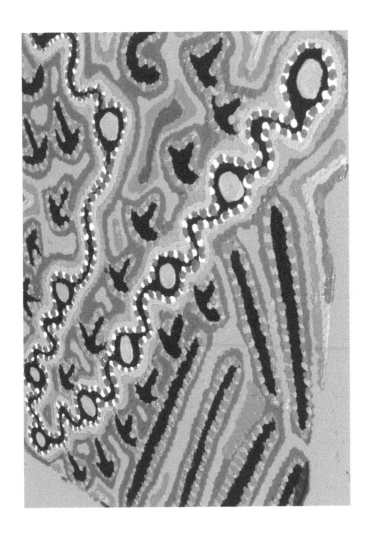

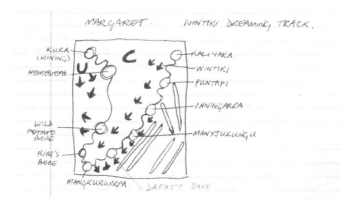

MARGARET. WINTIKI DREAMING TRACK.

KURA (MINING)
HOMESTEAD
KALI YAKA
WINTIKI
PUNTAPI
INNINGARRA
WILD POTATO BORE
MANYJUKUNGU
KIM'S BORE
MANGKURURRPA   DAKOTY BORE

Tanami Downs, 2013

It's already warm, and I feel the creeping lassitude that so often accompanies these returns — the desire to lie down in the freckled shade and let the day drift over me. The prospect of packing the car, negotiating the homestead, undertaking the long drive, paying my respects in Balgo and then Mulan at the end of the day, exhausts me.

What I experience, on this first morning at the lake, is something larger and less personal than grief, a responsibility to remember the people who have walked here. It's too intense to hold on to for long. It needs songs and rituals to create shared channels, along which it can flow through individuals without harming them.

By the time I walk back from the eagle tree to my car, the heat is beginning to set in. Although I don't have much to pack, it takes forever. There's a diesel moment when the new siphon hose refuses to flow, slipping out of the jerrycan and spraying me with fuel. I'm exasperated and cranky, stinking of diesel and convinced that this whole enterprise is evidence of a life squandered on quixotic idiocies. Pirate, who has seen it all before, pays no attention.

The only people at the Tanami Downs homestead are two Aboriginal women, the wives of the employees who are taking care of the station until the manager is replaced. The men are out some-where on the run, and the women have come over from Balgo for the weekend. They assume that I am travelling in a larger party, and are surprised that I'm on my own. It is still rare for women to travel alone out here. They assure me the bottom road is fine, hav-ing driven along it a few days earlier.

A couple of stud bulls graze the patch of couch grass between the workers' quarters and the main house, untroubled by the peri-odic spray of the rotating sprinkler. I top up my water container at the tap near the coolroom, keen to be on my way. The homestead looks forlorn and abandoned. How many different managers have I seen come and go in the past two decades? For some, it has been a stop-gap job en route to something closer to town or with bet-ter prospects. Others have brought passion and enthusiasm to the role, with dreams of how to enlist the energies of the traditional owners, improve the cattle herd, break in the half-wild descendants of the horse plant and return to mustering on horseback. There was a time when I came back every year expecting to find the place shut down, the cattle sold and the station abandoned. During those years the managers changed frequently, with some lasting only months. Most had no previous experience of management. Some were employed on the basis that underpins a lot of jobs with remote indigenous organisations: that you are available; that if you have a criminal record it's not for really bad stuff; that if you don't have basic literacy you have a spouse or de facto who does; and that the traditional owners are agreeable.

—There's nothing to it, I recall the young wife of one of the managers during this era saying. You just leave the cattle to get fat out in the paddocks, and then you sell them.

She was one of those exquisite northern Australian mixtures of European, Aboriginal, and Asian — in her case, Filipino — that infuses towns like Broome and Darwin with a population of exotic good looks.

—I don't like these desert blackfellas, she told me. They scare me. I don't let them come inside the house yard.

I wondered how this went down with the custodians of the country, who were responsible for employing her husband. I heard later that her fearful dislike of the local people provoked an incident at Rabbit Flat that earned her a belting from one of them, to whom she was just another cheeky yella fella.

In spite of the fact that the station barely turned enough profits to cover its running costs, let alone to provide its extended population of traditional owners with an income, and was at best an intermittent employer of local people, the Warlpiri owners of Mongrel Downs, as most of them still called it, had a deep and sentimental attachment to the cattle station. There was an unshakeable faith that their young men would come back one day and work the cattle, wheeling quad bikes and motorbikes with the same panache as their fathers and grandfathers had wheeled their stockhorses. And the Warlpiri were in the enviable position of having money to invest. When the first mining royalty agreements were brokered, and it became apparent that there was big money involved, astute decisions were made to invest a proportion of that income for the benefit of the communities of Lajamanu and Yuendumu, where most of the Warlpiri lived. While individuals still received substantial payments, the invested money was used for community education, sports facilities, employment, and the like.

Although there was periodic grumbling that the station should be paying its way, there was never any suggestion that it should be given up. In 2002 a decision was made to employ someone with professional station-management skills, and to put some of the invested money into improving the station infrastructure — in effect, to pull the station back from the brink of collapse. That was when the Napiers took over, and the slow haul back to some kind of sustainability began. The Napier years remain in my memory as good years. The last time I saw them here, things were unravelling, and although there was no connection to what was happening at Mulan, the coincidence of the timing was hard to ignore.

Driving west from the homestead along the familiar track, I note that the turnoff to Wild Potato Bore and the track south to Manjurungu looks well used. It seems the mine is destined to go ahead, although too late for the old man, who died a year ago. Too late for Dora, too. Like her daughter, she has made the decision to forgo the medical treatment for diabetes that might prolong her life a little but would take her away from country and family. Now it is only a matter of time, weeks at most, before she will go back into her country for the last time, taking with her the language that articulated it.

The language itself survives in a dictionary — an astonishing tome compiled over many years by poet and linguist Lee Cataldi. She has brought a poet's sensibility to the task, contextualising the words throughout, so that when you search for a word you find it embedded in its uses, its value, its social significance, its relationship to people and objects. Lee has recorded the language in its high form, with the help of a group of women, including Dora and her sister Peggy, for whom it is their mother tongue, and for whom as children the desert was their daily life.

I'm travelling across country as familiar to me as stretches of my own mind. There are the well-worn tracks whose every bend and hollow I can anticipate, the sandy and stony stretches that make for slow going, the flat, fast ironstone country cut here and there by eroded channels that require quick reflexes to avoid axle-breaking jolts. There are places I've explored in intimate detail, and places where I become disoriented and lose my way. There are places I know about but have not yet managed to visit, and places reached only through effort and preparation and perseverance.

Today, crossing the plains, I'm on the lookout for *Acacia pachycarpa,* which grows only in remote pockets of the Tanami and along the lower floodout of Sturt Creek. It is a fire-sensitive tree, and the grazing of cattle on the grasslands of its habitat has subdued the fire threat and allowed stands of the tree to mature and spread. I remember them for the powerful gidgee smell they give off when wet. I first encountered the trees as a teenager, mustering one day when the sky sheeted over with storms, and the smell of rain hitting dry earth mingled with the pungent stink of the shaggy acacias that we pushed the cattle through. The acacias are too rare to have a common name. Peter Latz, whose authority I would concede to in all things botanical to do with the central desert, calls them Tanami gidgee, and it's at his behest I'm checking on the current condition of the trees.

Peter and I go back a long way. He first visited the Tanami in the sixties when, as an opinionated young botanist, he annoyed my father with his opposition to cattle grazing. On another occasion, he and a travelling companion helped me start a recalcitrant generator at Chilla Well, a neighbouring property I was taking care of for a short time. Back then, before the mines re-opened and tourists became more intrepid, the Tanami track was little more than wheel-track access for the handful of people who lived out there. The surprise of coming across a solitary seventeen-year-old in a corrugated iron hut hundreds of kilometres from neighbours was an event Peter referred to often in later years.

The *pachycarpa* are thriving, and I take a number of photographs. It's an opportunity to make the point that stocking is actually improving the habitat for the tree. Peter says he never imagined the day would come that he would admit such a thing. Time and knowledge and deep attachment to country have moderated our positions, and these days we belong to the same tribe.

On the ridge to the south-east of Lake Sarah, I stop the car and let Pirate out for a run. The dry lake basin glimmers into mirage across the ochre-coloured distance, a phantom waterway that for a few short years was an inland sea, when Violet Sunset lounged on the shore and dreamed her transient dreams.

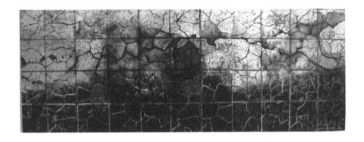

What is she searching for, out there among all that salt and
sand?

    If it's the sea, it's not the one that bites the shore with its
ragged teeth.

    It's another kind, buried deep under dune fields before
memory began.

    She's not looking for new lands to inhabit, but for somewhere
she knows already,

    some place she's been in her dreams.

(Do you remember those dreams, that took you by the scruff and
scared you into knowledge? It's things you didn't want to know,
not really, that pulled you towards them — a future that isn't
yours, or anybody's, if things keep going the way they are.)

The thing is, she found it in the end just by being there at the
right time.

    Walked over a sand ridge and there it was, stretching to the
horizon, silent and new.

    Not even the birds had found it, blue as an eye, curling round
the rim of the world.

As I navigate this subaqueous zone, I think about the time I brought Pam here to see the inland sea. There's a place north of the track where eroded sandstone cliffs mark the shoreline of the expanded lake. The formations of ancient red sandstone were not spectacular, but they were remarkable for what they revealed of a time when this was an active waterway. Along the receding water-line, the spiky remains of drowned shrubs were draped in scraps of beige-coloured paper. Formed by the breaking down and reconsti-tuting of some sort of water weed, the stuff had created dioramas of ripped sails and ruined encampments — an apocalypse in min-iature that was both captivating and sinister.

Pam had brought a new outfit for Violet, a mushroom-coloured satin slip and pink, fur-lined high heels, and a blue plastic reclining chair that she set up beside one of the sandstone pillars. She asked me to pose on the chair wearing the slip and high heels, and clutch-ing my GPS. Since Pam had established that the photographs and choreography were her property, I took a certain satisfaction in refusing to bring any animation to scenarios I thought were clunky and prescriptive. Passive resistance is a fine tool when you lack the moral fibre for argument.

Pam brought to her work an arsenal of post-colonial and femi-nist critiques that challenged the white-settler culture to which I nominally belonged. I didn't disagree with them exactly, but I thought they were blunt instruments to apply to a reality far more complicated than the critical tools allowed for. And there was an odd reversal at work. Of the two of us, I was by nature the more analytical. In everything but her art practice, Pam inclined towards the intuitive and empathetic, but art was the vehicle through which she was attempting to formulate an 'ethics of engagement' to describe her relationship to the country in which she identified as an outsider.

Her formal training at art school in the 1980s had taught her that ideas had to be interrogated and deconstructed through the prism of philosophical and political positions; that materials had inherent qualities which carried their own meanings, and should dictate the form of the work. For me, classically trained in the old-fashioned skills of life-drawing, tonal painting and clay sculpture, having been taught to observe the nuances of form and colour and light, art-making was all to do with the senses. It was observational, intuitive, haptic and emotional. That materials had their own integrity was self-evident — I had no quarrel with this — but to apply a rigorous intellectual approach to the making of the work afflicted me with a kind of claustrophobic horror.

Pirate and I continue across the desolate terrain, and pull in to the stock tank at Wilson's Cave, where I boil the billy for lunch. This road I'm travelling, which people refer to as the bottom road, used to be the only route through to Balgo before the new Tanami highway was established sometime in the 1970s. Some years I was the only person to use it, when the section from the border to Balgo was a corridor of whipstick wattle and sand, punctuated by eroded spines of laterite. The works manager at Balgo graded it about six years ago, much to the chagrin of Jim Napier. The intention was to reactivate the cattle enterprise at the Ngulupi outstation, but the outcome was to create an easy route to the Tanami Downs bullock paddock, and ready access to stolen beef.

Since that time the wattle has regenerated, and the cattle yards at Bloodwood Bore have been almost eclipsed by wattle scrub. The turnoff to Ngulupi is visible only if you know where to look. I've had no inclination to visit the homestead since the trip with Rachel and Pam, but I did once go back there alone. Pam had produced the series of photographs of Ngulupi that she called

Threshold (might be somewhere). They evoked a powerful and particular vision of dereliction and catastrophe, and having engaged closely with Pam's ideas on what Ngulupi represented, I needed to reclaim my own sense of the place.

+ + +

Ngulupi, 2008

The anthills crowd up to the edge of the road — small, massed, silent — as if they have been waiting for me to arrive.

—Hello, I say, nodding and smiling like the queen, but they remain impassive.

At the gateway where the road forks, I leave the vehicle and walk. I want to come to the place without insulation, with all my senses alert. In the sand and gravel of the old road, I make out the tracks of dingo and camel, kangaroo, python, goanna and bush turkey.

The iron roof is slumped and buckled, draped like heavy cloth over the pink stone walls. One end of the house is engulfed in crimson bougainvillea, and the white satellite dish has slid from the roof and nestles like an eardrum in the blaze of flowers. Sections of the roof are missing, all the interior windows are gone, the flywire ripped away from the verandahs that surround the building. A dozen Major Mitchell cockatoos have stationed themselves on an overhanging branch to keep an eye on me.

There has been a fire, and charred roof beams collapse into rooms that are middens of crumbling plaster. Ceiling fans hang from their entrails. In the office, filing cabinets have been overturned, documents buried under rubble. Tarnished sachets of condoms are scattered among the bleached bougainvillea flowers that pile in drifts along the corridors and verandahs.

A broken windowpane frames table-topped hills, refracting

them through the shattered glass. This morning the wind is moving the hills about, rippling them like banners of purple silk. In the foreground an ornate weathervane turns on its mount above a wrought-iron gate, and a lantern throws its hexagonal shadow across a sandstone barbecue. Long yellow grass pushes against the scorched iron of the verandah. On earlier visits the absences were sharper, the house full of the artefacts of ordinary life.

The small prefabricated houses have not suffered the same fate as the homestead. Purpose-built of concrete and steel and iron, they are almost indestructible. This is where Pam took most of the images she chose for the *Threshold* series — interiors with window glass painted over to keep out the light, walls inscribed with gnomic graffiti, naked wire bedsteads and eviscerated whitegoods. The outside, if seen at all, was framed by doorways and windows, or penetrated the rooms in strips of light sliced by metal louvres. The metaphor of the threshold, the sense of stepping from sunlight into a kind of desecrated twilight, was self-evident.

The photographs, exhibited in pairs that played flat surfaces against perspectival distortions, were difficult to read until you oriented yourself within the uneven picture plane. Mounted on aluminium, the diptychs were two-and-a-half metres in length, and the polished surfaces and geometric blocks of saturated colour appeared at first as architectural and abstract. A closer look revealed the corners of rooms, skeletal furniture, alcoves and windows and broken household fittings. The images that were not interiors — the weathervane, a baby jumpsuit on a barbed-wire fence, a structure that resembled a Hills hoist but was in fact a primitive merry-go-round — carried a theatrical, ambiguous charge. The missing human presence was supplied by the viewer's reflected image, hinting that he or she was implicated in this anonymous catastrophe.

The pink cockatoos track my progress. They are always here, moving en masse from vantage point to vantage point, reporting on the movements of visitors, their shrieks of outrage settling to a muttering commentary. I can never decide whether they are the resident spirits or the outriders that alert the spirits. I tell them I mean no disrespect, and have come to visit old friends and family.

The stone cottage that used to be the head stockman's house, built at the same time as the homestead and occupied by the Johns family when the Kershes managed Ngulupi, shows signs of a recent visit. Someone has made a fireplace in the front yard — a shallow pit straddled by a barbecue grill — and there's been a token attempt to tidy the detritus scattered around the house. Saddles and bridles and horse-breaking gear still hang on purpose-built racks on the verandah. They have remained sacrosanct — dried-leather memorials to the days before things fell apart.

Near the racks of stockmen's equipment I find a yellow packet of photographs — family snaps of people fishing, a teenage couple asleep on a coloured blanket, a small, naked girl howling on a dusty flat. There is something voyeuristic in these glimpses of ordinary Aboriginal lives. But I keep the photographs — the secret pilferings of the writer.

I make my way past the store and the coolroom to the big shed, which is built on a scale that could shelter a moderately sized aircraft. The steel and timber work-bench is solid and monumental, with a heavy vice bolted to the bench top. Tools and equipment have been taken away. The things that are left — machines with metal housings and fly wheels and drive shafts, pulleys and chains and concrete blocks — are too heavy to move. The solar panels that were never installed are deteriorating, their cardboard packaging rotted away.

The bones of the horses that fell down the mechanic's pit in the months after the place was abandoned have whitened, their hides dried away to fragments. Sheets of roofing iron hang like corrugated curtains. From high up in the rafters comes the rasp of a barn owl. I sense rather than see it — the rush of wings, a flying shadow against the rippled surface of the iron. This has been the owl's territory for as long as I can remember.

Ruins trigger a psychic anxiety and set the ghosts walking. A ruin like this, so substantial, so recent, and in so remote a place, requires more than ordinary homage. I feel as if I am a sense short, as if one needs a collective sense to face presences much too powerful to face alone. On every return visit I feel an accretion of time and memory that becomes deeper and more layered. It is not only my own memories that accumulate, but the memories of others, as if I have become a receptor for the events in which this place is saturated. To what extent I have imagined these memories, to what extent I have absorbed the traces they left, I can't say. Which parts of the story can I tell? The point of entry, or the aftermath? I know some things, but not others. Silences have accumulated in the house and in me.

The imaginary woman I encountered on the first visit is one of several ghosts — fictional creations who have acquired personalities and backstories in my absence, and occupy the ruined outstation with an authority that intensifies with the years. I feel beholden to the tangled skeins of their lives, and less and less competent to extricate them from the trap of my own imagination.

The owl has returned. I hear it ruffling and settling among the creaks and groans of the disintegrating building. The wind is up this morning, and the air is full of agitation. The extractor fan spins above the roof of the generator shed, dragging out the dark, diesel-saturated air. The Major Mitchells follow me back to the house and settle in the dead tree above the roofless bathroom. They are quiet now, but watch me all the time.

The place is becoming transparent. Light penetrates louvres and fills the rooms with bars of light and shadow, vehicle windows frame repetitions of anthills and yellow grass, powerlines and rafters make a blue geometry of the sky. Through the luminous architecture I search for the fragments of stories, gathering them up before they're lost for good, before they disintegrate in all this light.

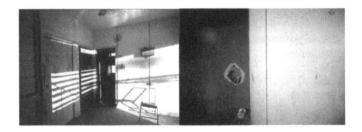

The house clicks and shudders around her, its history collapsed in on itself, the stories and memories she has brought with her seeking objects to which they can adhere.

She can hardly remember herself. She used to be so fearless. What happened to all that energy and confidence, the lack of caution?

Age and time have knocked the stuffing out of her. But there were other things, before that. Self-betrayals, moral cowardice, laziness.

Give it a break, she thinks. Human failings. Stop trying to elevate your ordinary shortcomings to the scale of fatal flaws.

But the place itself does that. Simplifies, elevates, intensifies. She is continually drawn back to it, as if it is only here that she can refine grief into meaning.

As Pam's art practice pulled her south to the rigour and challenges of academia, my own preoccupations pulled me out of that world and plunged me into an evolving enmeshment with the country and its non-imaginary inhabitants. My discomfort with the theoretical ground that underlay what Pam was doing put me on notice to work out where my own position lay. That I was out of step with the intellectual and academic temper of my time troubled me, but I could not submit to the reductionism that always seemed to place me in the role of a colonial usurper. It was more complicated than that, and always had been. Aboriginal people had always had more agency than such an interpretation allowed. And I knew white people who felt for the country as deep an emotional and physiological attachment as the traditional custodians, and were more like them in their social and psychological temper than they were like urban Australians of any race. The ghosts that haunted Ngulupi were their fictional kin.

2018

The road is well travelled, and I make good time, stopping at my customary spot near Pussycat Bore to boil the billy and enjoy the last opportunity for solitude that I will have for some time. When I reach Balgo I go directly to the women's centre to see Dora, who is swollen with diabetic oedema, too sunken in the discomforts of her dying body to do more than offer me a grimace that might be a smile. Her sister Peggy is in the bed next to hers, and chatters to her in Ngardi. Although Peggy has dementia, her cheerful disposition is unchanged.

—How did you come here? she asks me. In your own car? By your own self?

—Yes, I say. By my own self, in my own car.

—You not frighten? I'd be frighten!

At this point she laughs wildly and starts over.

—How did you come here? By your own self?

I sit for a while with Dora, but without the language of country to share there's nothing much to say. The other old ladies are in various states of survival mode. Maudie is strong and physically able, but prone to hallucinations. It's difficult to know whether she recognises me. The *kartiya* volunteer women who minister to the old women are saints. I hug Dora carefully, afraid of hurting her, assure Peggy that I came by my own self, in my own car, and am not frighten, and take my leave.

The drive from Balgo to Mulan, which I've done countless times over the years, is so familiar — the shining gravel plains, the fluted, curving, speckled hills, the old, hard, red country that appears to be flat but is a compilation of shallow valleys and subtle rises, the diminishing contours of the range I've painted several times but not yet begun to capture. I drive through the gateway, remnant of the fence-line that once marked the boundary of Lake Gregory station, and past Two Hills, the Nganpayijarra, where the ancestral brothers keep vigil over the country, their ancient mother hunkering in a low mound at their feet. The first sight of Mulan is the water tank perched on its elevated platform, visible above the hill now called Telstra Hill, being the point from which on a good day it's possible to pick up a couple of bars of reception on a mobile phone.

The lurch of recognition as I crest the hill is composed of anxiety, anticipation and gladness, along with a reluctance to face what must come next — finding the sorry camp, going through the ritualised hugging and wailing for Anna that feels like play-acting the grief I genuinely feel. But it doesn't happen like that. The first person I see is Anna's son Geoffrey, who hugs me like a brother, and then Julianne's son Lachlan, who calls me Auntie and embraces me with the same affection. I find Julianne and Rebecca, we talk, and they bring me up to date on funeral arrangements. The grandchildren come in clusters to hug me and cry a little, and wander off again.

I spend much of the first day unpacking the car and re-establishing my familiar niche, setting up my provisional home for the next couple of months. There's always something satisfying in creating a temporary, simplified order of my own within the less comprehensible forms of order and disorder that constitute the community. Although the door to my two-room demountable has been jemmied open, nothing has been damaged or stolen, so the break-in was probably kids on the hunt for food. Apart from sweeping out the dust and dead beetles, it's not too much of a task, but there's a point when I run out of puff and wonder again if there's something wasteful and ridiculous in the effort spent on this part of my life, whether I'm playing out an absurd folly to conceal the fact that I've achieved very little.

At this point Napurrula, ever the pragmatist, gets me out of the donga in search of Shirley and Evelyn, who I haven't yet seen. I find them watering their respective lawns and complaining about the rubbish that blows into their yards from the messy houses across the road. There's a civic pride being played out in preparation for the arrival of visitors for the Tjurabalan annual general meeting and for Anna's funeral, and the erecting of fences around most of the houses is creating a shift in the character of the community. There are more lush lawns and well-kept gardens around the Aboriginal homes than around most of the *kartiya* houses, although there are still a few dwellings in the community that maintain their reputation for squalor.

I sit and chat with them. Evelyn's strong, bony, beautiful hands tap my arm to accentuate a point.

—Did you bring my crowbar? Evelyn asks, meaning the crowbar with my name scored into it, a gift from the horseman. She has coveted it for years.

—I brought *my* crowbar, I say, and she grins her wicked grin.

We arrange to go out for a drive the next day to collect bark and firewood.

After dark, my unscreened donga fills with tiny flying insects, and I have to decamp to the IPA donga to cook some dinner, after which I watch several episodes of *Game of Thrones* on my laptop.

The following afternoon I collect Hanson, Evelyn and Shirley, and they direct me to an old hunting road where we find a *tinyjil* tree shedding its bark, and clusters of ripe *kumpupatja* and *parlapi*, bush tomatoes and bloodwood apples. The trip to the bush supermarket lifts all our spirits.

—That little AJ would like this, Shirley says, meaning Anna.

Later, watching the full moon rise from Two Hills, I remember watching the eclipse with Lockyer, stranded up here in the pitchy dark. We toasted the moonrise with a gin-and-tonic, and had a couple more while waiting for the eclipse. The earth's shadow creeping across the face of the moon was uncanny and primeval. For a short time it was a black moon rimmed in a halo of silver light, the craters and peaks on its surface weirdly visible as darkness etched into darkness. At this point, we realised that neither of us had thought to bring a torch. There was no question of trying to negotiate the steep and stony path down the hill, so we smoked Lockyer's kreteks and waited for the eclipse to pass.

Lockyer and Phil are driving up from Victoria for the funeral — a mad, quixotic thing to do — and I'm hanging out for their arrival. Smokes from hunting fires show in the west, and the breeze has shifted from the north-west and is now blowing from the south.

The moon is an immense orange semi-circle, and then it is up, round and perfect and reflecting the last glow of the sun. What a luminous, numinous object it is. No wonder humans have imbued it with the power and character of a divine entity.

I had flagged the possibility with Julianne and the family to paint Anna's coffin, as my family did for my mother's funeral, but the logistics of remote cold storage and the transportation of corpses proves too difficult to negotiate. Instead we make a banner several metres long to wrap around the coffin, using the motifs and colours of the Aboriginal flag, with the additional decoration of handprints made by her grandchildren. The kids come to the art centre, and take turns smearing their hands with paint and printing them on the canvas, the older ones managing the little ones. They cluster around and beg to be noticed.

The afternoon before the funeral there is a flurry of activity, as everyone descends on me to transcribe what they want read at the ceremony. They bring their handwritten statements of love and homage, and I type them on my laptop to be printed out. Anna's nephew George has written a powerful and poetic statement on his iPad, a more lucid and literary piece of writing than most of the students I know could produce.

—George, this is beautiful, I say. Where did you learn to write like that?

—Inside, he says, meaning in jail. I learned to write and I learned to think. I never went back.

Jamie Brown comes looking for paint to touch up the Madonna in the shrine at the cemetery. He tells me the CEO is away and has taken the key to the workshop compound with him, so Jamie has cut the padlock with bolt cutters and liberated the bobcat in order to dig the grave.

Lockyer and Phil arrive, and I'm so glad to see them I want to cry. And Tanya with her *lungkurta* twins, born after she rubbed the blue-tongue fertility stone. We are like some cobbled-together *kartiya* family whose lives are bonded to this place. On the metal plate welded to the white steel grave-marker, Lockyer prints the details of Anna's life in his neat architect's hand. Phil organises the masses of wildflowers we have gathered, arranging them in painted flour drums with a professional touch gleaned from his florist daughter. Days earlier I had collected the drums from the tip, risking injury as I clambered about in the smouldering pit of rubbish, and Lulu's eldest daughter, Noonie, painted them with Christian Aboriginal symbols.

Anna and Rex had been married in a Catholic ceremony, and now the bishop has flown in from Broome to preside over the funeral. It starts exactly on time, which catches me by surprise and foils my plan to wrap the banner around the coffin before the ceremony begins. Instead I find myself co-opted into the formal proceedings, handed a wad of texts to read, including many that I transcribed the previous day — among them the biography and eulogy I helped to write. I'm undone by my own well-crafted prose, so that by the time I come to read my personal homage to Anna I can barely get the words out.

This is ridiculous, I think. *I didn't break down like this at my own mother's funeral.*

But emotion is closer to the surface here. To weep openly is normal. There's no way I could have shown my love and grief more convincingly in this company.

Anna is to be interred beside Rex, and Jamie has done a good job of excavating a trench between Rex's grave and a close-buried relative. In her grotto, the Madonna's face and arms glow brick pink against her blue robe, as if she has a bad case of sunburn.

UNSTABLE HORIZONS

Horizon and ground, and the numinous zone between them of mirage and reflection ...

These words, first scribbled in pencil in one of my drawing diaries from the 1990s, flag a preoccupation that continues to haunt my work. The tension between ways of seeing the landscape — the perspectival view of foreground, middle ground and horizon, and the bird's-eye view of a schematic, inhabited topography — mirrors the tension between ways of being in the landscape. Even the term 'landscape' comes freighted with implications of a European imperial point of view. The eighteenth century saw the word coined to describe a 'master of all he surveys' aesthetic, but time and usage have opened it up to other meanings.

The philosopher Edward S. Casey writes, in *Representing Place: landscape painting and maps*, '[A]t the very least, landscape is something situated at the intertwining of earth and world ... It brings the dark earth to bear at the very places where the world begins to manifest clarity and order.'

In Casey's definition, 'earth' is the material substance of place, while 'world' is what we humans make of it. He takes 'landscape' to mean land shaped by and for all aspects of permanent human occupation, and thus offers a nuanced complexity equivalent to the way 'country' is now used in Australia to indicate an indigenous perspective of place:

> Beyond its power to combine earth and world as well as refuge and prospect, landscape is also a creature of surface as well as depth, of visibility as well as invisibility, of image as well as word, of nature as well as culture. It can be just as well painted as mapped. In addition to being perceived it can be actively imagined.

In this conception of landscape, the horizon regains its power as a space of mirage and imagination, a flux of changing light and atmosphere, a place where map and metaphor become the same — smoke and mirage, shadows and absences, through which meaning slips like light.

Casey goes on to describe the preparation undergone by the ancient Chinese painter of landscape before he embarked on painting a place:

> To begin with, the ancient painter identifies not with a person but with the landscape through which he wanders for years in preparation for painting; the purpose of the wandering is not just to note and observe but to make himself one with what he has

moved through. ... Moreover, this identification involves a strong
factor of internalization, even to the point of pathology: the
serious painters of previous centuries, says Shen Kua (A.D. 1031–
95), 'had streams and rocks in their vitals, and clouds and mists as a
chronic illness.' But the internalization of the landscape, whatever
its risks, remains necessary, so far as painting is concerned.

Casey draws a parallel between this incorporation of place into
the body of the artist with Freud's speculation that when a loved
person dies their presence is incorporated into the psyche of the
survivor, and if not properly mourned may become 'encrypted'
and psychically troublesome. The difference lies in the nature of
what is incorporated, since the internalised landscape finds its way
from the body into the painting, enriching the painting with the
nuanced sensibilities of that embodied knowledge.

Pam used the word 'dystopothesia', coined by Canadian anthropologist Christopher Fletcher, to describe what she felt to be a
fundamental condition of displacement for both black and white
Australians. It means, in the context Pam used it, 'the incompat-
ibility of bodies to the space they inhabit', or, more simply, feeling
out of place. The American Baptist in the bus at Tanami Downs
was undoubtedly suffering from dystopothesia.

But I am more interested in what happens when the unconscious mind experiences a fundamental displacement, triggered
by the opposite of feeling out of place — when the body feels
an almost cellular affinity to a place that has been constructed
by a different cultural imagination. The ancient Chinese painters, with streams and rocks in their vitals, and clouds and mists
as chronic illnesses, are painting a landscape to which they are
culturally and cognitively attuned. But if the landscape you are
learning to paint is the active site of a shared consciousness from

which you are largely excluded, does it remain encrypted?

Someone, somewhere, has probably coined a word to describe such a condition, but I don't want to know what it is. I wonder sometimes if the time I've spent in the desert has compromised my access to the deep psychology of my own culture — replaced the collective unconscious with the shadowy glimpses of a place-based collective consciousness, and sentenced me to wander in the borderlands between Jung and Geography.

The continuing discoveries of neuroscience offer hard evidence for what people have always known — that place, memory, and emotion are inextricably linked. In October 2014, the Nobel Prize in physiology or medicine is awarded to three neuroscientists for their discoveries about how the brain locates where we are and plots how we move through space.

One half of the prize is awarded to John O'Keefe who, thirty years earlier, discovered that certain cells in the hippocampus — the part of the brain that generates emotion and encodes new memories — form cognitive maps of the environment. The other half of the prize is jointly awarded to May-Britt Moser and her husband, Edvard Moser, who discovered that cells in the neighbouring entorhinal cortex fire in distinct, grid-like patterns. The 'grid cells' create a spatial map and fix the co-ordinates, while 'place cells' remember specific locations. It is clear evidence that cognitive processes have a physiological origin.

It seems that maps are a direct reflection of how our brains function. The template of the grid, with specific places located on it, mirrors the neural co-ordinates that let us find our way in the world. There's a continuous feedback loop between the interior self and the external environment.

Navigation, memory, and emotion are all located in the hippocampus, a seahorse-shaped sliver of matter replicated in both hemispheres of the brain. That the neural receptors which allow us to know where we are occur in the same nub of the brain that governs emotions and the laying-in of new memories suggests that these capacities are wired into the same circuit. Does a map, registering in the hippocampus as a navigational tool, send a sympathetic ripple along the nerve thread of memory and feeling? If this is so, if our ability to find our way and to know where we are is tied inextricably to feeling and remembering, it goes some way to explaining why certain places cast a spell of enchantment on us.

+ + +

A couple of years after my mother's death, I move from Manar and buy into some land north of Canberra. It is a dual-occupancy arrangement with a long-time artist friend and her partner, and a year after we move in we design and build a shed that houses two studios. For the first time in years, I am able to unpack boxes and crates of old or unfinished work, and in one of them I discover a stained and folded canvas with roughly hemmed edges. It measures two by two-and-a-half metres, and has been primed and stained with a thin wash of bitumen. Ancient hornets' nests crumble from the creases, spilling their contents of dead grubs, and the fabric smells of mice and earth and, faintly, of gum turpentine. I recognise it as a groundsheet I had made from heavy cotton duck canvas and taken on the first and second Tanami trips with Pam.

At the centre of the canvas is a clay-coloured imprint of my body framed by the oval shape of a coolamon. To the left of the body print, a wash of bitumen is pooled over a layer of white pigment. On the right, a shield-shaped grid blocked in with charcoal completes the trio of forms.

It's like opening a time capsule.

This is what I've lost track of, I think, as memory recalibrates and I remember the raw, unmediated relationship I once had between materials and ideas and country and the body.

The shapes and pigments on the groundsheet represent real places, but they are mapped onto the co-ordinates of emotion and imagination. In spite of having forgotten that I had made it, I know that this is the map I have been missing. To orient myself on this map, I must stand in the middle of it and see the country radiating out around me. Or, better still, lie down and feel the country radiating out around me. If I align myself with the body print, my head points south.

I tack the canvas to a timber frame and stand it up against the studio wall. The groundsheet reads like a text, from left to right, from east to west, the places organised in the sequence that I visited them — Lake Ruth, Bullock's Head Lake, Lake Gregory: Mangkurrurpa, Yanypurru, Paruku. Like the map Roger drew for Joseph Birdsell, south is at the top. With a coloured chalk pencil, I begin to map out the story that has been incubating for many years.

The fragments come together, the narrative takes shape. I remember the lessons of the Balgo mosaic, and leave space for all the elements to breathe. If I were to join the dots, it would create a lattice of tracks linking people, place, memory, and metaphor. This is my unfinished map, with all the stories not yet told, the stories that have not yet happened, the stories that aren't mine to tell. Each time I set to work on it, I feel something shift in my brain, an elation that here is a language that opens up inarticulate spaces, makes room for memory and dreams, elaborates both the purpose and the folly of setting out on an enterprise, holds together the quixotic and the heroic, the imaginary and the real. It's a plan that is never completed, an itinerary that isn't followed — and there's always the chance of meeting a lion.

UNDERTOW

Mulan, 2014

I drive to Billiluna to pick up Evelyn, Shirley Yoomarie, and Shirley's grandson, Junior. On the way back to Mulan, Evelyn tells me to stop the car. It's the season for *kumpupatja*, the prized bush tomato *Solanum diversiflorum*, and plants loaded with fruit flourish along the roadside. We are through the floodout country, with plenty of time to make it home before dark, so I pull off the track. Junior is still young enough to engage happily in food-gathering with middle-aged women, and he trots ahead of Shirley, spotting plants and picking the greenish-white fruit, undeterred by the protective brackets of spikes. Evelyn scurries down the road with a comical flat-footed gait, determined to be first to reach the special bush she's been keeping an eye on whenever she travels this road. It's a robust plant with unusually large fruit, dozens just ripe for the picking, and she strips the bush and bundles the tomatoes into a loop of her skirt.

We wander with intent, three women and a child, alone and in company, observing and absorbing, purposefully, without urgency.

Taking note of the tracks of lizards in the red sand, the slant of the afternoon light, the small purple tufts of the pussytail *Ptilotus calostachyus* nodding at the ends of their long fine stems, I am entirely content.

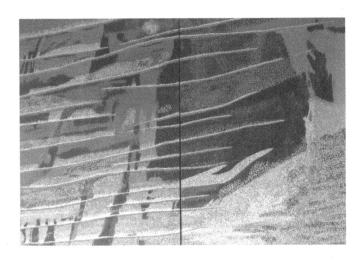

Lulu and I continue to paint together. We paint claypans and fire scars, and there are times, sitting side by side in the Mulan art centre, when the rhythm of dip, dot-dot feels as natural as breathing. It's still early days, and we are trying different strategies. When I'm in Mulan and we can work together on a daily basis, it allows for close collaboration. To counterbalance this, I send Lulu broad tonal underpaintings of the claypans in her traditional jurisdiction, and satellite printouts for her to use as a reference. We have exhibited some of the resulting works, and sold several. When Lulu accumulates a couple of thousand dollars, she buys a car. In the years that I have known her, she has purchased at least half-a-dozen cars — the best of them lasting a couple of years, the worst a few weeks — so that she can take her expanding tribe of grandchildren and great-grandchildren for regular visits to the lake, where they learn who they are and where they belong. On such foundations are built a sense of identity and authority, and the possibility of a future.

I've watched the older women raising their grandchildren — stepping into the gap left by parents who have died, or gone to jail, or succumbed to alcoholism and other kinds of substance abuse. It's through these women that I've come to know the kids, watch them grow up, see the personalities and character traits emerge, feel both fearful and optimistic for what awaits them. They are clever and beautiful and charming, like children everywhere. Belonging to the country is still paramount, and cultural prohibitions are still strong, but they know something of the world beyond the desert. A school group visited Melbourne not so long ago, and one of the boys was lost. He found his way back to the hotel, a distance of several kilometres, using the observational skills he had learned at home.

September 2015

When I visit Mulan to talk to people about my book, there's a sorry camp in progress for Julianne's three-year-old granddaughter, who died recently in Perth. She had an inherited condition that caused extreme obesity, and had been taken away from the family and placed in care, with fatal consequences. People are angry, and the welfare department is given short shrift when it tries to get Mulan to participate in a managed-income trial.

The child's mother, Delphine, is Julianne's eldest daughter, and has just borne a second daughter, who seems healthy, and has the distinctive features of the Yoomarie clan. I sit with the family and admire the new baby, as I admired the little girl who died, as I admired two-month-old Delphine when Julianne showed her to me at a women's ceremonial gathering in 1992, and as I admired newborn Julianne when Anna showed her to me in 1969. I promise Delphine to print the photographs I took of her with her first daughter, and give her some baby's clothes. There's a crop of new babies, and I have brought a couple of bags of clothes from Vinnie's to distribute.

Most of the Yoomaries, who comprise a significant proportion of the Sturt Creek mob, now live in Mulan, and I arrange to bring morning tea to the sorry camp and discuss the chapters I have written about the trip to Sturt Creek and the massacre. Evelyn represents the Clancy clan, and Julianne facilitates the conversation. Everyone listens avidly to the account of the trip, and to my rendition of Boxer Milner telling the story of the massacre. I'm nervous about suggesting that the popular version of the massacre story may be a compilation of several distinct events, but when I explain why I think so, people nod in agreement. Apparently this is not a new idea. They tell me I should talk to somebody in Fitzroy and to someone else in Wangkajungka — people who know more about the Sturt Creek killing times.

My tale of Riwiyarra's escape, imagined during the long night while Slippers is dying, draws particular approval.

This gives me confidence. Once again I provide fruit and biscuits and tea, this time for a gathering in the art centre. At Rebecca Johns' instigation, I also provide tinned meat and bread for a ceremony to release Jamie Brown from the food restrictions of sorry business. This is carried out before we embark on the discussion about my book.

I face the assembled group with my manuscript.

—I've been working with you for a long time, I say. I've written down your stories, I've mapped your country with you, I've made a radio program, I've helped to write books about you and for you.

Now it's my turn. I'm going to tell my side of the story.

I read everything that I think might offend or upset people. Bessie is not sure about the moment on the Canning Stock Route trip when we all say we stink, but the others laugh and tell her that it's really funny. Many of the people in the room are not literate, but the context, the animation I bring to the reading, the knowledge people have of the events and places, transcends the barrier of language. I read the story of Monica heading to Anna's house with a crowbar, and everyone howls with laughter.

—What? says Monica.

Rebecca shouts into her ear.

—You was looking for your niece at Mum's house. You had a crowbar. Mum was worried.

—I remember, Monica chortles. I was going to give that girl a hiding.

When I stop reading they demand more. Seeing themselves through my eyes is a beguiling novelty. The ancient authority of storytelling maintains its power to captivate.

After dark I go to the community office to use the internet. The little town is full of night sounds — the thud of a ball in the basketball court, children calling to each other, dogs barking, the crashes and explosions of an action movie playing at top volume in a house with all the windows open.

The office, windowless and silent except for the permanent hum of the air conditioner, is like a bunker into which the *kartiya* aspirations have retreated, taking refuge behind filing cabinets and computers and multiple sets of keys. It's not a place to linger, even in the daylight hours. I answer pressing emails, do some internet banking, and leave. As I lock the door, I hear a voice.

—Goodnight Kim.

—Who's that? I say.

—Theo.

A boy sits up from the bench where he has been lying, and waves a mobile phone to show me why he's there. The covered annexe in front of the office is one of the better spots for mobile reception. Theo is one of Lulu's grandsons, home on school holidays from the Perth boarding school where he and several other Mulan teenagers have been sent. He belongs to a family that values education, but homesickness is a powerful force that sabotages the secondary schooling of many of the children. He is poised on the volatile brink of his future.

—Goodnight Theo, I say.

Walking back to my little two-roomed donga with my laptop under my arm, I feel the heartbeat of the town — the connections between families, the feuds and alliances, the undertow of the desert. Mulan fits the demographic of small remote communities threatened with closure by the West Australian government. But I'm confident that it will endure. It is, in its unique way, too important and too ordinary not to endure. Part of the ordinariness is the effortless way in which people and country hold each other. To destroy that effortless belonging would be to destroy the heartbeat of the continent.

The *warlu* season has come early this year, and when I leave Mulan the Tanami highway is closed by fires burning south of Halls Creek and near the Territory border. The bottom road is not affected, but I let the Balgo police know I'm travelling that way. There's a hot fierce easterly blowing, and the country is tinder dry. The bottom road follows the route of the *Warlu* dreaming, and if anyone lights a hunting fire between Balgo and the border there's a real risk of getting trapped. I don't stop until I reach Wilson's Cave, the western-most bore on Tanami Downs. Once into the cattle country the fire risk is much reduced, and I let Pirate out for a drink and a run.

There's a more direct road from Wilson's Cave to the Tanami Downs homestead, but I take the long route past Lake Sarah. Although the track has been back in use for six or seven years, the vegetation is still stunted and woody, and the skeletal remnants of the original shrubs suggest there's been an environmental catastrophe. The drowned grader stands like a rusting monument to the unpredictable, the underside of its canopy packed with the tubular mud nests of fairy martins. Global warming may yet turn this country back into an inland sea. If I were to continue the metaphor of country as mind, and conflate it with Jung's notion of the sea as the unconscious, there's some fertile riffing to be made on the implications of a landlocked sea that most of the time is present only as the route of an ancestral being from another cosmology.

The station track runs along the northern edge of Landinyungu, a bluebush swamp in the middle of the cattle country. In the sixties it was almost devoid of trees, a treacherous place to gallop a horse because of the deep fissures in the clay. Now, after years of inundations, it is choked with well-grown *Melaleuca glomerata*.

Mangkurrurpa is as dry as I've ever seen it. Last year it was full to the brim. This year it's windswept and covered with horse and cattle manure. I can hear both Pam and Margaret telling me off for the state it's in. But it will fill again, next year or the year after, and I'll set up camp by the eagle tree to wait for Napurrula. Violet Sunset will teeter past on her high-heeled shoes, searching for the boat. Margaret will make damper, Dora will smile her ancient smile, and Pam will raise her beaker of wine to toast my return.

AUTHOR'S NOTE

Versions of several excerpts from *Position Doubtful* have been published previously as essays. A short version of 'Vertigo' was short-listed for the 2015 Nature Conservancy essay prize. A version of 'Testimony' was published as 'The River' in *Meanjin*, Vol. 72, number 2, Winter 2013, and in *Best Australian Essays 2013*, ed. Robert Manne. A short excerpt from 'Faultlines and Songlines' was published in *Griffith Review 28: Still the Lucky Country?*, May 2010.

I have used material from the essays 'Listening is Harder Than You Think', *Griffith Review 19: Re-imagining Australia*, Autumn 2008, and 'Mapping Outside the Square', *Journal of Aboriginal History*, Vol. 30, 2007.

Any inconsistencies in the spelling of Aboriginal words are due to alternate spellings in the orthographies of the different languages.

IMAGES

125 'Old yard bin right here' from *Postcards from the Tanami* series, Kim Mahood, 2006.

134 'On the day my dog died' from *Postcards from the Tanami* series, Kim Mahood, 2006.

136 'Sturt Creek' collaborative painted map, Jaru traditional owners and Kim Mahood, 2006.

145 Untitled from *Postcards from the Tanami* series, Kim Mahood, 2006.

152 Topographical map Australia, 1:250,000 series, with satellite image overlay of expanded Tanami lakes after 2006 extreme rain event.

166 'Warlukulangu', Dora Mungkina Napaltjarri, 2007. Photograph Pamela Lofts.

171 Satellite image of Sturt Creek flood-out, copyright Google Earth, 2015.

177 Map of Billiluna Station Lease, issued at Halls Creek in 1963 (no citation available).

189 Painting the Paruku section of the Canning Stock Route at Lake Stretch. Photograph Wade Freeman, 2007.

193 Martu elder Billy Patch's sand drawing of the songlines interrupted by the Canning Stock Route. Photograph John Carty, 2008.

197 Satellite image of fire scars, copyright Google Earth, 2015.

198 'Paruku' fire map, Veronica Lulu, Anna Johns, Shirley Yoomarie, and Kim Mahood 2008/2011. Photograph Kim Mahood, 2011.

212 'Parnkupirti Creek aerial view', Kim Mahood, 2008.

223 'Nyarna Lake Stretch' map, Daisy Kunga, Charmia Samuel, Shirley Yoomarie, and Kim Mahood, 2008/2009. Photograph Kim Mahood, 2009.

231 'Kilwa and Lirra' family map, Anna Johns, Rebecca Johns, May Stundi, and Kim Mahood, 2008/2009. Photograph Kim Mahood, 2010.

REFERENCES

Baume, F.E. *Tragedy Track: the story of the granites*. Wayville, S.A.: North Flinders Mines Ltd; Carlisle, W.A.: Hesperian Press, 1993.

Bohemia, Jack, and McGregor, Bill. *Nyibayarri: Kimberley tracker*. Canberra: Aboriginal Studies Press, 1995.

Casey, Edward S. *Representing Place: landscape painting and maps*. Minnesota: University of Minnesota Press, 2002.

Davidson, Allan Arthur. 'Journal of the Western Expedition'. In *Journal of Explorations in Central Australia by the Central Australian Exploration Syndicate, Limited, under the leadership of Allan A. Davidson, 1898 to 1900*. Adelaide: Government Printer, 1905.

de Ishtar, Zohl. *Holding Yawulyu: white culture and black women's law*. Melbourne: Spinifex, 2005.

Elias, Derek. 'Golden Dreams: people, place and mining in the Tanami Desert.' PhD thesis, Australian National University, 2001.

Feld, Steven, and Basso, Keith H., eds. *Senses of Place*. Santa Fe: School of American Research Press, 1996.

FORM. *Ngurra Kuju Walyja — One Country One People: stories from the Canning Stock Route*. Melbourne: Macmillan Art Publishing, 2011.

Harley, J.B., and Woodward, David, eds. *A History of Cartography*. Vol. 1. Chicago: University of Chicago Press, 1987.

Hoban, Russell. *The Lion of Boaz-Jachin and Jachin-Boaz*. London: Picador, 1991.

Latz, Peter K.; illustrated by Jenny Green. *Bushfires and Bushtucker: Aboriginal plant use in Central Australia*. Alice Springs: IAD Press, 1995.

Lewis, G. Malcolm. 'The Origins of Cartography.' In *A History of Cartography*. Vol. 1. Chapter 3. Chicago: University of Chicago Press, 1987.

Lofts, Pamela. 'A Necessary Nomadism: re-thinking a place in the sun.' Masters thesis, Australian National University, 2008.

Lopez, Barry. 'A Literature of Place.' In *Portland Magazine*, Summer 1997, pp. 22–25.

Mahood, Marie. 'On the Track.' In *The Stockman*, Chapter 2. Sydney: Landsdowne Press, 1984.

Marais, Eugène N. *The Soul of the White Ant*. London: Jonathan Cape, 1970.

Momaday, N. Scott. *The Way to Rainy Mountain*. Albuquerque: University of New Mexico Press, 1969.

Morton, Steve, Martin, Mandy, Mahood, Kim, and Carty, John, eds. *Desert Lake: art, science and stories from Paruku*. Melbourne: CSIRO Publishing, 2013.

Napanangka, Tjama Freda; Napangarti, Payi Payi; Napanangka, Martingale Mudgedel; Nampitjin, Kuninyi Rita; Napurrula, Nanyuma Rosie; Nampitjin, Millie Skeen. *Yarrtji: six women's stories from the Great Sandy Desert*. Canberra: Aboriginal Studies Press, 1997.

Urban, Anne. *The Wildflowers and Plants of Inland Australia*. Alice Springs: Paul Fitzsimmons, 2004.

ACKNOWLEDGEMENTS

This book has been a long time gestating, and has had support from various sources along the way. My thanks go to the Peter Blazey Foundation for the Blazey Fellowship that allowed me to marshal the narrative threads into the beginnings of a coherent form. The H.C. Coombs Creative Arts Fellowship, hosted by the School of Art and Social Sciences at the Australian National University, brought the stamp of intellectual gravitas to what was a wildly non-academic endeavour, and gave me the opportunity to work in a rigorous and creative environment. Finally, a grant from the Literature board of the Australia Council provided me with the means to focus on writing during the final months of pulling the book together.

Many thanks to Aviva Tuffield for her enthusiastic support and for convincing me that I had a book in the making. Ordinary thanks are not sufficient to acknowledge the herculean editorial task undertaken by Tamsin Wagner and Margot Rosenbloom in helping me to hammer a vast and intractible manuscript into shape. Thanks to my good friends Jess Jeeves and John Carty for the many conversations in which I teased out thoughts and ideas without censorship or moderation. Many thanks to Lee Cataldi for translating the recording of Dora Mungkina Napaltjarri's story from Ngardi into English, and to Dr Nic Peterson for sharing his professional knowledge of the Tanami. Karin Riederer read the manuscript at a time when I was losing confidence in it, and reassured me that it had some merit. There have been many others who have offered encouragement and support — among them Kate Grenville, Helen Maxwell, Ross Gibson, Jenny Taylor, Sue Fielding, and Kerrie Nelson.

Thanks also to Wade Freeman and John Carty for permission to use photographs, and to Helen Maxwell for her assistance in providing photographs from the estate of Pamela Lofts.

For the time that they lived on Tanami Downs, the Napier family gave me a second home, and the recent tragic death of one of the boys adds poignancy to my memories of those times. Gerard Waugh made the world of the goldmines accessible, and provided the demountable that became my permanent base in Mulan.

Most of all, my thanks go to the Aboriginal people of the Tanami, who continue to share their country with me, and through whom I have learned something of the living world of the desert.